POWER BALANCE

POWER BALANCE

Increasing Leverage in Negotiations with Federal and State Governments

LESSONS LEARNED FROM THE NATIVE AMERICAN EXPERIENCE

STEVEN J. HABERFELD

University of Oklahoma Press : Norman

Library of Congress Cataloging-in-Publication Data

Names: Haberfeld, Steven, author.
Title: Power balance : increasing leverage in negotiations with federal andstate governments : lessons learned from the Native American experience / Steven J. Haberfeld.
Other titles: Increasing leverage in negotiations with federal and state governments : lessons learned from the Native American experience
Description: Norman [Oklahoma] : University of Oklahoma Press, [2022] | Includes bibliographical references and index. | Summary: "Builds on traditional Native values and peacemaking practices to equip Native American nations and tribes with tools necessary for negotiating with federal, state, and local governments or with private-sector interests. A practical how-to for mastering six fundamental steps in the negotiating process, ranging from initial planning and preparation to hammering out a comprehensive, written win-win agreement. Useful for tribes and other organizations seeking to promote economic and community development and to protect and advance their legal and historical rights"—Provided by publisher.
Identifiers: LCCN 2021032859 | ISBN 978-0-8061-7651-2 (hardcover) | ISBN 978-0-8061-7626-0 (paperback)
Subjects: LCSH: Indians of North America—United States—Government relations. | Conflict management.
Classification: LCC E93 .H18 2022 | DDC 323.1197—dc23
LC record available at https://lccn.loc.gov/2021032859

The paper in this book meets the guidelines for permanence and durability of the Committee on Production Guidelines for Book Longevity of the Council on Library Resources Inc. ♾

Copyright © 2022 by the University of Oklahoma Press, Norman, Publishing Division of the University. Manufactured in the U.S.A.

All rights reserved. No part of this publication may be reproduced, stored in a retrieval system, or transmitted, in any form or by any means, electronic, mechanical, photocopying, recording, or otherwise—except as permitted under Section 107 or 108 of the United States Copyright Act—without the prior written permission of the University of Oklahoma Press. To request permission to reproduce selections from this book, write to Permissions, University of Oklahoma Press, 2800 Venture Drive, Norman OK 73069, or email rights.oupress@ou.edu.

I dedicate this book to all the Native leaders throughout the country who have been at the forefront of efforts to forge ahead, limit exterior governments' and private interests' control of their political and economic lives, and position their people to become the true masters of their own destinies. To the extent Native leaders have done this, they have been increasingly able to break the fetters of paternalistic control and dependence and enjoy greater internal autonomy and prosperity on every level of community life. I hope this book on improving negotiating skills and maximizing power in intergovernment transactions will serve as a useful tool in gaining even greater political and economic independence and prosperity.

CONTENTS

Preface — xi

Acknowledgments — xv

Introduction — 1
    A Selected Sample of Internal and External Conflicts — 2
    Indian Dispute Resolution Service (IDRS) — 8
    Outline of the Book — 9

1. Negotiation as a Strategy for Conflict Resolution — 11
    A Typology of Conflict Resolution Strategies — 11
    Adversarial versus Collaborative Forms
        of Dispute Resolution — 17
    Mediation versus Arbitration — 20
    The Concept of Win-Win — 21

**2. Traditional Native Approaches to Negotiation and
the Field of Dispute Resolution** — 29
    Consensus-Based Decision Making — 30
    Treating Others with Dignity, Respect, and Honor — 31
    Collaborative Negotiation versus Positional Negotiation — 35
    Relationship Building — 36
    Careful Selection of Community Peacemakers — 37

3. Planning and Preparation — 39
    Causes or Origins of the Conflict — 39
    Costs of the Conflict — 41
    Benefits of the Conflict — 42

Identifying Your Interests	44
What Are Interests?	45
Knowing Your Interests	46
Knowing the Other Party's Interests	46
Maslow's Hierarchy of Needs	47
What Are Issues?	49
Identifying Your Expectations	52
Building the Agenda	53
Developing and Exchanging Proposals	56

4. Creating the Three Satisfactions — 63
- Negotiate a Procedural Agreement — 63
- Creating Substantive Satisfaction — 71
- Developing Relational Satisfaction — 75
- Recap: The Six Stages of the Negotiation Process — 77

5. Meeting the Structural Challenges of Negotiating with Governments — 81
- Tribal Protection of Natural Resources and Ancestral Lands — 81
- Structural Challenges of Government-to-Government Negotiations — 86
- Vertical Negotiations — 87
- Internal Team Negotiations — 94
- Horizontal Negotiations — 100

6. Leveraging Power — 109
- Alternative Political Resources for Tribes — 111
- Other Legislative Sources of Leverage and Control — 115
- Tribes Should Champion Their Cause in the Public Sphere — 118

7. How the Timbisha Shoshone Tribe Got Its Land Back: A Case Study in Government-to-Government Negotiations — 135
- Historical Background — 138

The California Desert Protection Act	139
Round One of the Talks	140
The Tribe's National Political Organizing Strategy	146
The Second Round	150
Creating Substantive Satisfaction	156
Creating Relational Satisfaction	161

Appendixes: Improving Negotiation Outcomes with Better Communication Skills — 165

A. Exercises for Chapter 1: "Negotiation" as a Strategy for Conflict Resolution — 167

B. Exercises for Chapters 2–4: Implementing the Negotiation Methodology — 173

C. Exercises for Chapters 5 and 6: The Structural Challenges of Government-to-Government Negotiation — 183

Notes — 199

Bibliography — 213

Index — 219

PREFACE

This book is designed to increase people's understanding and skills in the discipline of negotiation. We—that is, I and my collaborators at Indian Dispute Resolution Services—have defined "negotiation" as "working things out by talking things through." It is not an esoteric activity reserved for a special class of people such as lawyers or other advocates. On the contrary, all of us negotiate on a daily basis from the time we get up in the morning until the time we retire at night. It is the way we normally decide what to do if more than one person needs to be involved in making a decision. We proceed within the context of some agreed-upon ground rules to discuss, share information, articulate our perspectives, consider options, try to persuade the other party of the merits of our point of view, and together decide what will work best for both of us. Seen this way, negotiation is indeed the most common form of conflict resolution used in our society.

Of course, these negotiations do not always go smoothly. Sometimes we encounter issues that are not easily resolved, or individuals and organizations that are not easy to communicate with and persuade. But this does not mean that negotiations are out of the question. It means simply that we need to approach these more challenging negotiations systematically and with increased forethought. This book, among other things, focuses on how negotiators can design and implement a process that anticipates the pitfalls and builds in the appropriate safeguards and strategies to ensure that the difficulties in reaching a negotiated agreement can be overcome.

Not every conflict can be resolved through negotiations, but most can if approached with the benefit of the lessons learned and applied by experienced practitioners down through time. We lay out an approach that breaks down the discipline of negotiation into its constituent parts and provides a step-by-step methodology for practitioners to follow. The discussion of our methodology begins with consideration of some age-old practices and principles that Native American communities used successfully many generations before European conquest. These are blended with an approach known as interest-based negotiation (IBN). The two have a lot in common. Both are based on the "win-win" principle, as well as the understanding that since negotiation is designed to elicit agreement from both sides, it generally will not happen unless all the parties perceive that they are winning something of significant value to them (the win-win). Both of these approaches are based on collaboration and persuasion rather than coercion and intimidation, and on finding common ground and what is good for the whole rather than what is good only for a part.

This book takes a positive approach toward conflict, consciously choosing to see it as an opportunity for creativity and change rather than as a disaster that will come to no good. Typically, one of the things we do in life is wait for things to happen to us and then we try to get our act together so that we can handle the new situation. Instead of being reactive and having to play catch-up, we need to take a proactive approach, reach out, establish and nurture new relationships, and proceed with an understanding of our underlying interests—all with a vision of the conditions we want to create. Through negotiations we can expand the sphere of our influence and, while not stuck on any one position, explore with the other side what concrete steps we can take to create a better future.

The primary feature that distinguishes negotiation from other forms of dispute resolution (e.g., litigation and arbitration, among others) is that it puts the parties in the best possible position to be change agents and in control of the conflict and its ultimate resolution. It is not turned over to outside, impartial, third-party decision makers who decide our fate.

This book approaches the subject of negotiation primarily from the vantage point of Native nations in the United States. Negotiation skills are powerful tools that Native leaders can use to protect and advance their communities' interests on an everyday basis, and help shape their people's destiny over the long run.

The approach promoted in the book is intended to complement rather than replace other forms of conflict resolution that have been used in Indian country. Native nations have also relied on litigation and political lobbying to assert their legal and historical rights and win important legal and legislative victories. This approach accelerated in the 1960s when American Indian tribes began to have access to subsidized legal services through the federal Office of Economic Opportunity (OEO)–funded legal assistance programs. For the first time, Native peoples had access to the courts and competent and independent attorneys. They were no longer dependent on attorneys in their local areas who were reluctant to assist tribes because they were beholden to hostile local political and economic interests. These legal victories have been important in leveling the playing field and expanding the areas in which tribes could enjoy more political authority and control over their own destinies.

As important as these victories have been, litigation and legislative initiatives have their limitations. Not all of tribes' disputes revolve around legal questions that lead to legal remedies. Second, the climate and receptivity to new legislation for Native American issues is not always present in Congress. In addition, both strategies often require a substantial outlay of tribal funds and take an inordinate amount of time to wind their way through the process.

Negotiation skills are important to Native nations for another reason. While they are key to tribal governments being able to effectively communicate, cooperate, and collaborate within their own communities, these skills are also essential to Native nations being able to hold their own with entities in their external environments. American Indian tribes have entered a new historical period; more now than ever, "No tribe is an island." As tribes expand the size and role of their governments and take steps to develop their economies, a growing number of their projects and activities spill over the boundaries of their reservations and impact the interests of external jurisdictions. Unless they establish and actively manage these relationships, tribal leaders will miss important opportunities to generate significant benefits for their members. Moreover, proactive engagement is one of the few ways they can prevent these external entities from extending their jurisdictions at the expense of tribes, and prevent them from encroaching upon, interfering with, and limiting tribes' inherent rights to self-determination and the full exercise of their sovereignty.

This book is intended for tribal leaders, including those elected, those who are directing and managing a broad range of tribal programs and institutions, and many others who are serving in informal positions of leadership in their communities. It is also designed for tribal attorneys, legal scholars, and law students. Moreover, it is written for future leaders of Native communities who may currently be students enrolled in tribal and community colleges, and in law schools and university and college programs. Other students, Indian and non-Indian alike, who are taking courses in Indian studies, American history, and negotiation and mediation will also benefit.

Government officials can also benefit from this book. It is one of the few step-by-step guides to negotiations in a field where how-to manuals are rare. Very few American government officials in local, state, and federal government agencies have any training, expertise, or experience sitting down and negotiating with people outside their own agencies. Typically, they operate within their own hierarchies as semiautonomous silos and are accustomed to having it their way. It is well known that little interagency coordination takes place, and even less with organizations in the private sector. Most glaring is their lack of experience and sensitivity to cultural differences when interacting with Native governments.

We hope that in reading this book, people will now have the opportunity to learn from actual experiences of tribes and government agencies that chose to resolve their differences not in extended court battles, but by sitting down together to resolve their differences in dignified and mutually respectful bilateral negotiations.

Currently, a compelling need exists for a broad spectrum of the American public to be versed in negotiation skills and processes. As this book was being written, American society was experiencing increasing polarization and distrust among citizens. Many people are not willing to discuss their different points of view with people with whom they disagree. Others choose to cut off certain personal contacts altogether. Instead of agreeing to disagree and accepting the presence of different perspectives, people often do not focus on the problem but instead choose to engage in ad hominem attacks: name calling and personal insults. They reject and condemn those who hold different opinions, rudely dismissing their opponents as irrelevant. Unchecked, this growing hostility will result in not only a failure to address and resolve the urgent problems confronting our society but will also pose the danger that the increasing anger and frustration will create more division and turn more violent and destructive.

In this book we present the discipline of negotiation as an effective antidote to the current breakdown in our communications. We offer specific skills and a step-by-step negotiation methodology that people from every walk of life can use to bring people together, create understanding, listen and discuss their differences in the spirit of mutual respect and dignity, and ultimately reach agreements in our places of work, families, communities, civic organizations, and local and national governments. Negotiations can provide a problem-solving process in which we ultimately appreciate that when we are open to having our ideas challenged in a constructive way, the final product is a more workable, refined, and nuanced solution than one that reflects only our own point of view.

ACKNOWLEDGMENTS

First and foremost I want to acknowledge my indebtedness to two nationally prominent negotiator-mediators who trained and mentored me in the early years of my career. Thomas Colosi, who served as the Director of Education for the American Arbitration Association (AAA) in Washington, D.C., and was the principle in The Colosi Group. Tom was my primary teacher, joined Indian Dispute Resolution Services (IDRS) periodically as one of our trainers, and served on our initial Board of Directors as the representative of AAA. I was also trained and certified as a professional mediator by William Lincoln, the Executive Director of the Conflict Resolution, Research, and Resource Institute in Tacoma, Washington. Bill was involved extensively throughout the world in conflict resolution as a trainer and practitioner. I had the honor of serving as part of his small training team in Cuba and during national reconciliation efforts after the civil war in Guatemala.

I also acknowledge three Native leaders with whom I worked closely over long periods of time. I am especially indebted to Pauline Esteves, the longtime leader and ardent chief spokesperson and negotiator for the Timbisha-Shoshone Tribe in Death Valley, California; Jeff Mitchell, a dedicated leader and negotiator since his teenage years for the Klamath Tribes, and an organizer and executive of the Klamath River Intertribal Fish and Water Commission in southern Oregon; and David Lent, prominent leader of the Bishop Paiute Tribe and Owens Valley tribes on the eastern Sierra Mountain Range in California. During his career, he found time to serve as IDRS's Board Chair, Executive Director, and staff mediator in the 1980s. These remarkable leaders have had in common during their lifetime a steadfast commitment to be on the front lines and lead the fight for their community's recognition and rights to self-determination. Despite facing from time to time both external and internal opposition, these three leaders persisted with patience and ultimately prevailed in making significant and transformational improvements in the quality of their members' lives.

I also want to thank Mark Thompson, the current IDRS Executive Director, with whom I have worked side by side for the past eighteen years. Everyone familiar with Mark's work habits knows that he has a boundless commitment to the purpose and mission of Indian Dispute Resolution Services, to long hours and hard work, and to the well-being of the Native nations we have had the honor of serving for the past thirty-plus years.

Finally, this tribute would not be complete without mentioning the fine people I have had the pleasure of working with at the University of Oklahoma Press in preparing my book for publication. Alessandra Jacobi Tamulevich, Senior Acquisitions Editor, accepted my book proposal; arranged for two outside reviewers (anonymous), who gave it a welcomed thumbs up; and helped to promote the manuscript among the major decision makers at the Press. Steven Baker, Managing Editor, worked closely with me and freelance copyeditor Bob Land to prepare the book for final publication and was always helpful and respectful in guiding me and gently answering my questions.

Thank you to all the above and many others too numerous to mention. Thanks to the University of Oklahoma Press, we now have a book available to the public that shares real-life examples and important lessons we have learned about how negotiators can improve the balance of power and can best structure and manage the negotiation process to advance and protect their interests.

INTRODUCTION

When Indian Dispute Resolution Services (IDRS) was first being organized in 1989, the executive director (ED) had a conversation with a group of Native leaders about the plans under way to start a national organization and program that would train and assist tribes to be more effective in resolving conflict. The ED spoke about internal conflicts and conflicts with outside entities in the private and public sectors that were undermining Native Nations' efforts to successfully pursue their community and economic development goals.

There was unanimous agreement among the leaders in attendance that conflict in Indian Country was a huge problem and something had to be done. Unresolved conflict was standing in the way of progress. But when the ED suggested that negotiation and mediation be the strategies that tribal government use to resolve conflict, one gentleman spoke up: "Excuse me, you don't understand, we are dealing with 'life and death' matters. We cannot afford to give an inch more."

It became clear that he and others associated negotiation and mediation with "compromise," as in "splitting the difference." They believed that the moment they agreed to enter the negotiation process they would be having to give up something of significance. After more discussion, it became clear that, aside from educating people about the ins and outs of the negotiation process (and that negotiation is not about compromise), an important challenge our new organization would have to overcome is persuading the disputing parties to enter the negotiation process. This in itself would be part of the "negotiation," and not all parties would be immediately ready and willing to do that.

Since those early days, we found that parties involved in internal and external conflicts may resist participating in negotiation for a number of different reasons.

A Selected Sample of Internal and External Conflicts

Timbisha Shoshone Tribal Council election conflict. One common internal conflict that Native communities including the Timbisha Shoshone and many others have grappled with revolves around their tribal council elections. Tribal constitutions typically concentrate all power over legislative, executive, and judicial functions in one small elected Tribal Council. As a result, the council members are able to exercise almost complete decision-making authority over every aspect of community life without institutional checks and balances. Because they are for high stakes, giving the winners almost total control, tribal council elections are highly competitive and carefully scrutinized, and the results will often be challenged by the defeated candidates. With no neutral tribal institution to appeal its concerns to, the disgruntled parties often take things into their own hands by conducting their own election, and insisting that its winning candidates are the only legitimate tribal government.

How is this dispute between two allegedly legitimate councils resolved? In the case of the Timbisha Shoshone Tribe, the conflicting factions turned for resolution to the federal Bureau of Indian Affairs' (BIA) internal appeal process. Under this appeal process, the BIA investigates and then makes a win-or-lose decision on behalf of the tribe. Tribes that appeal through this adjudication process typically discover that it can often take two to three years to wind through the system when the losing party, as it often does, appeals the BIA's decision to its Area Office, then to the BIA Regional Office, and then to the Department of Interior's Board of Indian Appeals (IBIA) in Washington, D.C.

The major problem with this approach is that, while tribal members wait for the BIA's final decision, there is a power vacuum with no one clearly in charge. The adversaries then often behave in a number of ways that fan the animosity among community members. This may include padlocking the doors to tribal administrative offices and businesses, moving the official tribal headquarters to a new location, taking possession of or emptying tribal bank accounts, absconding with office equipment and important files, destroying property and committing violence, and so on. Under these circumstances the impediment to negotiations exists as long as the competing factions are waiting on the BIA to resolve their dispute for them and believe that it will decide in their favor. They have little incentive to sit down and negotiate their own agreement.

Winnemucca Tribal Council election dispute. This tribe was engaged in a long and bitter battle over (1) which of two tribal councils vying to be officially recognized was the legitimate tribal government, (2) who were legitimate tribal members, and (3) who were the legitimate tribal judges.

The IDRS executive director received a request to serve as a pro tem judge to hear the case. He agreed provided that he would first have the opportunity to try and persuade the tribal factions to sit down together and attempt to reach a negotiated agreement, with him serving as the mediator. He suggested that the three issues in contention would be best resolved by the members themselves and not by some outside authority. He also believed that whatever decision the pro tem judge made would be appealed by the losing party, and that there would likely be no end to the appeals.

Both factions refused to enter mediated negotiation. The impediment was that both parties believed that they had such a strong case that they would win in adjudication and therefore did not need any agreement from the other side. They bet on the win/lose approach. The trial lasted more than six months, an extensive ruling was issued, it was immediately appealed, and that decision too was appealed. The conflict was not resolved for many years, during which time the tribe was at a standstill, major decisions were delayed, and tragically one leader was shot and killed.

The Wilton Miwok Tribal Negotiation to settle internal factional dispute. In 1958, when the U.S. Rancheria Act stripped numerous tribes of their federally recognized status, the Wilton Miwok Rancheria was among them. This congressional act was rescinded in 1970, and most tribes that had lost their federal recognition throughout the country were reinstated. However, the Wilton Miwok Rancheria was left out. This meant that it would continue to have no federal recognition, with no land of its own and no federal resources to support tribal programs and services for their people.

In 2000, the tribe was contacted by the BIA and offered an opportunity to be part of a group of terminated tribes that would be included in a tribal restoration bill being submitted in the U.S. Congress. The condition they were asked to meet in order to be included in the pending legislation was that they had to come in "undivided." For the Wilton Miwok, this meant negotiating an agreement that would resolve a conflict between two major factions that had been brewing for the previous ten years—over the tribal name—criteria for tribal membership, and the structure of their tribal government.

In this case, the BIA declined to get involved in the tribe's internal dispute and instead recommended and paid for mediation services. This decision plus the additional motivator, the lure of federal recognition and restoration, persuaded the two factions to agree to enter negotiations with one another using two mediators from IDRS to help them negotiate. After five full days of emotional sessions they reached a negotiated agreement that resolved all the outstanding issues and qualified them to be among the other tribes that were included in the congressional legislation.

Unfortunately, the bill never passed in Congress and it was not until 2009 that the tribe was officially restored and given back federal recognition. Nonetheless, the negotiated agreement the factions reached in 2001 was lasting and became the authority they relied on to live in relative harmony for many years thereafter.

Torres Martinez dispute over toxic dumping on tribal lands. There was a bitter dispute within this tribe between a faction that was contracting with outside companies that were paying some tribal members huge amounts of money to dump and remediate toxic soil from former gas stations on their assigned parcels of land. Other members were strongly opposed and brought in representatives from established non-Indian environmental organizations (e.g., Greenpeace) and freelance protesters to help tribal members stop these activities. Picketing on county roads to block access to and prevent dump trucks from entering reservation land, physical altercations, law enforcement involvement, and full coverage by the not-so-friendly media all took place.

In the middle of this confrontation a scheduled biannual tribal council election was to take place. The tribal chair was apprehensive based on a history of past contested elections that had left the community without an agreed-upon government that had the authority to maintain law and order. She requested that IDRS, as an impartial third party, administer the election on behalf of the tribe.

In order to avoid allegations by the losing faction after the election that it was fraudulent and unfair, IDRS mediators brought together representatives from the main factions before the elections to negotiate an election process that would be acceptable to both: "The Torres Martinez Tribal Elections Procedures Agreement." All the members involved in the negotiations placed their signatures on the negotiated document. Then IDRS election administrators conducted the election in full compliance with the agreed-upon procedures. People from all sides were allowed to be present to monitor the process and observe the vote count. No candidate appealed the election afterward, and without precedent, the losing candidates formally thanked the chair in public for having made sure that the election process was implemented with "transparency and fairness." The chair claimed that these elections negotiations set the precedent for successful negotiations that eventually resolved the toxic dumping dispute.

Fort Independence tribal elections dispute. The tribe had two main factions that claimed to be the legitimate tribal government. When they appealed to the BIA to determine which faction was to be recognized as the legitimate governing authority, the Central California Area BIA Office once again responded in an unpredictable fashion. It informed the factions that the federal government could no longer have a government-to-government relationship with the tribe because it was not clear who the legitimate tribal government really was. It suggested that the factions commission the services of a mediator to help them negotiate an agreement among themselves.

The tribe agreed to bring in two IDRS mediators who over five consecutive days mediated between two five-member negotiation teams. They reached a comprehensive written agreement that included creating one tribal council that would give equal representation to both factions. This agreement was taken back to the entire membership for ratification. Twelve years later, the tribe was back in contact with IDRS with another issue, whereupon IDRS learned that all the provisions of their negotiated agreement were still being honored and had been used as the authority to settle most every subsequent disagreement over these years.

During these negotiations another potential impediment to the parties being willing to negotiate emerged and was sidestepped. Three days before the mediation was scheduled to begin, IDRS mediators were contacted by the chairman of one of the factions who informed them that he would not be participating. It became clear that he was afraid to participate in the negotiations because he did not feel safe from insults and abuse from the chairman of the other faction. Once the mediators told the resistant chairman that the parties would start by negotiating some rules of engagement that the mediators would help enforce, and he was asked what rules he would propose be included, he agreed to participate.

Owens Valley Indian Water Commission v. Los Angeles Department of Water and Power (DWP). The Owens Valley Tribal Water Commission consists of representatives from five tribes, situated in the Owens Valley watershed at the base of the Eastern Sierra Mountain Range. Over the years since the 1930s, these Native nations had been illegally stripped of hundreds of thousands of acre feet of water by the Los Angeles Department of Water, which diverted and channeled the tribes' water hundreds of miles south to support the growing population in the Los Angeles Basin. The tribes' lawyers from California Indian Legal Services (CILS) had been in litigation for eleven years and had sought over $300 million of relief from DWP. Finally, anticipating being on the losing end, DWP offered to sit down with the tribes to try and reach a negotiated agreement.

Despite this new opportunity to finally negotiate an agreement with the DWP a long-standing personality dispute with the primary leader of one of the five tribes became the impediment to pursuing the matter further. Two of the tribes refused to include him and his tribe on the Tribal Commission's negotiation team. Subsequently, the DWP indicated it was not willing to negotiate with only a portion of the tribes at the table. The negotiations never began, and the court case was dropped without any settlement or payment for damages. A procedural agreement could not be reached because of the tribes' inability to agree on the composition of its negotiation team and meet DWP's request that all five tribes be involved at the same time.

In 1995, the Department of Interior formed a federal water rights negotiation team to fashion an agreement with the DWP without the tribes playing a significant role in the negotiations. Ultimately the tribes refused to ratify what was referred to as the 1997 Principles of Agreement because the department declined to address numerous questions and concerns the tribes had about the proposed settlement, and it also lacked the usual benefits found in water settlements. With the tribes' refusal to ratify, the federal government withdrew its support, dissolved its negotiation team, and negotiations once again came to a standstill.

The Fort Independence Tribe v. State of California Department of Transportation (Caltrans). The agency and the tribe were in a disagreement over how a particular tribal economic development project would interface with a state highway (Highway 395) adjoining the reservation. Discussions had already bogged down when IDRS was contacted by a Caltrans official with the request that it make contact with the tribe and explore the possibility of initiating mediated negotiations. When contacted by IDRS the tribal representatives indicated that IDRS should work through the tribe's legal counsel. The tribe's attorney then indicated that the tribe would not participate in negotiations and accused IDRS of secretly working for the agency. He indicated that he would on behalf of the tribe pursue litigation and under the pressure of a lawsuit compel the agency to agree to the tribe's demands. In this case, the impediment to the tribal leadership entering government-to-government negotiations with the agency was presumably the tribe's choice to rely on its attorney to do its bidding for it rather than getting directly involved in the resolution process.

Four Eastern Sierra tribes and the China Lake Naval Air Weapons Station (NAWS) negotiation. These four tribes had been interested for many years in resolving a conflict with the NAWS over its management of the Coso Hot Springs, which was located on the naval base. These hot springs had been traditionally used for hundreds and perhaps thousands of years for health and spiritual purposes by Native people coming from a large area in eastern California and western Nevada. The conditions of the hot springs had deteriorated, which some believed was in part due to the existence of a geothermal plant adjoining the hot springs and other navy practices and policies. Under the existing conditions, traditional use of the hot springs by the Native people was no longer possible.

For many years, the tribes had been frustrated by the Department of the Navy's lack of cooperation and its unresponsiveness. The tribes wanted to discuss, in the context of a government-to-government negotiation, the causes, possible remedies, and responsibilities for reversing the deteriorated conditions, and to discuss prevention and mitigation measures as well as the existing restrictions on their access and use. They wanted to negotiate a memorandum of understanding (MOU) that would resolve these and other related issues. Because the Coso Hot Springs had been designated as a Cultural and Historic Preservation Site, the State Historic Preservation Office (SHPO) and the Advisory Council on Historic Preservation (Washington, D.C.) had been contacted by the tribes and were involved in resolution efforts.

The U.S. Institute of Environmental Conflict Resolution contacted IDRS to inform it that the four tribes had requested an IDRS mediator to assist them and the navy to negotiate an agreement that would resolve the outstanding issues. After reviewing the credentials and track record of the designated IDRS mediator, the navy agreed to participate. IDRS entered a contract with the U.S. Institute. Over the next six months in four separate all-day mediation sessions, an MOU was successfully negotiated to the mutual satisfaction of all the parties. There was no impediment to the tribes' willingness to use mediation because many of the tribal leaders were already familiar with the disciplines of negotiation and mediation and had participated at one time or another in IDRS training and as beneficiaries of its dispute resolution services program.

The Klamath Tribes–Winema National Forest negotiations, and the Timbisha Shoshone Tribe versus a team of four federal agencies. Both of these were large-scale government-to-government negotiations that required multiple years to work through. We deal with these two major conflicts extensively in chapters 6 and 7, and use them to take a close look at the full sequence of steps tribal negotiators can follow to overcome typical impediments and launch successful win/win negotiations with the federal government.

Indian Dispute Resolution Service (IDRS)

This book has been prepared by Steven Haberfeld, Ph.D., the associate director of conflict resolution services and senior negotiator/mediator at Indian Dispute Resolution Service (IDRS). He is one of the organization's founders and has been integrally involved in designing and delivering the program since the organization's founding in 1989.

IDRS is a national Native-governed nonprofit corporation that has been working in Indian Country for the past thirty years. It provides a comprehensive leadership training program and direct services in conflict resolution to Indian tribes, government agencies, and others throughout the lower forty-eight states and Alaska. It is led by a board of directors that has been made up of prominent Indian leaders from throughout the United States.

IDRS has two areas of emphasis. First, it works to increase leaders' skills in resolving conflicts within their own communities. It has trained over twenty-five hundred elected leaders, staff, community members, and government officials in cross-cultural communication, negotiation, and mediation. This includes training and certifying professional mediators. It has also provided direct services to tribal governments, Native organizations, and government agencies in mediation, arbitration, fact-finding, election administration, and negotiation coaching.

IDRS also trains and coaches Native leaders to be more effective in their transactions with external entities in the public and private sectors. It has worked closely with Indian leaders who have been at the forefront of efforts to negotiate agreements with these entities. IDRS has addressed issues including reacquiring tribes' ancestral lands, securing Native Peoples' historical water rights, protecting and accessing tribes' cultural resources and sacred sites, managing and restoring the health of natural resources on federal lands, developing protocols for negotiations between states and tribal governments, working with public school districts and tribal communities to improve the quality of educational services for their Native students, and more.

Outline of the Book

We begin the first chapter with a description of negotiation as a distinct form of conflict resolution and contrast it with twelve other forms of dispute resolution used in societies today. We then focus on the important differences between "collaborative" and "adversarial" forms of dispute resolution. In this section, we also take an in-depth look at the concept of "win/win" negotiations.

Chapter 2 describes aspects of the traditional Native approach to negotiation. We focus on five specific principles and practices commonly embraced by Native communities in North America prior to European conquest and federal government domination and interference. These principles and practices are extremely relevant today and are foundational elements in the methodology we propose.

The third chapter of the book addresses the question of how to negotiate. We offer a methodology that is a blend of traditional Native practices; some principles and practices promoted by interest-based negotiations (IBN), a negotiation method encouraged in non-Indian society; and additional practical lessons that we have learned during working in the field of conflict resolution in Indian Country during the past thirty years. We finish this chapter with a summary outline of a sequence of six stages of the negotiation process that negotiators can follow.

Chapter 4 presents the concept of the "three satisfactions." It examines in-depth how to design and implement a negotiation process that creates satisfaction among the negotiators on three different dimensions: procedural, substantive, and relational.

Chapter 5 focuses on how Native Nations that are engaged in complex government-to-government negotiations can overcome the structural and cultural challenges presented by remote multilayered bureaucratic agencies that typically do not have a great record dealing in good faith with Native communities.

Chapter 6 discusses strategies that tribal negotiation teams can use to maximize their leverage and improve the balance of power when negotiating with outside agencies. This subject of generating and using power in negotiation has rarely been addressed on a systematic basis. Two strategies are elaborated: using Indian tribes' special legal and historical rights as separate sovereign entities to leverage the treatment to which Native nations are legally entitled. Also discussed are complementary political strategies that take the negotiation out from behind closed doors and into the public sphere. A wide range of direct actions are identified that can be used to educate and influence public opinion to weigh in behind the tribe. Real-life examples appear throughout the narrative.

Chapter 7 presents a case study of the precedent-setting government-to-government negotiation between the Timbisha Shoshone Tribe in Death Valley, California, and a federal team of four agencies (the National Park Service, the Bureau of Land Management, the Bureau of Reclamation, and the Bureau of Indian Affairs). IDRS helped to shepherd the tribe and the federal government team through a lengthy process that began as a very contentious and bitter confrontation and ended in a win/win agreement. This resulted in congressional legislation that restored part of the tribe's ancestral land base, established a permanent homeland, and defined water rights and economic development opportunities for the Timbisha people.

In three appendixes, we address the need to develop intercultural communication skills in order to be effective negotiators. Emphasis is on improving both proactive listening and constructive speaking skills. Numerous exercises are provided.

1

NEGOTIATION AS A STRATEGY FOR CONFLICT RESOLUTION

Conflict exists in every social setting. It cannot be eliminated entirely. At best, we can learn how to minimize, contain, and better manage conflict to reduce its negative impact and to maximize its potential benefits. Because of the prevalence of conflict in our lives, it should not be surprising that all social systems have devised a number of ways to deal with it.

While the negotiation process is the central focus of this book, it is just one of a number of different approaches to conflict resolution that parties throughout the world choose to address their differences. The strategies they adopt and when they adopt them depend on what they regard as acceptable practice in their communities as well as on their own assessment of what is possible and what they believe will work to their greatest benefit.

A Typology of Conflict Resolution Strategies

In the following discussion we offer a typology of the different approaches people use throughout the world to try to resolve a conflict in a fashion most favorable to them—that is, strategies by which they successfully get the changes they want. The approaches are listed in order ranging from the mildest presentation of their case to the most violent, aggressive, and disruptive form of making their issues prominent.

Ignoring the Conflict

A party consciously or subconsciously refuses or fails to acknowledge the conflict. The problem is walked around and not spoken about.

Non-engagement

In this case, a party to a conflict acknowledges the conflict but consciously decides not to engage in trying to resolve it. As a strategic move, a party may decide to unilaterally walk away—for example, through divorce, resignation, retirement, or suicide. Alternatively, a party may want to try and resolve it but as a strategy decides to wait and prepare for a better moment (e.g., when things are much calmer, or when "all its ducks are in a row").

Conciliatory Gestures

These gestures consist of an initiative taken by one side on its own in the interest of improving a situation. Conciliatory gestures can include substantive unilateral concessions, apologies, gifts, prayers, honoring ceremonies, and so on. Some unilateral activities can also be intended to make oneself more acceptable to the other party (e.g., counseling, therapy, cosmetic surgery, or a personal makeover).

Negotiation

Negotiating is the process by which disputants seek to resolve their differences through direct, face-to-face discussions. It is a process in which the parties try to work things out by talking things through. Negotiation requires that both parties acknowledge their interdependence and realize that neither party can prevail unilaterally. The problem will not go away without both parties addressing it together and finding a way of resolving their differences.

Mediation

This process is essentially an extension of the negotiation process. The disputants bring an impartial third party into their deliberations (the mediator or facilitator) because negotiations between them have reached an impasse. The third party brought in is known to have expertise in helping parties negotiate and resolve their differences. The prototype mediator does not have the authority from the parties to either make recommendations or impose solutions. The mediator's role is to help the parties negotiate their own agreement.

Peacemaking

Peacemaking is the traditional approach to dispute resolution. It relies on the skills, judgments, and decisions of elders and other persons who are highly respected within a given culture. Peacemakers prefer that the parties reach agreement through negotiation. However, the peacemaker may recommend that the parties resolve the matter in a certain way. His suggestions are generally authoritative and upheld by virtue of his standing in the community and by virtue of a consensus on what are acceptable values, norms, and behavior in that community. The peacemaker is impartial with respect to the disputants, but exercises more authority than a mediator. The peacemaker is committed to restoring harmony and what is in the interest of the whole community.[1]

Today, many Native nations are working to restore traditional peacemaking processes in their institutions, programs, and communities. They intend to resurrect traditional cultural values and emphasize harmony and healing instead of division and punishment. The restorative justice model is intended to replace the adversarial, adjudicative, win/lose, punishment-oriented model of conflict resolution. The Navajo Nation's Peacemakers Program may be one of the best known and comprehensive.

Arbitration

This is a quasi-judicial win/lose process used to determine right and wrong, or guilt and innocence. It is characterized by a semiformal hearing process in which parties present evidence to an arbitrator who acts in the capacity of a judge. Parties can represent themselves or have counsel represent them. In arbitration, the parties select the arbitrator by mutual agreement, distinguishing it from litigation in which a court's administrative section assigns a judge. The parties sign an arbitration agreement that spells out the issues to be decided and the range of possible solutions, and authorizes the arbitrator to hear the case and rule within these parameters. The rules of evidence are less stringent in arbitration than in litigation. For example, an arbitrator can consider hearsay evidence that would be inadmissible in a court of law. Arbitration is typically quicker and cheaper than litigation and is therefore often written in as the designated dispute resolution process in many insurance policies, commercial agreements, and employee grievance policies and procedures.

"Med-Arb" (Mediation-Arbitration)

In this process, an impartial third party starts with an "Agreement to Arbitrate" that the disputing parties sign. However, before conducting a formal hearing, the med-arb functions first in the role of a mediator, assisting and facilitating the communication and negotiation between the parties. If the parties fail to reach a mediated agreement, then the mediator switches hats and begins the process of arbitration. At this point, the arbitrator conducts a formal hearing—receiving evidence and testimony from the parties, accepting the testimony of witnesses, and rendering a decision that may or may not be binding, depending on the degree of authority the parties have given to the arbitrator beforehand.

The med-arb form has the benefit of motivating the parties to craft their own solution to the conflict. They know that if they are unable to come to an agreement, the arbitrator will immediately step in and impose a ruling, and they are not sure what ruling she will come up with and how favorable it will be to them. In mediation the parties still are in charge of the solution.

The med-arb form is not used very often because the constraints on the mediator's and arbitrator's roles are so different. This makes it difficult to transition from the role of mediator to arbitrator if the mediation effort fails to produce an agreement. For example, a mediator who is trying to bring the parties together can initiate private conversations with each party freely outside the presence of the other party. In contrast, the arbitrator is prevented from holding separate (ex-partite) conversations with the parties. But what happens when the mediator/arbitrator has already spoken separately to the parties at the point he puts on the arbitrator's hat? In addition, on his own initiative a mediator pieces together an understanding of the case. In arbitration, as in the case of litigation, the parties make their own case in their testimony. That is not the role of the impartial decider.

Administrative Hearing

In this quasi-judicial process, government agencies hear grievances initiated by the agencies' employees or clients regarding the agencies' performance in implementing statutes, regulations, and policies as part of an agencies' mandate. A typical case may be an employee's allegation that the agency he was working for unfairly terminated him or bypassed him for a promotion. The plaintiff or grievant can choose to be represented by counsel. The hearing officer is assigned by the agency and has the authority to make a ruling. This process produces winners and losers.

Litigation

Litigation is designed to determine which party is "right" or "wrong," "innocent" or "guilty"; then the parties are penalized or rewarded under the law. Lawyers represent the parties in a formal court hearing before a judge or jury, or both. Adhering to strict, preestablished evidentiary rules is required. The parties to the conflict typically do not talk to one another once they have submitted their case to the judicial system. Any negotiation takes place through the attorneys. This process is adversarial and also produces winners and losers.

Direct Action

This process consists of various strategies, undertaken within the law, designed to pressure the opposition by depriving it of crucial resources and support in hopes of inducing it to negotiate and settle the dispute. Ways to engage in direct action include the following:

Deprive the opposition of its workforce. Examples include organizing the employees into unions, work stoppages or slowdowns, and labor strikes.

Deprive the opposition of its market. Examples include appealing to consumers of the adversary's goods and services and launching an economic boycott, engaging in a secondary boycott, and making official complaints with regulators regarding allegedly unsafe products or illegal business practices.

Deprive the opposition of critical support in an election. Examples include getting voters to favor your candidate over an opponent and passing specific ballot initiatives, referenda, or recall petitions. Activities associated with elections consist of developing and circulating campaign materials, raising money, making speeches, staging candidate debates, running paid advertisements, getting endorsements, running door-to-door campaigns, and so on.

Deprive the opposition of favorable public opinion and support for a program or policy. Examples include public demonstrations, picketing or leafleting, writing open letters to the public, speeches, petitions, letters to the editor, printed articles, editorials, talk-show interviews, documentaries, direct mail campaigns, special public hearings and investigations, and coalitions of like-minded interest groups.

Violence against Property

This strategy is designed to damage or destroy property in order to convey to the owners the seriousness and determination of their opposition. This approach is no longer persuasion but rather intimidation and coercion. In addition to the unwanted costs of replacing damaged or destroyed property, these strategies are intended to create an atmosphere of insecurity, fear, and unpredictability, thereby introducing a sense of greater urgency and inducing people to work harder to resolve the conflict. Violence against property may also create the opposite effect and lead to the hardening of positions. Examples include vandalism, sabotaging equipment or products, painting graffiti, setting fires, stealing valued items, and desecrating gravesites or other religious symbols.

Violence against Persons

This coercive strategy is designed to have similar yet greater impact than violence against property and is also designed to create fear of further loss and impress upon the broader public the urgency of the problem. Such violence can take the form of terrorism, intended to appear unpredictable and make everyone feel like a potential victim of indiscriminate violence, with the purpose of inducing people to act more quickly and decisively in giving in to the demands of the perpetrators. Violence against persons can have the opposite effect and harden the other side's resolve to resist. The acts themselves are often hard to forget and forgive. Examples include death threats, blackmail, beatings, torture, rape, kidnapping hostages, beheadings, strategic assassinations, and the indiscriminate murder of innocent civilians.

War

War is characterized by wholesale and systematic aggression against persons and property. Violence, coercion, intimidation, retaliation, and subterfuge may all be part of the encounter, until one side submits or is destroyed.

The forms described above are all dispute resolution strategies. While listed separately, they are often used in conjunction with one another or in various sequences. For example, even though a dispute may ultimately be resolved through face-to-face negotiations (e.g., peace negotiations between adversaries after a war), the effort to resolve the conflict may not always start with negotiations. One party may initially believe that it does not need to concede anything. In this case, the party will only come to the table if the other party, in the course of the confrontation, is able to establish that "winning" without negotiations is unlikely, and the cost of doing nothing to resolve the matter may be greater than the terms of negotiated agreement. A lawsuit or a series of direct actions may precede negotiations, either because the other party has to be convinced that negotiations are necessary, or the party that is engaged in these actions is interested in softening up the other party and convincing it that a certain amount of damage can be done if they do not enter into good-faith negotiations.

Adversarial versus Collaborative Forms of Dispute Resolution

Judicial forms of dispute resolution—litigation, administrative hearings, and arbitration—are referred to as "adversarial" because the parties involved are competing and both are seeking a win for themselves and a loss for their adversary. From the preceding discussion, we know that direct action, limited forms of violence against property and persons, and all-out war are also nonjudicial forms of adversarial dispute resolution.

For our purposes, the focus here is only on the judicial forms of the adversarial approach and on contrasting them with collaborative forms. When selecting which form will serve us best, we need to understand the very important differences between these approaches, and ensure that our behavior is consistent with the form we have chosen.

One of the primary differences between these adversarial and collaborative forms for dispute resolution is the presence or absence of a third-party decider. In negotiation, mediation, and facilitation, no third party makes the decision. Mediators and facilitators help the parties negotiate, but lack the authority to decide. In all three of these collaborative forms, the parties should not see themselves locked in a battle with an adversary but instead as one of the parties trying to persuade the other of the merits of their case and committed to reach an agreement.

A common error among inexperienced negotiators is to bring adversarial behavior into a negotiation. It behooves us to understand the different dynamics of collaborative and adversarial forms of dispute resolution, and why adversarial behavior is counterproductive when negotiating.

Litigation, a common adversarial process in American society, is set up for the two opposing parties to battle it out in court to try to persuade the judge that one party is right and the other party is wrong. The parties are represented by attorneys who advocate on their behalf, unless they have chosen to represent themselves, which is discouraged.

The attorneys follow the classic educational methodology as they present their case to the judge and jury. They declare in their opening statements what they are about to prove, what facts they intend to establish, and what evidence they will provide in the process. They then put on their case, bringing forward witnesses and documents to support their assertions. While presenting their case to the judge, attorneys are logical, polite, respectful, and cooperative. They are not about to do or say anything that would alienate the judge, who is the ultimate decider.

At the same time they are educating the judge about their cases, the adversaries challenge the case that the opposing attorney is presenting. Behavior toward the lawyer representing the other side is nothing like the one they display with the judge whom they are trying to convince, influence, and persuade. Opposing lawyers are argumentative, often rude, intimidating, insinuating, and accusatory. They are likely to be full of surprises, trying to knock their opponent off balance, and they are not above trying to make their adversary look bad in order to look good themselves. By design, their entire strategy is to question and discredit their adversary's case by creating doubt, uncertainty, and incredulity. To state the obvious, this behavior is not designed to create a good, long-term, trusting relationship with the other party, nor ultimately to reach a mutually acceptable agreement.

But in litigation, the ultimate goal is for the judge to issue a ruling. In the courtroom the adversarial behavior between the litigants' attorneys is regarded as "vigorous advocacy" and a proper and essential part of the competitive game plan. The third-party decider (judge, arbitrator, hearing officer, referee, etc.) steps in after both adversaries have presented their best case for winning, and his job is to review the testimony and other evidence presented, determine the facts, distill the truth, and make the final decision about who wins and loses.

So, what type of behavior is most conducive to reaching an agreement in a negotiation? Should it resemble the adversarial behavior exhibited by attorneys in the battle against one another in a courtroom, or the strategy that the attorney uses to educate and influence the judge and jury? The answer is the latter. In negotiation, the parties need to be cooperative, polite, respectful, and responsive. They have to educate and influence, convince and persuade one another. The negotiators have to share information and not play the game of hiding the ball. Moreover, not only are negotiators having to persuade the other party of the merits of their proposals, but they must make a simultaneous effort to understand the interests as well as the constraints of the other side and what it will take to satisfy them. As a general rule, experienced negotiators are soft on people while hard on problems.

Before leaving this subject, we should try to understand why, even though it is neither logical nor helpful for the negotiator to act in an adversarial manner, that behavior is often what the inexperienced bring with them into negotiations. Parties in conflict are often angry and feel justified in their stance. They may feel that they were taken advantage of and abused. In the heat of battle, things were likely said that questioned the person's integrity and were hurtful. Real harm may have been done that is difficult to forget and forgive. The parties then are ready to continue to do battle and get even. But when negotiating, these feelings have to be set aside or overcome if the negotiation is to be successful.

Reaching an agreement will likely be difficult if the parties' behavior is only competitive and dismissive of the other's interests and needs. Being overtly or covertly hostile and disrespectful is also counterproductive. Even if a party feels that her personal attacks on the other party are valid, true, deserving, and therefore justified—and getting this off her chest makes her feel better—this behavior will not move the process any closer to an agreement. Instead, it will likely doom the effort to fail. In the final analysis, participating in negotiations is voluntary, and parties can withdraw whenever they feel that it is not serving them. Each party has to ultimately perceive that it is gaining something of value before it will be willing to remain engaged and in the end reach across the table, shake hands, and enter into an agreement.

The remaining chapters of the book take into consideration the potential combative nature of the parties as they initially enter the negotiation process. We offer a methodology that can be used to turn this approach around, defuse the conflict, and create a context that begins to establish the type of cooperation and collaboration upon which a negotiated agreement can be reached.

Mediation versus Arbitration

On the surface, "arbitration" and "mediation" sound similar. Indeed, in both cases, the disputing parties voluntarily choose an impartial mediator or arbitrator to hear both sides' cases—but the similarity ends there. Since some people mistakenly use the terms interchangeably, clarifying the differences at the outset is important.

Mediators help parties probe the causes and conditions of the conflict—and the interests and values of the disputants—identify issues, and explore alternatives for resolution. In contrast, an arbitrator can respond to or address only those issues or questions that the parties have jointly agreed to submit for adjudication. In their arbitration agreement the parties also place a limit on the range of remedies that the arbitrator can consider.

In mediation, the disputants rarely submit evidence or have a witness testify. Such testimony holds little weight where the emphasis is not so much on who is right or wrong as on what the parties can agree to that will work to resolve the dispute. In contrast, arbitration is an adversarial process in which the disputants make their case before the arbitrator by submitting testimony and documents, presenting witnesses, and perhaps being represented by an attorney. Here, winning over the other party is of central concern, and who wins depends on the decision of the third-party decider.

The disputants design the mediation process and establish the procedural ground rules. In contrast, the disputants in arbitration do not participate in developing the procedures or rules of engagement. Standard procedures are set by the arbitrator, or consist of rules established by the American Arbitration Service that the parties stipulate will govern their arbitration process.

In mediation, a mediator can have private confidential meetings—"caucuses"—with each disputing party to try and move them closer to resolution. In contrast, an arbitrator cannot have private meetings with the disputing parties. These conversations have to be in the presence of all parties so that the other party can challenge and try to discredit points it feels will prejudice the judge when making a decision. But in mediation there is no such fear that the mediator will be prejudiced since the mediator does not make the decision. The parties are expected to come up with their own solution, and to do so they need to persuade one another, not a third-party decider.

In addition, adversarial forms of dispute resolution look backward to resolve a past problem by determining who was guilty and who was innocent, who will be penalized and who will be rewarded. In contrast, mediators help parties look forward and come up with an agreement about how they will behave toward one another in the future. In other words, they do not look backward to resolve a past problem but rather forward to what will work better in the future.

In mediation, with the help of the mediator the disputants agree on the procedural ground rules, resolve their substantive differences, and craft their own agreements. In contrast, in arbitration the disputants do not participate in the decision-making process regarding substantive and procedural outcomes. Their role is to answer questions posed by the attorneys and the arbitrator. The disputants are limited to answering questions, offering testimony, and letting the arbitrator decide.

Mediators have no authority to render a decision or make recommendations. In contrast, arbitrators have authority that the disputants—by signing an "Agreement to Arbitrate"—have granted to render a decision.

The primary purpose of mediation is for the parties to reach an agreement between themselves. In contrast, in arbitration the primary purpose is for an arbitrator to resolve a dispute by making a decision.

Mediators are primarily interested in the parties finding common ground and coming up with a mutual gain resolution (win-win outcomes). In contrast, the arbitrator determines right and wrong, innocence and guilt, winners and losers. The arbitrator generally does not care whether his decision satisfies the parties.

The Concept of Win-Win

We have characterized our negotiation methodology as one that is based on win-win principles, ensuring that both the process and the results make winners out of both parties. This concept is not new. As we have pointed out, it resembles "consensus-based decision making" in which the opinions and needs of many different people are taken into consideration and incorporated into the final decision. Traditional Indian and other communities have practiced this for thousands of years.

Today, "win-win" is an expression referred to frequently in everyday speech. But what does it mean, what are its implications, and how do you achieve it in practice? This is a good place to start our analysis of negotiation, given that both the traditional Native approach to conflict resolution and interest-based negotiations (IBN) are premised on the principle of producing agreements that give each party a win.

Win-win negotiators are committed to ensuring that their agreement provides value to both parties. This does not mean that negotiators who practice the win-win method are simply nice people trying out of the goodness of their hearts to make everyone content. While that is a possibility, we want to emphasize that pragmatism rather than altruism is the chief motivator. Win-win negotiators for each side realize that the other party is much more likely to cooperate and be willing to respond in ways that will increase the benefits they are seeking if the other party perceives it is winning also. Both parties get more of what they are seeking through this type of collaboration, and the total number and size of benefits distributed among the parties by the agreement will be greater.

But what happens when negotiators behave differently and are competitive and confrontational—when they are only concerned about getting the most they can without any concern for the other party? Typically, when a party feels that a settlement was imposed or forced by a heavy-handed negotiator, then that party may be tempted not to comply at all, to comply with only part of settlement, or to drag its feet by doing only what is absolutely essential at the last possible moment.

Additionally, if the party is pressured to agree—for example, by public embarrassment, bad press, or economic boycott—an agreement may last only as long as the pressure continues. Once the threat has been removed, the party that agreed under duress will generally revert to its former behavior and the situation will return to the status quo ante. In contrast, when a party who has been persuaded has bought into the logic of the proposition or proposal and understands how it will serve him, he will recognize that, after negotiations are over, it is still in his interest to keep and abide by the agreement.

Similarly, an agreement reached under duress may be difficult to implement. For example, in old-style labor-management negotiations, when employers secure agreements by leveling such threats as terminating employees or cutting their fringe benefit packages—or unions make such threats as going out on strike, staging worker slowdowns, sabotaging equipment, or encouraging consumer boycotts—the parties discover that the fights are really just beginning when it comes time to implement the contract's terms and conditions. Every subsequent decision that has to be made between management and the union becomes a lengthy and unpleasant fight. In these circumstances, there is no amicable and trusting relationship established that the parties can rely on during implementation, when it would be helpful to give the other party some slack or the benefit of the doubt.

When tempted to pursue a win-or-lose strategy to reach a negotiated agreement, the parties need to anticipate the consequences over the long run. What looks like a win over the short run may indeed transform over time into a substantial loss; if the other party came out looking and feeling like a loser, the so-called win may soon disappear. Losers often become preoccupied with trying to get even. Their hostility and sense of incompleteness and unfairness may drive them to become dedicated opponents, rejecting any proposed solution.

This logic also applies in other internal conflicts. Organizations, institutions, and communities in which members are wedded to majority rule and dedicated to win at all cost, by hook or crook, will likely experience perpetual conflict. Winning and being in control become more important than the higher value of what is good for the internal relationships and the health of the entity as a whole. A minority that feels that no forum exists in which to make its interests known and considered generally becomes increasingly angry and resentful—and in the end may rebel.

These battles can be avoided when parties are also committed to a higher good, and to what, in the long run, will benefit the entire entity. Things can only improve when people develop the habit of taking discussions one step further than unilateral decisions or decisions by majority vote. A simple question—"How can we make this work for you too?"—can lead to a win-win agreement that is accepted without future strife and that will endure.

How Does a Party Know It Had a Win?

IBN proponents generally suggest that (1) whether a party has a win is subjective and primarily in the eyes of the beholder, and (2) whether it is a win is determined by the party's assessment of whether her interests were satisfied to an acceptable degree.

Another dimension should be considered as part of this process in order to properly capture the dynamic of the negotiations. A party's subjective assessment of whether he had a win is affected by his expectations. Parties, once they are clear about their interests, assess what appears to them to be realistic and possible within the context of the particular negotiation. In other words, a party typically looks at what he thinks are the realistic opportunities and constraints to determine how much and which of his interests he can expect to satisfy as a result of the negotiation. In the final analysis, he considers the negotiation to be a win to the extent he has come close to fulfilling his expectations.

A Party's Expectations Change as Negotiation Progresses

A party's interests remain the same but expectations are not fixed at any point in the negotiation process until an agreement is signed. At the outset, neither party knows much about how the negotiation process will unfold and what the ultimate outcome will be. Nonetheless, expectations are increasingly clarified and change as the negotiator learns more about the other party and sees how it responds to what is happening during the exchange of information and to the proposals being made and agreed to. The process is dynamic and subject to many changing variables.

A Negotiator's Expectations Become the Standard by Which a Win is Determined

During a negotiation a party goes through at least three phases in determining expectations and what will be an acceptable level of satisfaction.

First, a party must identify and understand its underlying interests with respect to the conflict at hand. This exercise is important because too often people go forward without being clear about their interests. Undefined, their interests will likely not be satisfied because they will not receive the required focus and attention. Moreover, if a party does not adequately identify and understand his interests beforehand, he will lack the criteria for evaluating whether the agreement being reached is satisfactory or not. If he is not anchored well in his own interests, he may strive longer and harder than is necessary or productive.

The first phase of identification is undertaken by the party in isolation, prior to the face-to-face stages of the negotiation. Identification is part of a party's preparation and focuses on its underlying interests and what it wants satisfied in the process of resolving the conflict.

The second phase of the negotiator's assessment of expectations also occurs during the preparation and planning period. She is concerned with what she can reasonably expect to attain, which is based on what she perceives to be the interests of the other side, the overall balance of power between the parties involved in the dispute, her own ability (i.e., resources) to sustain her active participation in the negotiation process, and her perceptions of the resources potentially available for distribution in an agreement. The negotiator acquires this information as she prepares for the negotiations, assessing what might be possible by conducting research, consulting others about their perceptions and information, brainstorming with members of her own side, and so on. What she learns during this investigation and analysis may cause her to modify her earlier strategy by expecting to satisfy fewer, more, or different interests than defined in the first phase.

The third phase of forming expectations occurs during active face-to-face negotiations. At this point, the expectations the party had coming into the negotiations are refined further based on firsthand information gained during discussions across the table. Information is shared, statements are offered, and questions are posed and answered by both sides.

Managing Expectations

When parties actually sit down face-to-face, they usually try to manage (i.e., lower) the expectations of the other side. A negotiator tries to limit the other side's expectations to discourage him from anticipating too much and then being disappointed that he did not receive all to which he felt entitled. A good negotiator wants to keep the other party as happy as possible so that it will be cooperative and accommodating. Moreover, if the negotiator is going to give something up, he wants to get maximum credit for his gesture rather than have its importance minimized because it was expected anyway. He would rather lower the other party's expectations and then, with a generous gesture and some fanfare, exceed the other party's expectations. If our understanding of human nature is correct, getting more than you expected is usually valued more highly than getting what you expected.

Negotiators have real constraints and need to convey them to the other party. Statements like the following are meant to lower expectations:

"We have limited resources."
"It has been a bad year for the business."
"We did not get the grants we hoped we would."
"We do not have, under the agency's enabling legislation, the authority to negotiate that."
"Recent court decisions tie our hands."

"You would have to get all the people with leasehold interests to agree to that."

"You are asking for too much."

A word of caution, however: these messages are not to be taken wholly at face value by the other side. A negotiator wants to hone her perceptive abilities and conduct research into how valid and reliable these statements are, and how they can be challenged, overcome, or circumvented. She will ask the other side for data and data sources to support its contentions. She will do research on her own by searching the internet and other sources of information.

Managing the Other Party's Expectations

It is especially important for an Indian nation to manage the expectations of the other party, particularly when engaged in government-to-government negotiations. Nothing may be more important from the beginning than to have the other party take you, your interests, and your issues seriously. Historically, this has not been easy for Indian tribes when dealing with external public and private entities, especially government agencies at the federal, state, and local levels. These entities usually have been tone deaf and accustomed to doing things their way without taking the interests of Indian Tribes into consideration during decision making.

The way to manage a government agency's expectations is to convince the agency representatives that it is in their interest not to trifle with you but rather to sit down and negotiate in good faith. There are approaches you can use to convey to them that they will lose more by being uncooperative and disagreeable than if they make themselves available and earnestly work things out by talking things through. We discuss in a later chapter some possible sources of negotiating power that Native nations have by virtue of being sovereign government entities.

Challenging the Other Party's Efforts
to Manage Your Expectations

The following example helps to illustrate the interplay between interests and expectations. The Timbisha Shoshone Tribe had been living in Death Valley, California, for hundreds, perhaps thousands of years. In 1933 it was displaced when the federal government established the

Death Valley National Monument and ignored the presence of the tribe. In 1994 the tribe finally got a chance to redress its grievances when it entered negotiations with a team of four federal agencies: the National Park Service (NPS), the Bureau of Land Management (BLM), the Bureau of Indian Affairs (BIA), and the Bureau of Reclamation (BOR). The tribe's major objective was to secure a permanent and recognized right to establish residential communities in the heart of its ancestral lands, in an area the NPS controlled. Such an outcome would satisfy multiple tribal interests: among them, a sense of equity after over sixty-five years of neglect and opposition, formal recognition as a legitimate entity with historical rights to the land, and the security of having a place to build a home and community and raise a family.

When the tribe entered these government-to-government negotiations, the NPS, the lead agency on the federal negotiation team, maintained that there was not enough water in the park to sustain another residential settlement on the land. The tribe's expectations of finally getting a tribal homeland were being managed—lowered—by the NPS. However, several members of the tribe's negotiation team had a conversation with an NPS hydrologist that altered the picture the agency was painting. He revealed that the Furnace Creek Hotel in the park drained and replenished the water in its swimming pool three times a day to compensate for the fact that it did not have a modern filtering system—a waste of hundreds of thousands of gallons of water each day. After the tribe shared this revelation with the federal negotiation team, the so-called shortage of water was never again raised as a reason for rejecting the tribe's proposal for a homeland in Death Valley National Park. Congress finally granted the tribe their lands together with water rights when it passed the Timbisha Tribal Homeland Act in 2000.

Knowing When You've Won

In the end, each party must decide and define for itself what is acceptable and therefore alone know whether it has a win. Clarity about one's interests and expectations put the negotiator in the best possible position to truly know how to answer this question.

Win-win may not always translate into a big win for both parties. In the discussion above, we suggested that, in addition to interests, expectations factor into the equation. It is more realistic to say that not every party can expect a big win. Because there may be a significant power imbalance between the parties, a difference in the amount of resources to sustain involvement during the negotiations, or a real constraint limiting one party's ability to satisfy the other party's interest, there will be situations in which a party may only be able to expect a small win. On the other hand, the negotiator may secure a loss that is less than what he initially expected, which is a "win" of a different sort.

2

TRADITIONAL NATIVE APPROACHES TO NEGOTIATION AND THE FIELD OF DISPUTE RESOLUTION

Chapter 1 provided general observations about the negotiation process. We offered a typology of different forms of dispute resolution, outlined the essential differences between collaborative and adversarial forms of conflict resolution, and expounded on the concept of win-win.

In this chapter we shift directions and focus on "how to" questions, providing tools for practitioners that can enhance their effectiveness when engaging in the negotiation process. We describe five conflict resolution principles or practices that traditional Native nations commonly followed many generations ago, before their ways of life were severely disrupted by the European onslaught. These aspects of the traditional approach are foundational elements incorporated in our recommended methodology.

Then we describe additional negotiation principles and practices that are integral components of our methodology and are based on interest-based negotiations (IBN) that are popular in non-Indian society. These principles and practices are consistent with the traditional approach to nonadversarial consensus building, where the parties talk until they have discovered common ground and can reach agreement.

Finally we present a summary outline of six stages of the negotiation process, offering a brief reminder of where to begin and where to end, and the steps that should be taken to keep things on track and move the parties forward toward resolution.

Native communities followed a common peacemaking approach many generations ago, before the European invasion. While today this approach is not generally in common use, it disappeared not because it was irrelevant but because most traditional Native American social systems and institutions were destroyed by the foreign forces, and then replaced with so-called Western democratic institutions and practices by the U.S. federal government.

Indian Dispute Resolution Services (IDRS) has identified five Native peacemaking principles that we have incorporated as foundational elements into our negotiation methodology. The underlying reasons for including them is, first, they still work effectively in minimizing, managing, and resolving conflict. Second, these principles still resonate today among Native people, particularly in those communities that are currently interested in reforming their constitutions and institutions to more closely reflect authentic Native cultural values and principles. The five principles are as follows.

Consensus-Based Decision Making

Building and sustaining consensus was the way most traditional Native societies in North America made decisions. Today, when "consensus building" is defined, it is often operationalized as requiring that it meet the following conditions: (a) everyone in a group is actively involved in making the decision, (b) the group searches for a decision that everyone can agree with, and (c) while everyone may not embrace the decision with equal fervor, they all agree they can go along with it and support it. In the true sense of the concept, everyone walks away with a win.[1]

The IDRS's leadership training program favors consensus-based decision making over a reliance on majority rule. Decisions by consensus encourage people to take the interests and opinions of a broad range of people into consideration before a decision is reached. In contrast, decisions by majority rule stop short of trying to satisfy minority interests when the majority perceives that it has enough political support to win. While majority rule may be a quicker process than finding consensus, majority rule actually results in a certain segment of the people being left out of both the process and the solution. Majority rule creates winners and losers, which can undermine the cohesion and solidarity of the group and eventually inhibit participation in the political process, especially when the minority consistently finds itself on the losing side. Then it is common that the losing party becomes determined to "get even." The relationship can become increasingly adversarial, and the conflict is perpetuated rather than resolved.

Decisions by consensus are inclusive, giving everyone an ongoing stake in the problem-solving process and the results. Genuine consensus is built when even the group's majority, which could otherwise determine the outcome alone, takes the extra step of agreeing to a solution that also satisfies the needs of the minority. As a rule, parties that have participated in making the decision are much more likely to abide by the decision reached than if it had been imposed on them—even if the decision is not wholly to their liking.

Despite the fact that traditional societies made decisions by consensus many generations ago, today we find very few Native organizations using consensus decision making as the preferred approach. The most common reason given for not using consensus is that it takes too long to get everyone on board. In the interest of efficiency, organizations just take a vote and go with the majority will. Reliance on majority rule is promoted in *Robert's Rules of Order*, which spells out a series of procedural ground rules that most organizations in American society adhere to today.[2]

Majority rule was formally introduced into Indian Country in 1934 when the federal government urged tribes to use a uniform template for governing themselves under the Indian Reorganization Act (IRA). Since then, many tribal communities have experienced serious internal conflict, resulting in deep cleavages within the body politic, and in unresolved anger, frustration, and stalemate among their members. We can speculate that, while there are many other factors, this result partly comes from a foreign system of self-government that was adopted and sometimes imposed from outside, and because old tools such as decisions by consensus that had worked for thousands of years were abandoned.[3]

Treating Others with Dignity, Respect, and Honor

At one time, before tribal societies were severely disrupted by the European onslaught, there was widespread consensus among people in traditional societies about common values, acceptable norms of behavior, and the need to enforce them.[4] It was generally understood that physical contact, verbal assaults, personal attacks, interrupting others, lying, bullying, intimidation, bluffing, and so on were not socially acceptable ways of relating to another tribal member. While for understandable reasons these practices are less prevalent today in many communities, they are nonetheless still regarded in Indian Country as reflecting important values and essential to maintaining internal harmony and balance and resolving differences.

Today, there is not the same degree of conformity with the traditional norms of behavior because Indian communities have become increasingly less isolated socially and geographically over the past several hundred years. Their members have been exposed to new and diverse outside influences. However, the story is not complete unless we understand that today's lack of internal agreement about behavioral norms is another unfortunate result of the severe disruption to Native social systems and institutions brought on by the European invaders during their western expansion and their "discovery" of America.

The story should not be unfamiliar. Many Indian people who were not murdered outright were physically abused, raped, starved, or relocated by forcing them on long marches to their new homes that only the strongest were able to survive. Perhaps the most familiar example of the forcible relocation of Indian tribes (Cherokee, Chickasaw, Creek, Choctaw, and Seminole) has been referred to as the "Trail of Tears." It was a series of forced relocations between 1830 and 1850, when the federal government abrogated its treaties with tribes in the southeastern part of the country and forced approximately sixty thousand of their members off their native lands to relocate to the Oklahoma Territories west of the Mississippi River. This initiative was taken with the active complicity of the non-Indian inhabitants and the state governments of Mississippi, Georgia, Alabama, North Carolina, Florida, and Tennessee. The people were marched over 5,043 miles of rugged land. Over four thousand of these Indians died on their way from disease, famine, and warfare.[5]

This is just one example of forced relocation: there were many others throughout the country, resulting in further disruption to their societies, and much more suffering was to follow. Many Native survivors were rounded up and placed by the federal government together on the same reservations and rancherias, often on isolated and what was believed to be worthless land with people who were from different tribes, cultures, regions.

Forced off their lands, deprived of their natural resources and traditional subsistence activities—such as fishing, hunting, gathering, and harvesting—they then faced the added challenge of having to live with Indian people from other tribes and regions with a limited foundation on which to build community cohesion and solidarity. They lacked a familiar leadership and system of government, not to mention a common history and set of beliefs, values, and standards. Added to the traumatic experiences of their dislocation was the extra pressure of persistent internal conflict without the leaders and institutions upon which they could rely to help mediate among differences and restore harmony. This has made it very difficult to this day for many of these same communities to work together and negotiate fair, lasting, and enforceable agreements.

Native nations during this time also had to deal with threats from the surrounding population—from both existing residents and the steady flow of European settlers, homesteaders, ranchers, farmers, prospectors, and adventurers who headed westward seeking a new life and the promise of greater prosperity. Pressure built to eliminate or displace the Native communities that the newcomers perceived as in the way of their gaining access to their coveted lands and resources.

The disruption of Native communities was particularly extreme in California.[6] The severity of the onslaught there has been explained as due to the massive migration to the state by tens of thousands of people seeking the bounty of California's minerals and natural resources. The discovery of gold in the Sierra foothills in 1848 was a particularly strong attraction.[7]

Many of the tribes that were living for generations in the Sierra foothills were treated brutally by the lawless invaders during a time and in a place still lacking organized law enforcement. The fact that the tribes in California had been living in small and scattered villages made them particularly vulnerable and unable to put up significant resistance. To appreciate the size of the disruption in California, consider the state's large Native population. Today, there are at least 108 federally recognized tribes in California, more than in any other state of the lower forty-eight states.

Their forced removal was undertaken to make way for the sale and resettlement of their former lands. This was coupled with official government policy to round up "landless Indians" and resettle them elsewhere. The Round Valley Indian Tribe is an example of how many current "tribes" were formed. It is a confederation of the Yuki, Wailacki, Concow, Little Lake Pomo, Nomlacki, and Pit River Tribes. To this day, many of the members of this tribe retain primary loyalties to and are politically aligned with members of their original tribes. These divided loyalties are still sources of deep internal divisions and a struggling government.[8]

The devastating experiences of these tribes within the northwestern part of the new state of California was totally consistent with California State government policy at that time. The state facilitated the formation of 120 private militias to participate in killing Indians. Private citizens received payment from the state in exchange for producing evidence of their deeds in the form of heads, scalps, or ears of their victims. The policy was backed up by forceful pro-extermination statements in regional newspapers and by the first American governor of the state, Peter Burnett. In his first State of the State address on January 6, 1851, he declared that "a war of extermination will continue to be waged between the two races until the Indian race becomes extinct."[9] California was declared a state in 1850, and one of its first official acts was to pass an "Act for the Government and Protection of Indians," essentially an Indian extermination act—legalized and publicly subsidized mass murder.

According to a PBS special—*An American Experiment*, which aired on November 6, 2006—"In the twenty years after the discovery of gold, 120,000 Indians, four-fifths of the California Native population, would be wiped out from starvation, disease, and publicly subsidized mass murder."[10]

During this period, federal, state, and local government leaders and the media joined together in promoting a narrative that dehumanized Native people. They portrayed them as inferior to whites and subhuman savages. This depiction gave their opponents the justification to declare open season to hunt them down and eliminate them with impunity.[11]

Claims that Indian people were subhuman and inferior to whites further prompted the federal government policy of ripping young Indian children from their parents and communities and sending them to be "civilized" in government boarding schools, often located thousands of miles away from their families. These children were prevented from speaking their native language, as well as wearing traditional hairstyles and clothing. These and other policies were deliberate attempts by the U.S. government to impose white culture, and by taking them away from their families, to interrupt the verbal transmission of Native culture from one generation to the next.

This traumatic period of history of the American Indian had serious repercussions that are still evident. Conversations with many tribal leaders and academics today reveal traces of what is commonly referred to as "historical oppression." Research suggests that many Indian people internalized the negative stereotypes held by their oppressors. As a result, Native peoples lost respect for themselves and for the dignity and humanity of other members of their communities. This is believed to still manifest itself in the form of destructive behavior against themselves, family members, and other people in their communities.[12]

IDRS's training program reinforces the importance of people "honoring and respecting" themselves and one another by encouraging negotiators to agree to create and adhere to a set of procedural ground rules when they first enter negotiations. Such procedural agreements are essential to people feeling that they will be treated with respect and will be safe from abuse as they engage in collaborative problem solving. Starting with a procedural agreement is one of the distinctive features of IDRS's negotiation and mediation methodologies. This exercise of agreeing on acceptable ways of talking and interacting with one another is an opportunity for the parties to ensure that traditional peacemaking values such as respect, harmony, and balance once again become part of existing relationships and the negotiation process.

Collaborative Negotiation versus Positional Negotiation

Collaboration respects traditional communal values by emphasizing the importance of meeting the needs of others as well as one's own through a process of give and take. Native people's commitment to win-win outcomes was based on their communal value system that emphasizes taking care of everyone in their community.

The value placed on consensus-based decision making—that is, taking care of the needs of the entire community—was based on the reality of societal conditions at the time when Native communities were geographically isolated and vulnerable to externally initiated hostilities. Their ability to defend themselves would be weakened with fewer numbers each time that disgruntled factions splintered off and abandoned their people. This was an incentive to maintain the solidarity of the community by relying on inclusive rather than exclusive approaches to problem solving; on collaborative, consensus-based decision making rather than on adversarial, positional decision making; on satisfying the unique needs of everyone rather than just the needs of those who might be powerful enough at the time to have it their way; and on processes that were based on "you and me" instead of "you or me."[13]

In most traditional societies, people's first loyalties were communal and not to their own personal interests. Among some traditional peoples, a stigma remains today on looking out for one's own needs. Nonetheless, we consider here the situation in which the tribal negotiator is representing the interests of his entire community vis-à-vis an outside entity. To treat one's community's interests with little vigor and as anything less than of paramount importance would be to fail to represent one's community properly. The tribal negotiator must be assured today that what distinguishes collaborative from positional negotiators is their commitment to serving their interests in addition to the interests of the other side. Negotiators should be vigorous in promoting their own interests at the same time they are gaining an understanding of the other side's concerns and working creatively to satisfy those without sacrificing the need to attend to their own community's priorities.

Relationship Building

In traditional societies, self-conscious steps were taken by the opposing parties to get to know each other and to build trust and respect as part of their conflict resolution process. As a general rule, parties in conflict do not trust or respect one another when they start the negotiation process. They have to build that relationship with what are commonly referred to as "confidence-building" measures. Once the parties establish a trusting and respectful relationship, they are more willing to work creatively shoulder-to-shoulder to try and solve the problems together.

Traditional societies understood that part of their negotiations involved building trust and preserving relationships. They typically entered negotiations with other tribes and entities by first giving gifts, sharing food, playing competitive games, storytelling, ceremonies, visiting, and so on. They used this time to get to know one another and to determine whether the other party's behavior demonstrated a commitment to fair play, discretion, trustworthiness, and respect before they sat down to negotiate agreements.

Today, there appears to be an increasing recognition that relationship building is an essential part of the conflict resolution process, especially if the parties—for example, family members, coworkers, union and management—have an ongoing relationship with one another. Whether the negotiators can begin to establish and sustain a close working relationship during the negotiations will vary depending on at least three variables: the degree to which the negotiators make an effort to nurture one, the personalities of the participants themselves and how open and personal they are by nature, and how long the negotiations extend over time. When interactions last a significant amount of time, people generally experience increasing familiarity and comfort with one another

While not always a priority among negotiators in Western industrialized societies, establishing a more holistic (functionally diffuse) relationship is particularly critical in Indian Country, where this value of knowing the whole person remains very important. To this day, the first topic of discussion among Native people when they meet for the first time is to whom they are related. The examination of their kinship ties and whether they are "family" is a way to gather critical background information, come to know each other on a more than superficial level, and determine whether they can be trusted.

Getting to know one another is still operative when tribes engage in negotiations. A number of years ago, the nine federally recognized tribes in Oregon were invited by Governor John Kitzhaber to negotiate with twenty-two state agency directors to establish a standard protocol for future government-to-government negotiations. IDRS was invited to train the Native negotiators and help them propose a process to follow during three days set aside for these negotiations.[14]

The state agency directors proposed beginning immediately with substantive negotiations without any preliminary formalities. This suggestion was met with strong objections from the Native leaders, who insisted that these state directors generally ascribed to the myth of homogeneity by lumping all the tribes together and had little information about any of them. This made the tribal leaders feel disrespected. After an exchange of procedural proposals, the Native nations were successful in having the entire first day of the upcoming negotiations set aside to get to know one another, to talk about their tribes and how they differed from one another, describing their unique histories and their current activities, interests, and strengths. The remaining two days of negotiations went very smoothly after the tribal leaders' presentations.

Experienced negotiators know that once trust and respect have been established between the parties, there is often a visible shift away from a focus on one another to a focus on the problem. At this stage of the negotiation, one can often see the negotiators' physical postures change: they listen more attentively, project their voices, move to the front part of their chairs, and lean forward into the conversations. This corresponds with an acceleration in agreement making. In contrast, when the negotiators lack trust, their body language reflects it. They often sit back in their chairs, respond more slowly, and are not available for small talk or personal revelations. Their bodies are what might be characterized as "closed off." If this behavior persists and the persons are reluctant to let their guard down, reaching an agreement can be very difficult.[15] Later in this book we explore how tribal negotiation teams can build relationship satisfaction into their government-to-government negotiations.

Careful Selection of Community Peacemakers

Leaders in Native societies were traditionally not elected, as they are today, on the basis of their popularity with a majority of voters. They were identified, trained, mentored, and appointed by elders and clans whose job was to select the community's leaders. Leaders were chosen who were perceived to have the aptitude for leadership and who had demonstrated exemplary skills and character. Moreover, they were chosen because the elders observed that they enjoyed the confidence and would generously serve the needs of the whole community. Today, this traditional system of selecting government leaders has been mostly abandoned to be consistent with the so-called democratic principles of the popular vote proposed by the federal Indian Reorganization Act (IRA).

What choice do Native communities have today when they need leaders who are competent in peacemaking and qualified to represent their people in negotiations with government agencies and other external entities? Should they automatically rely only on their elected leaders to fill these roles, or should they look to other leaders as well who may have been informally mentored by their elders and have already demonstrated experience and expertise in communication and negotiation skills, can think strategically, and who enjoy the respect and confidence of their community?

Each tribe answers this question for itself. However, in selecting negotiators, Native nations should be encouraged to consider leaders who may or may not hold elective office and who have already exhibited the necessary character and skills, and whom the community trusts. If the negotiators lack traditional leadership training and mentorship, tribes should be encouraged to compensate by sending them, whether elected or not, to formal leadership training in collaboration, consensus building, negotiation, and mediation skills.

Finally, in the interest of self-determination and protecting and enhancing tribal sovereignty, Native groups are encouraged to rely on their own people to speak on their behalf rather than counting on lawyers or other technical experts. Indigenous leaders are generally taken more seriously today and can best understand and present the interests of their people. What's more, they remain in the community long after the lawyers go home.

3

PLANNING AND PREPARATION

One of the first steps parties take during the preparation and planning phase of the negotiation process is to perform their own assessment of the conflict. In doing so, negotiators should answer three separate questions: What are the origins and causes of this conflict? What are the costs of this conflict? What are the benefits of this conflict?

In addition to lists we include here that you can complete by yourself, we offer some additional exercises for you to deepen your understanding of the materials. They are in Appendix A and can be used for self-study as well as topics for group discussion.

Causes or Origins of the Conflict

How and when did the conflict start? Who cast the first stone, and what stone or stones were cast? What was the reaction, and from whom? Why did the conflict persist? Before deciding what to do, it's necessary to tackle the more fundamental problem of highlighting and comprehending what is happening.

During the first face-to-face negotiation session, both parties should be asked to provide an opening statement that describes their own version of what they think happened. One result is that both sides are heard from, new information is shared, the parties develop a broader understanding about what actually happened, and a composite picture begins to emerge.

Parties usually have different ideas of what caused the conflict. In fact, multiple causes may need to be addressed during the ensuing discussions. What also generally occurs is that each of the parties begins to realize that each comes from its own vantage point and has its own experience and perspective. With this background, it is harder to cling to the idea that "my way" is the only way of seeing and understanding the conflict. This may be the point already where the parties begin to move from "me" to "we," and start to comprehend that both of them, from different yet valid perspectives, are needed to solve the problems.

Many factors can cause, influence, escalate, affirm, or support conflict. Following are some possible sources or causes:

Different values and belief systems
Misinformation—including disinformation, inaccurate information, and outdated information
Incomplete information or lack of any information
Unfamiliar information, such as technical information
Information regarded as not credible because of the values, experience, or reputation of the source
Contradictory information
Unpleasant or disturbing information
Complex information not yet integrated or fully understood
Deception and chicanery
Domination and coercion
Discrimination and prejudice
Lack of resources
Income disparities
Competition between entities
Personality clashes—even between organizations and nations
Unpredictable or erratic behavior
Laws, regulations, and policies
Gender and age differences
Customs, patterns, and practices
Habits and egos
Physical appearance
Geographical differences
Unresolved disagreements
Change without explanation
Not allowing grief or reconciliation to occur
Jealousy, envy, anger, suspicion, distrust, and other unresolved feelings

Costs of the Conflict

Negotiators should consider an additional question when they begin to plan and prepare to enter negotiations: what is being gained and what is the conflict costing us, both in the short and long term, if the conflict persists over an extended period of time?

The costs should be raised to the level of awareness also because they need to be factored into each party's negotiation strategy—to make sure it furthers rather undermines its interests. Conflict is costly on many different levels (see the list below). It is disruptive to normal routines and is associated with inconvenience and hardship for as long as it lasts. Conflict also causes stress that leads to emotional reactions that are often difficult to contain and control. If not resolved, the conflict is likely to escalate—drawing in additional people, which adds to the complexity, fans emotions, and increases the negative impact on the individuals involved and on the community as a whole.

Some costs of conflict are as follows:

Emotional stress and turmoil among people directly involved

Avoidance or disengagement behavior, for example, absenteeism; tardiness; work slowdowns; withdrawal of time, effort, and resources

Physical ailments; psychosomatic conditions; deteriorating physical, emotional, and spiritual health; anxiety; sleeplessness

Significant financial loss

Self-destructive behavior (substance abuse, smoking, fighting, exaggerated risk taking, suicide)

Sabotage and destruction of physical property

An undermining of relationships and reputations through spreading rumors

Incomplete and distorted communications, resulting in bad or no information and ill-informed decisions

Involvement of innocent bystanders, either because of proximity to the conflict or because the disputants seek to draw in allies

Dampened morale, energy, enthusiasm, and motivation

Reduced productivity, leading to decreased quantity and quality of output

More organizational time, energy, and resources devoted to managing conflict

- Need for reorganization, reassignment, replacement, recruitment, and retraining—all of which translate into increased costs of operation and reduced effectiveness
- Decreased ability of the organization to respond to available opportunities in a timely manner
- Jeopardizing stated self-interests
- Instability and unpredictability in personal, social, and work lives
- Inability to adapt to change
- Hindering of efforts to implement needed change
- Formation of lasting grudges
- Escalation of conflict, resulting in physical violence and emotional abuse
- Loss of public support
- Locking people and organizations into public stands or positions that cannot be rescinded easily or quickly
- Promoting action or reaction instead of carefully considered responses
- Tarnishing credibility
- Causing disunity and breakdown of alliances and coalitions
- Escalating, accelerating, and broadening the conflict, making it harder to contain
- Disrupting routines and predictability
- Undermining trust, confidence, and understanding
- People becoming secretive and dishonest
- Records lost and destroyed
- Death and physical injury

Benefits of the Conflict

Conflict is not all bad, and actually has benefits. On the one hand, people might be discouraged from entering negotiations because they believe that emotions are running so high that the situation will only get worse. On the other hand, people might be encouraged to engage in negotiations when they see that they will be guided and contained within a framework of agreed-upon ground rules that will move the fight off the street, cut losses, contain strong emotions, and provide an orderly way to reach agreement on how to restore peace and move forward constructively. One encouraging development is that, perhaps for the first time, parties can listen to one another in a safe environment without interruption.

Conflict also has potential benefits. They include:

Providing the first opportunity to sit down and hear the perspective of the other side—uninterrupted
Surfacing existing problems that were ignored and unattended for too long
Getting people talking and thinking about alternatives
Providing parties with the opportunity to face and overcome old fears
Creating new sense of urgency and energy
Refining one's own ideas and positions
Fostering consciousness of commonality when other people reveal the same or similar interests or values
Creating greater understanding within and between people and groups
Temporarily defusing or setting aside other conflicts
Setting new priorities
Promoting new values and a new moral order
Serving as a safety valve for the release of emotions in a safe and constructive environment that has procedural ground rules
Stimulating creative and innovative thinking
Allowing development of useful interactions with others
Stimulating the development of equitable conflict prevention, management, and resolution systems for addressing misunderstandings in the future
Bringing about constructive change and cooperation
Bringing new groups into decision making and broadening the base of power and influence
Providing opportunity for new leaders to emerge and acquire experience and confidence
Providing opportunities to learn and practice new organizational and leadership skills
Establishing new relationships and alliances
Promoting healing of age-old wounds and unresolved grievances
Wider distribution of system benefits
Catharsis, giving people an opportunity to get things off their chest in a safe environment

Exercise 1. Add to the list above. What are some additional causes of conflict?

44   CHAPTER 3

Exercise 2. What are some costs of unresolved conflict in addition to those presented in the earlier list? List additional ways in which conflict leads to dysfunctional results.

Exercise 3. Add to this list. In what other ways can conflict have functional benefits?

As pointed out earlier, negotiation is a voluntary process. One of the challenges is overcoming a party's initial resistance to participating and motivating the party to enter serious face-to-face discussions. There also may be times during the negotiation that progress is slow and problematic, at which points people may become discouraged from continuing to participate. Sometimes an assessment of the origins, costs, and benefits can be an effective way to get parties to slow down, moderate their emotions, and make a rational and practical assessment of whether their current behavior is consistent with their true interests. These exercises can be used at the outset or at any time during negotiations with the other side and with one's own team and constituents.

Identifying Your Interests

Interest-based negotiation (IBN) was popularized by Roger Fisher and William Ury in their 1981 book, *Getting to Yes: Negotiating Agreement without Giving In*.[1] IBN was offered as an alternative to what was observed to be widespread use of negotiation strategies that were unnecessarily confrontational and self-limiting. Interest-based negotiation added a new dimension to the process: in the course of the conversation, parties share information about the underlying interests that are their reasons for making their proposals. When IBN negotiators make proposals, they try to educate the other side about why the proposals are important to them. They make an effort to persuade the other side rather than exert pressure or make threats when their proposals are resisted and rejected.

The IBN practitioner also is encouraged to think of proposals in a new way. No proposal should be seen as the only way a party's interest can be satisfied, but rather as just one among others that could be put forward by the negotiator to advance his interests. This puts the negotiator in a position, if a proposal is rejected, to come up with alternative proposals until one is acceptable and agreed upon by the other side. Thinking in this way encourages the negotiator to be more flexible and creative in finding solutions. He is less inclined to assume that his proposals are identical to his interests, and less likely to view his proposal as the hill he is willing to die on.

Again, one of the first tasks for the negotiator during the preparation phase is to clarify his underlying interests, and then to keep these in mind throughout the negotiation process. At the very end, when reviewing the written agreement, he can use his interests and expectations as evaluation criteria to determine whether he had a win. If we are not clearly anchored in our interests, we run the risk of fighting over the wrong things—or even winning something that really does not serve us.

Approaching the negotiation from this perspective can also make our negotiations more productive for the other party. She will have more flexibility in responding to us because she is being offered additional ways to satisfy her interests when she cannot agree to our first proposal. She may not have to shut us down with a no. In addition, when we articulate our interests, the other party better understands what we want, our underlying reasons for being there, and thus is better positioned to work with us to figure out how she might be able to satisfy our interests.

What Are Interests?

We have already made numerous references to "interests" without clarifying what exactly we mean by this term. Many years ago, social psychologist Abraham Maslow listed seven basic needs or drives that he found to motivate all people to varying degrees.[2] This list is an excellent starting point in our consideration of what our own interests might be in a given situation. It should also sensitize us to what might be motivating the other side. Maslow's list, to which we have added an eighth, is as follows:

1. *Basic physiological needs*—water, food, warmth, shelter, sleep, health, cleanliness, air, exercise, and space.
2. *The need for safety and security*—stability, predictability, protection, dependability, structure, order, rules, laws, fairness and equity, boundaries and limits, freedom from fear and chaos, and financial resources.
3. *The need to belong and be loved*—intimacy, affection, support, trust, family, friends, group affiliation or membership, partnership, and interdependence.
4. *The need for respect and to be counted*—dignity, recognition, standing, acknowledgment, appreciation, understanding,

strength, mastery, competency, confidence, reputation, prestige, status, and fame.
5. *The need for self-actualization*—fulfillment of innate talents, gifts, and purpose; the chance and opportunity to become and fulfill our destiny, to be what we truly are, to achieve our potential. It is about securing some autonomy, opportunity, social space, or elbow room.
6. *The need to know and understand*—satisfying our curiosity; gaining knowledge; understanding rationales and reasons; insight, meaning, and purpose.
7. *The need for an aesthetic quality in our life*—beauty, order, symmetry, system, and structure.
8. *The need for spiritual values, beliefs, and disciplines*—having concepts of a higher being and nonmaterial reality, immutable laws, and the Divine's expectations of human beings and their behavior toward the Divine and their fellow men and women. (This is our addition to Maslow.)

Knowing Your Interests

These needs—Maslow's and our addition—serve as interests that drive and motivate us. They underlie what we do and pursue. Their relative importance and how they are met may vary from person to person, and from culture to culture. They also may vary for each of us, depending on our circumstances and the time in our lives (e.g., our age).

These interests are nonnegotiable in the sense that we cannot do without any of them. However, flexibility may be present in how and the extent to which we need the needs met, and in how we order or prioritize them vis-à-vis our other interests. We may also be willing to take less of one interest if it is balanced by more of another. For example, security may be less important if we are given the opportunity to be more fully self-actualized. At certain times in our lives, affection and close personal intimacy may be less important if in other spheres of our lives other needs (e.g., recognition, reputation, and success) are being met.

Knowing the Other Party's Interests

When negotiating, we need to understand the underlying interests of the other sides as well. What interests or needs lie behind the other party's proposals? Answering this question requires us to use our expertise in understanding people, to listen carefully, and to ask questions of the other side, such as "Why?" or "Why is that important to you?" When we know what the other party's interests are, we have information about how we can satisfy those interests without having to give up any of our own vital interests.

Some people we negotiate with are not clear about their interests. Our questions can help them in this regard. A good example is when an employee asks for a raise. In his mind, he may not actually be motivated by wanting more money. Instead, the salary increase may represent to him an employer's appreciation of the quality of his contribution to the organization. Understanding this employee's motivation is important, because if he cannot be given more money, perhaps he could be given recognition in any number of other ways that would provide the feeling of significance and validation he is seeking. This is a good example why negotiators should not assume they understand the other party's motivation without asking the question explicitly. In this case, increased recognition from the employer may satisfy the employee and reduce the risk that he will leave his job.

Maslow's Hierarchy of Needs

In addition to providing us with his list of basic human needs or interests, Maslow maintained that everyone has the same "hierarchy of needs." In other words, he suggested that we all order or rank the importance of his seven different needs in the same way, regardless of our culture, personal histories, or individual idiosyncrasies—but we have not found that to be the case.

People may differ from one another in how they order the importance of their interests. Consider, for example, career military personnel compared to entrepreneurs. An officer who has chosen to make a career in the military likely has a tolerance and perhaps even a preference for security and predictability, order, structure, and hierarchy. He is expected to follow orders, and his discretionary authority is limited. In contrast, entrepreneurs have a strong preference for independence and autonomy, wanting to be able to do what they want—when and how they want. They have a lower tolerance for order and structure than career military people, who are more comfortable in a more prescribed environment. Entrepreneurs are more likely to be risk takers. The typical entrepreneur considers what Maslow calls "self-actualization" (lots of latitude to realize their potential) more important than security and predictability.

The ordering of our different interests may change with age. For example, people's interest in self-actualization may count heavily as a driving force when they are young and ready to make their mark. However, as they grow older—when their options are fewer, or when they have a family with a number of dependents—financial and physical security may begin to take precedence over autonomy and free expression. Their priorities may change yet again when they are older and no longer have the responsibilities of raising a family. When they are ready to retire, they may be ready to sell their house and car, give away the family pets, become footloose and carefree, buy a motor home and travel, and move from place to place without any major responsibilities or permanent home. In stark contrast, as people get older their financial situation may deteriorate once they stop working and their health may be in jeopardy: conditions may make a person more cautious and security-oriented. Which interest is it? You have to ask.

An additional observation regarding interests is that parties may be willing to make trade-offs among them during negotiations to get more of something in exchange for accepting less of something else. This is critically important from the perspective of a negotiator, who, when aware of the other's preferences, has much more flexibility in satisfying the negotiator's interests.

For example, consider the employer introduced earlier who is negotiating with an employee. Financial security may be less important to certain employees if they are given the opportunity to be more fully self-actualized. They might be willing to forgo a salary increase if they are offered a new position with more responsibilities and independence, a shorter work week, or the permission to gain important experience by working elsewhere (e.g., as a private contractor) in another area of their interests during part of the week. Similarly, these employees may be willing to give up some financial security—in the form of no salary increase—in exchange for more recognition, appreciation, and prominence on the job. They may also be willing to accept no salary increase in exchange for other forms of financial remuneration, such as family health benefits, membership in a health club, free parking and bridge tolls, an annual bonus, or a larger employer contribution to the employee's 401(k). These alternative ways of satisfying the interest in financial security may have different tax implications and be more acceptable to the employee and the employer.

Moreover, people often have many interests, and in some situations their proposal will serve one of their interests while undermining another. If we listen carefully, we can hear the contradiction and get people to consider an option that better satisfies their competing interests while coming closer to meeting ours.

Consider, for example, a couple that is divorcing and battling over who gets physical custody of their three children. The mother is demanding full custody, because she believes that "no self-respecting mother would have anything less." She has an interest in her family and friends seeing her as a good mother. She feels that her reputation is at stake. But economic security may also be very important to her. She may want to become financially independent, but she may not have the time and energy to find and hold a good job if she also has to be a full-time mother.

The father may also have competing interests to reconcile. By taking the children part of the time and providing his ex some financial support for a specified time, the father can help the mother meet her needs and his as well. He can fulfill his need for love and relationship (being with his children), a reputation as a good father, and his own long-term economic security (an eventual end to his wife's financial dependency).

In the final analysis, while we do not accept Maslow's hierarchy as standing up cross-culturally or even for all people within a culture, his list by itself provides an excellent window into what motivates human beings and a huge contribution to understanding which interests are important to us and to other parties in a negotiation. For that contribution alone, Maslow's list is well worth committing to memory and keeping in mind when we are trying to resolve differences. We can use the list when we prepare an inventory of our interests and when we listen to the other side and try to identify its own underlying interests that it wants to satisfy. Maslow's words often come up naturally and explicitly during the negotiation, and we can learn by listening carefully and asking clarifying questions about what interests or needs lie behind the other side's proposals.

What Are Issues?

Issues have been called the "what" of negotiations, with interests and needs being the "why." Issues are the problems that we list as agenda items for discussion in the course of resolving the conflict. They are much more tangible than interests.

When we are defining our negotiation strategy, it will be helpful, once we know our interests, to ask ourselves, *What are the problems that have to be surfaced, addressed, and resolved so that our interests are met and this conflict will be resolved?* Asking ourselves this question is also valuable when selecting agenda items.

Taking the earlier example of the divorcing couple, the mother's multiple interests and issues (possible agenda items) can be shown as follows:

INTERESTS/NEEDS	ISSUES (Agenda Items)
Respect/reputation	Physical custody of children
	Parenting responsibilities, for both parents
	Time commitment required
Economic security	Acquisition of a good job
	Dependable salary/income
	Financial support from children's father
	Financial independence for the mother
	Length of postdivorce transition period
Relationship	Time spent with mother and father
	System for exchanging and coordinating transfer of children
	Mechanisms for resolving logistical details, misunderstandings and changes in schedules, and so on.
	Involvement of relevant others (grandparents, boyfriends and girlfriends, doctors)
Self-actualization	Financial support and sharing in child care while mother is training for a job

As another example, before negotiating for a new job or for changes at an existing job, start with some thought about your underlying interests and needs, and about the issues (that is, the agenda items) you would like to discuss.

Next, define some explicit proposals regarding each agenda item to ensure that your underlying interests are met. With a fuller understanding of your interests and the issues you can raise, you can be more creative and flexible in how to follow up on the initial proposal with a second and third, and how to define your fallback and bottom-line positions. Below are some ideas for negotiating with a potential or existing employer.

INTERESTS	ISSUES or AGENDA ITEM PROPOSALS
Financial security	Salary/wages
	Compensation time
	Bonuses
	Tax-sheltered annuity
	Fringe benefit package
	Stock options
	Administrative leave
	Company car
	Free parking
	Health club membership
	Hardship pay
Self-actualization	On-the-job training
	Training stipend
	Job rotation
	Mentorship
	Educational leave time
	Merit system
	Special projects assigned
	Job responsibilities redefined
	New assignments
Safety, security	Seniority rights
	Retirement benefits
	Prior notice of layoff
	Union representation
	Process for changes in assignments
	Relocations
	Buyouts
Respect, recognition	Achievement awards
	Employee evaluations
	Office location and amenities
	Special assignments
	Employee input
	Job titles
	Organizational charts
	Performance evaluation criteria defined

Equity, fairness	Established salary structure
	Fair employment practices and policies
	Clear chain of command
	Grievance procedures
Safety	Health and safety standards
	Workers' compensation policies
	Health benefits program
	No-smoking areas
	Limit on hours worked
	Nearby parking in safe areas
	Regulation of apparel
	Regulation of equipment

After studying the lists above, consider how different the negotiations would be with the employer if the employee's only agenda item was compensation and his proposal was limited to an increase in salary. There would be no further place to go with the negotiations if the employer refused to agree. On the other hand, if the employee had started the negotiation by citing his interest in "greater financial security" rather than making a specific proposal for a salary increase, the employer would be informed that additional ways were available to reward the employee financially. Short of giving a salary increase, the employer could satisfy the employee's interest in greater financial security by increasing his monthly disposable income in other ways. This could include paying for bridge tolls, daily parking, free lunches, child-care costs, gym membership, health insurance coverage for the family, an increase in the employer's contribution to his 401(k), the use of a company car, a contribution to your children's college tuitions, and so on.

Identifying Your Expectations

In discussing win-win in chapter 1, we talked about developing an inventory of interests as one of the first things that negotiators do to prepare. These interests are what you want to achieve in the negotiation and therefore the underlying reasons for making your proposals.

While typical discussions of interest-based negotiation leave it at that, we pointed out earlier, in describing how to achieve win-win results, that another factor intervenes in the process of using interests as the guide in formulating the negotiation strategy. A negotiator's expectations are based on a realistic evaluation of what seems possible within the context, and they limit the type and extent to which one's interests can be satisfied.

We defined three distinct steps a negotiator takes in defining "expectations" as she plans for and then actively engages in the negotiation. We suggested that the negotiators' expectations change as the process between the parties plays itself out, all the way up to the signing of the final agreement. Whether the negotiator concludes that he had a win is determined by the extent to which her final expectations were met.

The reader is encouraged to review discussion of the win-win concept in chapter 1 before going forward.

Building the Agenda

After you have begun to clarify your interests and realistic expectations, you are ready to work with the other party to build an agenda that will serve as part of the framework for your negotiations. The primary purpose of creating an agenda is to break the conflict down into manageable and understandable parts: a list of specific problems that have to be resolved. The parties work together to establish one common agenda they can agree on, even though each party may have different items they want to place on the agenda.

The act of putting an agenda together at the outset has the effect of giving the parties the first opportunity to explore jointly the general dimensions of the conflict and the areas that should be addressed that can provide solutions. Another function of an agenda is providing one important way to satisfy the parties' interests in having order, safety, and predictability during the negotiation. Even if a party's greatest priority is not the first being discussed, he has the assurance that it has been placed on the agenda and will be addressed. Developing an agenda is especially important when the parties are just entering a process that may still be unfamiliar and they are experiencing anxiety and distress about it. The need for order and predictability are among the basic human interests or needs that Maslow identified.

As logical as it seems that parties would create and follow an agenda to frame their discussions, many parties in negotiation and mediation fail to spend the time to design an agenda, or after they have formulated one, they fail to follow it scrupulously during the discussions. In either case, these parties who try to resolve the dispute by launching into the discussion without following an agreed-upon agenda frequently waste a lot of time moving from one subject to another—in no particular order and with little progress to show for the effort. This approach can increase confusion and frustration among the parties when the atmosphere is already tense and still quite unpredictable. Of course, another risk of not following an agenda is that certain important issues may not be addressed and the agreement reached will be incomplete. This outcome may instead extend the conflict.

Think of the agenda as the road map for negotiators to identify the specific points of interest along a designated route that must be visited before the parties to the conflict can reach the final destination—which is, of course, conflict resolution. Just as you do not generally take a trip with no idea of where you are going, an agenda is essential to using your time as effectively and efficiently as possible and not inflicting yourself with unnecessary anxiety and confusion.

Now let's take up the questions of when and how to formulate an agenda.

Parties begin to formulate the agenda early on when they start discussing the possibility of resolving the conflict, either in person or in writing. At this stage, a tentative agenda is prepared, and affirmed later when the parties come together in their first face-to-face negotiation session.

Alternatively, if the parties do not have contact prior to the negotiation and they are using the services of a mediator/facilitator, the mediator usually takes the lead role in pulling together a tentative agenda based on preliminary discussions with each party before they arrive at the mediation session. The mediator/facilitator also gets another look when the parties make their opening statements during the information-gathering stage. The mediator/facilitator repeats what he heard and asks the parties to confirm or modify the list of agenda items before proceeding.

Once agreeing on a list of agenda items, the parties decide on the order in which the items should be addressed. Often a logical order emerges, based on the need to resolve certain items before others. At other times, the parties may prefer to take on easier and less emotional matters first so that there can be some early successes and an opportunity to build up goodwill and trust before tackling the more intractable issues. In still other instances, the parties might decide to take on the hardest issue first because it is viewed as central to the dispute.

In determining how to formulate an agenda, it is crucial that the items are properly worded. They should be stated in general, objective, and value-neutral terms rather than in ways that could irritate the parties and end in a lengthy and heated argument about whether an item is valid and even belongs on the agenda. At this initial stage of the negotiation, the agenda should be used just to help frame the process: it is too early to be distracted by an argument. The following are examples of how to frame or reframe the agenda items so that they are conducive to constructive problem solving rather than stated in ways that could disrupt the process.

Here are some ways that the parties can be irritated if an agenda item is poorly written:

- *Reflecting a point of view of one of the parties and not the other.*

    Examples:

    Bad: The agency's exclusion of the Wabash Tribe from the Tribal Forum.
    Reframed: The agency's policies and practices for inviting participants to the Tribal Forum.

    Bad: John's disrespectful behavior at the meeting.
    Reframed: Acceptable procedural ground rules for meetings.

- *Assigning one of the parties the responsibility for the problem.*

    Examples:

    Bad: Mary's lack of commitment to the relationship.
    Reframed: Parties' commitment to the relationship.

- *Stating a conclusion that has not yet been reached.*

    Examples:

    Bad: John's theft of the office petty cash fund.
    Reframed: Circumstances surrounding the missing petty cash fund.
    Reframed: Improved petty cash management strategies.

    Bad: The university's racist and sexist admission policies.
    Reframed: The university's admission policies.

- *Phrasing one party's proposal before a full discussion and consideration of alternatives.*

    Examples:

    Bad: Firing Ed for his incompetence.
    Reframed: Performance criteria and evaluation process for staff.

Bad: Rescinding Mr. J.'s forced resignation.
Reframed: Reevaluating Mr. J.'s resignation.

Even though we are discussing agendas in the context of a negotiation, what is said here applies equally to any business meeting. Participants are generally wasting time if there is no agreement at the outset about the agenda items to be discussed, in some agreed-upon order, and if they are stated in an inflammatory way.

Developing and Exchanging Proposals

Each party typically starts the discussion at the table by making an opening statement that outlines each party's view of the problems, their opinions of the causes and origins of the conflict, their underlying interests, and what results they want to achieve as an outcome of the negotiations.

While listening to these opening statements, the parties gain insights into the other party's underlying interests as well as into the problems they think should be listed on the agenda. After these opening statements have been made, the agenda can be finalized.

The next step is to take each agenda item one at a time and discuss it thoroughly with the other party. Then the focus becomes developing possible solutions and making specific proposals that are then discussed, modified, added to, or subtracted from before they are accepted as part of an agreement.

In this section of the chapter, we consider some guidelines for formulating and offering proposals and counterproposals. In old-style confrontational negotiations, proposals were often referred to as "demands," which in itself reveals a lot about the combative dynamic of the relationship between the parties. That style of negotiation is referred to as "positional negotiation." Demands are made, and when resistance arises to meeting those demands, the party making them typically resorts to actions designed to pressure the other side to accept them.

Positional negotiation unfortunately has also become the primary style of negotiation in American politics over the past few decades with the decline in bipartisanship. Rather than collaborating, finding common ground, and coming up with agreements that satisfy mutual interests, the political party that can muster a majority too often acts unilaterally. Meanwhile, threats, name calling, misrepresentation of what the other side said, and forcing the majority will upon the minority have replaced deal making.

A slight variant of making demands has been to call them "proposals," which sounds like a kinder and gentler approach to settling differences. However, presenting demands as proposals has often not resulted in any better results, especially if the proposal makers become more persistent, threatening, and coercive when their proposals are resisted.

A different approach that works better—one that does not draw a line in the sand but relies on searching for common ground and persuading the other side of the proposal's merits. Keep the following in mind when adopting this approach.

- *Make sure that proposals are accompanied by an explanation or justification.* Proposals should be wrapped in a narrative that describes the underlying interests the proposal is intended to advance. Inexperienced negotiators often just drop the proposal on the table without giving some context or rationale for having made it. This error in judgment usually is an indication that the negotiator is not comfortable speaking or does not ascribe to the art of persuasion. In this case, a more confident and experienced communicator should be asked to present the proposals.

  Recall that one of Maslow's basic human needs is to know and understand, and giving explanations and their underlying reasons is the way to try to satisfy this interest. Gone are the days when it was enough to say, "Do it because I said so." This doesn't even work with one's children anymore. People need to understand the reason they are being asked to do something. They want to be persuaded. At the very least, the people the negotiator is representing in the negotiation will want an explanation and a justification for acceding to the proposal, and the negotiators should be prepared to provide it.
- *Win-win negotiation doesn't just consist of compromise.* Parties who compromise split the difference between them and receive only a part of what they each wanted. In contrast, win-win negotiators can pursue and consummate agreements in which both parties can fulfill all their interests by virtue of the fact that they usually have different interests or wants. They can be satisfied in a host of different ways without just getting a portion of what they are requesting. Through win-win collaboration, parties can agree that if they have something the other party wants, they can offer it to the other party in exchange for getting something they want.

The only time compromise might be used is if both parties want the same thing, it can be broken down into numerical portions, and no other principle can be used to allocate it. For example, take an inheritance left by a father to his children. If it is only a financial amount, such as the deceased father's investment portfolio of stocks and bonds, splitting its total market value among the children according to some predetermined formula would be a logical distribution scheme—a compromise. Then a deal might be struck between the parties, with each getting a portion anywhere between 1 and 100 percent.

In contrast, if the parties looked at the investment portfolio along with other things available for distribution that the children are suited for and interested in (such as the deceased father's home, his car, a family-owned business, a management position in the family business, a time-share vacation retreat, or jewelry), there might be a distribution plan that would satisfy everyone's interests without just receiving a portion of the value of the portfolio.

- *Avoid getting stuck promoting a proposal that the other side is rejecting.* That negative response can inhibit further discussion. To avoid this, a negotiator should have a backup plan that includes being ready to make other proposals that also meet his interests. These are often referred to as "secondary" and "tertiary" proposals. The message the negotiator wants to convey is that any proposal is just one among many others that might work as well or better in meeting the mutual interests of the parties. This approach to sharing proposals makes it more exploratory than demanding and rigid.
- When you are ready to formulate your proposals, remember that *a good proposal meets three criteria in win-win negotiation:*

    1. It promises to satisfy your interests and expectations, and in your presentation you show how it does.
    2. It promises to satisfy (or at least does not violate) the interests of the other party, and in your presentation you show how it does.
    3. It is based on data and an information source that is credible to the other party as well as you.

- When making proposals, *make sure that you have people's attention,* the time and place are right, there is time to reflect and

respond, and you are addressing the right people: those in a position to make a difference and contribute to a solution.
- *If possible, it is best if negotiators not try to pressure the other side into changing its position.* Instead, enlist the other side in working together with you to identify a third option that can work for both of you. This approach raises less resistance and can be a more constructive way to achieve a win-win.
- *The most effective way to get the other side to change its proposal or position is to raise questions about her underlying assumptions and thereby create doubt and uncertainty about the merits and viability of her proposals or positions.* To do this successfully requires that the negotiator asks his questions from the standpoint of seeking information rather than being seen as trying to trip up and embarrass the other party. Of course, this line of questioning has to be acceptable to you too. You also have to be open to the other side questioning your underlying assumptions.
- *All proposals should be ones you can justify logically.* Avoid making pie-in-the-sky proposals simply as a starting point in hopes that you will get part of what you want. The other side will not take it seriously and may begin to do the same with your other proposals. Better to build credibility by being able to justify all your proposals in rational terms with persuasive arguments, even when you are asking for the maximum you think you can expect but may not get.
- *When you are exchanging proposals, make sure an agreement is in place to maintain confidentiality.* When proposals are being discussed it is a very dynamic phase of the negotiations. You want to make sure that no content of the discussion is being shared with anyone (e.g., the media, constituents, family) outside of the room who is not directly involved at the negotiation table. There is no agreement at this point, just the consideration of various proposals. It is too easy for people who are not present to take things out of context and treat something as done before there is agreement. Breaches in confidentiality undermine trust, inhibit creative thinking, and discourage negotiators from being willing to explore a variety of different ideas with one another. Most state legal codes protect the confidentiality of the negotiation process for this reason.
- *When you make proposals, know the difference between concessions and quid pro quos.* A "concession" is a proposal designed to

satisfy the other side's interests. Presumably you are making the concession to appear generous, collaborative, and in hopes that the gesture will move the negotiations one step closer to an agreement. At the same time, make sure that your concession does not sacrifice any of your vital interests.

- *Know that making a concession it is not a quid pro quo.* "Quid pro quo" is Latin for giving something up in exchange for getting something specific in return, or "this for that." When making a quid pro quo proposal you are spelling out in explicit terms what you want the other party to do in exchange for the concession that you are making. Quid pro quos emphasize reciprocity and are effective in getting the other side to begin to make concessions too. This can create a momentum for ensuring that the agreement will be one in which all the parties have agreed to do something.

  Even the most experienced negotiators can make the mistake of assuming that their concessions will be reciprocated with concessions from the other side. Often negotiators become angry if these expectations do not materialize. The thinking goes, *If we are generous and nice, they will be also.* Take heed, however, if that is what you want, you have to get their explicit agreement to reciprocate before you assume they will do it on their own.

- *Proposals should generally be phrased in conditional language:* "If you will do X, then we will consider offering Y." This is a quid pro quo proposal: something offered for something else given in return.

  Other suggested language for offering proposals are as follows; these examples promote the win-win concept:

"We might consider X, if you would consider Y."
"If we were to offer X, what might you offer to meet our interest in Y?"
"If you were to modify your proposal by inserting language to the effect of X, we would consider meeting your previously stated interest in Y."
"Would you be willing to consider proposals other than the one you offered that would meet your interests as well or better, and that would satisfy our interests as well?"
"We might be willing to consider accepting your proposal if we heard some new ideas and proposals on how you might meet our interests concerning X."

"Would you be willing to modify your proposal if you heard some new ideas and proposals on how you might meet our interests concerning X?"
"Can we agree on X?"
"Do you have any objections to Y?"
"Can you take our proposal and tell us how it can work for you?"

- *When the negotiators keep talking and show that they sincerely want to reach an agreement that works for all parties, there usually will be a shift* from coming only from one's own point of view to be willing to view the problem together and try to resolve it collaboratively. They are moving away from just making statements and beginning to have a conversation. This is a very important moment in the negotiation.
- *Negotiation provides people with the experience of being heard, perhaps for the first time, since the conflict broke out.* Being heard helps people feel validated, reduces resistance, and encourages collaboration. Writing proposals down that the other party offered can also be validating. This can either be done on an easel, flip chart, or whiteboard in the front of the room, or by projecting comments recorded on the computer on the front wall. This literally changes the focus to the problems at hand and to what you are building together. When you display the proposals visually you are literally focusing all eyes on the proposals and the evolving agreement.
- *Negotiators are encouraged to ramp up their skills at proactive listening.* Hearing is passive; listening is active. Proactive listening consists of the following activities:

  a. Repeat and clarify in their language what you heard.
  b. Rephrase or paraphrase in different words that capture the intent but may be shorter and more to the point.
  c. Verify whether you understood the message that the other party intended to send: "This is what I am hearing, is it correct?"
  d. Ask lots of questions, specific and general, to make sure you understand.
  e. Sometimes it is helpful if you ask what the other party heard you propose, giving you the opportunity to repeat and clarify.
  f. Engage in periodic summarization to remind people of the proposals or agreements already placed on the table, and to demonstrate that progress is being made.

- We referred above to the possible problem of people not being ready yet to make definitive proposals and to agree to any of them. They may still need more time before they trust the process, themselves, and the other party. *Know that you can do things to get through this transitional period and still be moving forward.* For example,

    a. Consider proposing for the time being an agreement in principle, which may capture a concept that will need to be defined further at a later stage of the negotiations—for example, "Can we agree in principle that we are both committed to work for the best interests of our children?"
    b. Consider reaching tentative agreements with the understanding that they will not be finalized until there is a whole package that wraps a number of the agreements together.

- *Don't reject out of hand or ignore any proposal coming from the other side.* If it is not totally suitable, ask permission to modify their proposal to better meet your interests as well. Work with it, massage it, revise it, and then send it back for further comment and discussions. View their proposal as a starting point on which you can build. When you look at proposals as the starting point, an organic process begins in which the proposal evolves into an agreement that both parties contribute to and that meets both parties' interests.
- *Keep notes on any conciliatory gesture you heard during the discussions, and ask the other side, when the time seems right, if it would be willing to make it into a proposal.* Do not be surprised, though, if the party was not aware of making the statement or has forgotten. This is quite normal, and do not push it if there is resistance.
- *You do not have to respond immediately to any proposal offered.* Take time to reflect and respond. Don't react. Ask if you can take some time to consider their proposal. Extend the same courtesy by giving the other side time to respond to your proposals.

4

CREATING THE THREE SATISFACTIONS

Whether parties can sit down and discuss their differences and ultimately reach and uphold a clear, fair, and lasting agreement depends on the degree of satisfaction they have with the process by which problems are being discussed and resolved, the substance of their written agreement, and the type of relationship the parties establish during the negotiation. A distinguishing feature of the negotiation process, in contrast to all other forms of dispute resolution, is that negotiators have it within their power to create satisfaction along these three dimensions.

In this chapter we examine in detail how parties working together can build procedural, substantive, and relational satisfaction.

Negotiate a Procedural Agreement

Almost all conflicts are emotionally charged and characterized by some degree of uncertainty and apprehension about the other side's behavior. In this context, parties experience varying degrees of anxiety, insecurity, distrust, and anger—all of which frustrate open communication, an exchange of information, and creative and resourceful problem solving.

The courts know full well that people who attempt to resolve disputes in litigation are often driven by strong negative emotions (e.g., fear, frustration, anger) that they might act on during the proceedings. This is why there is a security system in the courthouse and a bailiff in the courtroom with the legal authority to keep order. This is also part of the reason there are such strict courtroom procedures to follow and the option for the judge to hold people in contempt if procedures are violated. There are additional devices intended to create an atmosphere of awe and respect for the sanctity of the formal proceedings, including having people stand up when the judge enters the courtroom, the judge sitting in an elevated position dressed in a black robe, having attorneys address the judge as "Your Honor," and attorneys being under instructions to ask special permission to approach the bench before they are permitted to leave their desks. Finally, these strong negative emotions motivate parties to select an attorney to represent them in court because it removes them from having to face, speak, and deal directly with their adversary. They hire an attorney to be their mouthpiece and go to battle on their behalf.

When parties try and resolve their conflict through negotiations they also have to deal with disputants who have these same strong negative emotions. However, in contrast with litigation, which has an established procedural framework to rely on, the negotiation process has no such framework unless the negotiators create one themselves. They would have to devise a way to subdue and transform, and at the very least, contain these strong negative "feelings" by creating their own framework of rules that is conducive to safe, calm, deliberative, and informed decision making. The challenge for negotiators is to create the same kind of awe and respect for the process and the parties that is present in a court of law.

Four Important Rules for the Negotiation Process

There are four important rules to keep in mind when coming up with a process design for your negotiation:

1. There are no procedural rules or an established process in negotiations unless the parties themselves establish them.
2. These rules are jointly established by the parties at the beginning of the negotiations. They should not be unilaterally determined and imposed by either party. Government agencies typically commit this error. When all the parties have a hand in establishing the rules, they become co-owners of these understandings and can be expected to share in the responsibility for following and enforcing them consistently.
3. Parties should not try to resolve the substantive issues (agenda items) without first having a procedure in place that they all are willing to enforce. If there still is no order, then the parties can revisit the procedural ground rules at any time, and come up with additional ones that will address whatever behavioral problems remain.

4. It is highly unlikely that the negotiation will produce a substantive agreement without these procedural rules.

Reflect a moment about meetings and other situations you have participated in where people tried to negotiate and resolve differences without first defining a fair and safe process they agree to follow. What were the substantive results? Was there any personal satisfaction? Was it an efficient use of your time? Were matters made worse or better?

In some situations, certain procedural issues have already been defined before the first face-to-face meeting between the parties. In this case, the parties did so during the preparation phase through an exchange of letters and phone calls. When the first face-to-face meeting is convened, the parties formalize these initial agreements along with additional procedural issues that still may need to be addressed. When a mediator is involved, preliminary discussions with each party before they are brought together can include the kind of ground rules they would like to have in place. This can be an effective way of giving them the assurance that the process can be safe and productive, and thus serve as a way to persuade them to agree to participate.

There often will be a wide range of these procedural issues that should be considered. Moreover, getting agreement on these issues might take considerable time. For example, in the government-to-government negotiations between the Timbisha Shoshone Tribe and the federal government (see the case study presented in chapter 7), it took seven months of exchanging correspondence to agree on some key procedural issues before the first joint meeting was convened. During the peace negotiations that began in Paris in 1968 to end the Vietnam War, it took over one year for the parties just to agree on the shape of the negotiation table before they could begin their substantive discussions. In both cases, despite the delay, these preliminary procedural negotiations were integral to the negotiation process and it was time well spent.[1]

Typical Procedural Issues

The procedural issues can be divided into categories upon which agreement must be reached:

- *Agree on the purpose of the discussions.* "Can we agree that we are both committed to negotiate (rather than consult) and continue to work together toward developing a written agreement that resolves our differences and meets our mutual interests?"

- *Agree on the setting.*
    a. **Location of the sessions.** Will it be accessible, comfortable, private, quiet, and viewed as neutral by all the parties?
    b. **Times and duration.** Will these times be convenient for all? Will there be sufficient time allowed for a full exchange of ideas and options, and for preparing a detailed written agreement? A minimum of two hours is required to get anything done in the most basic interpersonal negotiation, and many days are often necessary for interorganizational and intergovernmental negotiations, depending on the number and kind of issues that have to be resolved.

        In addition, it is often helpful at the outset to schedule times for future sessions to anticipate the possible need for additional time to get together, thereby assuring the parties that they will have all the time they need and satisfy their interest in predictability.
    c. **Stakeholders participating.** What parties will be invited to send representatives to the negotiating table to resolve the issues? Who needs to be represented to ensure that the conflict will ultimately be put to rest?
    d. **How many from each side?** There must be a balance struck between having the numbers small enough to get the job done, and meeting the need to have each side feel that its team will be properly representative of its constituents' different perspectives. Moreover, the number of representatives from each side should be comparable. Five to seven negotiators on each side is close to the ideal size.
    e. **Specific individuals to be involved?** If more than one person is representing a party, the other side needs to know before the first session who specifically will be at the table. Team leaders should exchange the names. Avoid surprises and prevent strong reactions (e.g., objections to certain individuals) that could sabotage the entire proceeding. Adjustments may have to be made in the original cast to avoid personality clashes that could undermine the process. These kinds of considerations should be discussed with the leader of the other team.
    f. **Room arrangement?** What type of furniture will be made available, how will it be arranged, and who will sit where? Parties often have strong preferences that need to be

worked out. The parties usually prefer to sit with members of their own team, facing the other side across the table. Also, putting physical distance between the parties may help diffuse some of the tension. If the situation is volatile, placing a table between the parties can provide them with a sense of protection and safety.

- *Agree on procedural ground rules for the meetings: the rules of engagement.* Possible basic rules of courtesy and decorum include the following:

a. Being on time.
b. No interruptions.
c. No cursing or name calling.
d. No intimidation, threats, yelling, or personal attacks.
e. No physical contact.
f. No weapons in the room.
g. Treating people with respect, as defined by each side.
h. Use of caucus (private, confidential session)? A caucus allows parties to withdraw from the table to meet with their people to cool off, refocus, reenergize, discuss new information, and plan their next move. Agree on time limits, methods for requesting and extending time limits for the caucus, and sometimes even the number of times each party can call one.
i. Agreement on specific times for meals and breaks during the negotiation.
j. Placing limitations on the use of cell phones, emergency calls during the negotiation sessions, and so forth.
k. Negotiating a confidentiality agreement. This is very important to the success of the negotiation because the parties should be able to consider a variety of proposals without necessarily ending up accepting them. If they cannot rely on confidentiality, and have to worry that they will be publicly exposed for just considering these proposals, it inhibits full exploration of the options. As pointed out earlier, most states have laws protecting the confidentiality of the negotiation process. Sometimes parties are required to have had explicitly included a confidentiality provision in their procedural agreement in order for the courts to enforce it. There are different levels of confidentiality that the parties can agree on when it concerns communicating

with people outside the negotiations (e.g., press, constituents, friends and family, other staff):
* Parties can choose to share information with these outsiders about the issues being discussed without sharing the content and who said what.
* Parties can choose to share only the specific agreements that were reached.
* They can choose to share only the fact that an agreement was reached.

l. Creating a record of the proceedings. What form should the record take? What are the implications of each option?
* Voice recording of the entire proceeding
* Written transcripts of the entire proceeding
* Minutes approved by all parties
* Private notes
* Summary letter or memo
* Narrative report
* Record of only the written agreement prepared by the two teams

m. Using the services of an impartial mediator or facilitator during these negotiations to help move discussions along in an orderly way. If the parties use a mediator or facilitator, is there agreement on who that would be, and how the service will be paid for?

- *Agree on an agenda for the session(s).*
  a. What issues will be discussed? In what order?
  b. Will time limits be assigned to each issue?
  c. Agree to add issues upon mutual agreement at a later time if needed.

- *Once the negotiations are complete, agree on what is to follow.*
  a. What type of agreement do we intend to create?
     * A verbal agreement?
     * A tentative agreement?
     * An agreement in principle?
     * An agreement on a process to follow to resolve substantive issues?
     * A behaviorally specific written agreement that addresses and resolves all the issues? We believe that all that is

necessary is to record the explicit agreements that the parties made. That alone is the record to which parties can be held accountable.

b. Define the steps and timing of the process for ratifying the proposed agreement. Who else must review and approve recommendations before they can be legal and binding? How long will each additional ratification stage take after negotiations, and when will it be scheduled?

Integrating All Parties' Cultural Preferences

The fact that the procedural agreement or process design is negotiable gives all parties the assurance that each of them has an equal share and a sense of ownership in the process. They are able to participate without being dominated by the other party. This assurance is particularly welcomed by groups that historically experienced a one-sided relationship in its negotiations, American Indian tribes being a case in point.

Serving to enhance the parties' sense of equity and ownership are negotiations that build into their procedural agreements the accommodation of the cultural differences that exist among the parties involved. We define "culture" as the way we do things around here. Cultural differences exist among and within tribes, and also among and within government bureaucracies. The culture of the negotiations should ultimately be a blend of the cultures represented by the parties at the table.

Often we are not aware of these cultural differences at the outset. In that case we have to make a special effort to articulate them from the beginning and to spot and address them whenever they appear during the discussion. If these differences are allowed to remain submerged, people may talk past each other with words and expressions that mean very different things to them. They will miss important cultural cues and may create significant distrust, costly misunderstandings, and bad feelings.

Some of the provisions of the procedural agreement (e.g., locations, times and length of the negotiation sessions, who will be invited to participate, acceptable language and behavior) may elicit different cultural preferences. Other cultural values and practices that might be taken into consideration when crafting a procedural agreement may be elicited through the following questions: Will the elders play a special role? What language(s) will be the official one(s) spoken? Will interpreters be invited to be part of the process? Will the meeting begin with a prayer? How will meals be handled? What values, traditions, or interests will be reflected in the seating arrangements? How long will the working sessions be? What subjects will the agenda address or not address and in what order, and will there be a special way of addressing them? What role will relationship building play in the process? How much of a need will there be for active listening to ensure that people are understanding each other? In the end, the procedural agreement will not result from your way or my way. It will be a blend of each party's cultural preferences: our way.

At Indian Dispute Resolution Services (IDRS), we do not have an opinion about what constitutes Indian values and traditional negotiating practices and processes that should be incorporated in all negotiations involving Native people. Instead, the principle that should be promoted is that negotiators in each community should define these preferences and values for themselves, and to make sure that the negotiations accommodate the cultural preferences, values, and practices they consider important.

Functions of the Procedural Agreement

The need for negotiating procedural ground rules at the outset can only be fully appreciated when we understand the multiple functions they serve. A procedural agreement has the following benefits:

- *The agreement defines the framework in which the conflict will be resolved.* It confines and focuses the attention and energy of the disputing parties in a constructive direction.
- *The parties are given the assurance that the process will not be a free-for-all.* In the spirit of satisfying some of Maslow's basic human needs (see chapter 3), rules are designed to assure the parties of an orderly approach, personal safety, predictability, respect, dignity, fairness, a place to hear and be heard, and a place to gain understanding and meaning.
- *The agreement sends a clear message that the negotiation process belongs equally to all the parties.* These ground rules are negotiable, so no party alone can design the process and determine how the discussion should proceed. This is an essential message for government agency officials who might think they are in charge.
- *Taking the time to systematically negotiate a procedural agreement at the outset slows the parties and the process down* and brings

relative calm at a time when the parties are most prone to quickly react rather than thoughtfully respond.
- *The agreement provides the parties with a structured setting* in which to listen and talk to, cooperate with, and agree with one another, perhaps for the first time since the outbreak of the conflict.
- *The agreement encourages the parties to take personal responsibility* for protecting the resolution process by anticipating, planning, managing, and putting in place what will be needed to ensure that their negotiations will be productive.
- *Agreeing on procedural ground rules is easier than agreeing on solutions for contentious substantive issues.* Starting with these easier procedural issues can help establish some momentum behind agreeing. Parties often observe at this point in the negotiations, "At least we are agreeing about *something.*"
- *Procedural ground rules give negotiators the opportunity to anticipate and accommodate cultural differences* between the teams, constituents, and leaders, and to design a process that works for everyone.
- *An agreement creates mechanisms that can serve as confidence-building measures in a context in which the parties initially did not trust one another.* When the parties keep their procedural agreements, these become concrete ways to measure trustworthiness. As a proposition to be tested: "If you can trust them to keep their procedural promises, you probably can trust them to keep their substantive agreements."

Creating Substantive Satisfaction

This book is devoted to teaching skills and outlining a step-by-step process by which negotiators can create a secure and predictable setting for problem-solving, surface important differences, build an agenda that identifies the important substantive problems, generate options, satisfy mutual interests, and reach agreements to resolve their differences. In effect, negotiators use all these tools to achieve a satisfying outcome.

However, the agreement language itself should be crafted in certain ways to lock in these gains, and to ensure that substantive satisfaction is protected and promoted into the future. These ways include the following:

- *Make sure you spend the time and effort to craft a detailed written agreement.* Only a written agreement can properly capture and memorialize what you and the other party have agreed to orally. If agreements are only oral, the parties will inevitably interpret and remember them differently—or not at all. In fact, in the very process of writing down specific language you are able to identify the omissions and potential loopholes of your oral agreements.

- *The agreement should be a carefully written document to avoid misunderstandings and further conflict after negotiations are finished.* It should leave nothing undefined and be crafted so that it is completely understandable to all those who participated. Only a written agreement can serve as the official record that you, not to mention others who were not directly involved, can refer to well into the future during the fulfillment of the promises you exchanged.
- *Create balance in the final agreement so that there is apparent fairness in what you are agreeing to,* so that everyone is assigned part of the responsibility of keeping the agreement. You can do this by alternating between what each party agrees to: "Mary agrees to X. Ed agrees to Y. Mary agrees to Z."
- *Express the promises being made in specific behavioral terms.* Address who, what, when, where, how, and how much. The more explicit and concrete the agreement is, the less likely that false and unfulfilled expectations are being created. Moreover, the parties will better understand what they are agreeing to, with less likelihood that there will be "conflict aftermath" (i.e., additional conflict over provisions in the agreement and additional disagreements that arise). Expressing these provisions in complete sentences forces people to be clear. People may get tired or lazy at this point, but this is no time to resort to shorthand.
- *All the issues identified as agenda items should be resolved or otherwise disposed of in an agreed-upon manner.* In the last stages of crafting the agreement, you and the other party should revisit the agenda together and review whether you feel that each agenda item was addressed one way or another. Some items may no longer have the same importance or urgency once other items have been resolved and agreements were reached. On the other hand, some items may have been overlooked in the excitement of having successfully resolved the other issues. In either case, try to establish an explicit agreement to

drop such items, and incorporate some specific language in the agreement to this effect. It will enhance both parties' sense of completeness—and satisfaction.
- *Avoid using vague language.* Some negotiators and mediators intentionally use vague agreement language because they feel that attempts to get more precise at that time might jeopardize getting any agreement at all. Others just have bad habits and do not fully appreciate the need to be specific in order to avoid future misunderstandings. The problem with vague language is that it means different things to different people, revealing a lack of agreement. Some examples of poor agreement language include the following:

    "Good-faith effort"
    "Reasonable facsimile"
    "Of similar value"
    "In a reasonable amount of time"
    "With all deliberate speed"
    "As quickly as possible"
    "A significant amount of"
    "To the satisfaction of"
    "An acceptable substitute"
    "Approximately"
    "Adequate"
    "Demonstrate every effort"
    "Considerable"
    "Substantial"
    "Comparable"

    List others.
- *Make sure that the agreement has been reality-tested.* You and the other party should closely examine the agreement together before it is finalized to determine whether it is realistic and feasible. Do each of you have the resources, the time, the agreement of others not at the table, and so on, to actually fulfill the commitments you are making? Are you taking the time to think through thoroughly the implications of your agreements?
- *Include a "future dispute resolution clause" that defines a step-by-step process for resolving unanticipated disputes that may arise* during the implementation of the agreement or at any time in the future between you and the other party. Agreeing now on a

process when things are cordial is better than trying to define a process when things may have heated up again. Consider the following as an example of agreement language:

> In the event a new matter arises pertaining to this dispute, or there is subsequent disagreement over the language or the interpretation of any provision in this agreement, the parties will implement the following steps:
>
> a. We agree to notify each other whenever either of us has a problem we want to discuss. We will then agree to sit down together to try to work things out by talking things through.
> b. In the event our efforts to negotiate are unsuccessful, we will commission the services of a mediator. [As part of this provision, you can agree on a specific mediator or program or organization that provides mediators.]
> c. In the event that we are unable to resolve one or all of the issues through mediation, we will agree to binding arbitration to resolve remaining problems. We will select a mutually acceptable arbitrator to conduct a hearing and make a decision for us. If we are unable to agree on a particular arbitrator, each of us will select one—and the two persons selected will select the third person to serve. The panel of three arbitrators will decide the case.

- *Include in the final agreement the understanding you previously reached about keeping confidentiality.* Some provisions may apply to behavior that still must be honored after the negotiations are complete.
- *Include a paragraph generally affirming that the agreement fully addresses and resolves all the matters in contention.* As an example, "We agree that this Agreement, and all the provisions contained herein, fully resolves all the disagreements between us. We further agree that we have entered this Agreement on our own volition and will fully comply with all the terms and conditions expressly agreed upon."
- *Consider including a preamble or concluding paragraph that makes explicit the parties' purpose for coming together to negotiate*

a mutually acceptable agreement. This statement establishes the broader context and serves as a reminder to the parties what is truly at stake. An example of possible language for such a provision is as follows: "We, the undersigned, agree that we have entered into the above-listed provisions of the Agreement on our own volition with the intention of resolving some major conflicts that have limited the effectiveness of our organization. Our intent is that this Agreement resolve past conflicts once and for all and that we move forward together to create a healthy and prosperous community for all our members."

- *Remember that the parties can always negotiate breaks if participants are getting tired and are not able to give full attention to the discussion.* The process can be exhausting, and chances are that if one party is running out of steam, the other is also. A good game of volleyball might be a great way to refresh, unwind, and build relationships.

Developing Relational Satisfaction

What happens between the parties during negotiations will have a direct bearing on how successful they are in their negotiations and are able later to work together during the implementation phase. When they are still suspicious of one another's intentions, are reluctant to reveal their reactions and concerns, and do not volunteer crucial information, they may still be able to be cordial and muscle through the negotiation/mediation process to arrive at a final agreement. On the other hand, the results will be far different when people have developed a positive chemistry, have candid or humorous exchanges, accept differences in perspectives, reveal heartfelt hopes, get to know each other during breaks, and are able to sit down together for meals and recreational activities.

Building relationships between the parties in a negotiation has not been a top priority in contemporary American society, particularly within the business community. Members of corporate America have typically skipped this relationship-building phase and assumed they could get down to the nitty-gritty business decisions immediately. They have not set aside ample time to develop goodwill, and then they often resort to forcing the issue (e.g., creating false urgency) in order to reach an agreement.

The neglect of relationship building has been particularly apparent with U.S. corporate leaders who have tried to enter into business relationships (licensing agreements, franchises, partnerships, etc.) with their counterparts in developing nations. Thinking they can fly in and out of a foreign city the same day, U.S. business leaders have failed to allow the time needed to meet the social customs and traditional practices in these other cultures. Businesspeople from these areas typically want to spend time together with other businesspeople, eating meals, taking in cultural and entertainment events, and introducing their foreign guests to their family members. They are offended if their gestures of hospitality are rejected. Sometimes U.S. businesspeople are bewildered by this behavior of their foreign counterparts, but this is all part of wanting to get to know each other better before getting down to the task of negotiating a deal.[2]

Relationship building between parties in a negotiation may not always be easy or successful, but trying is important, especially in situations in which parties in a conflict have an ongoing relationship and must interact after the conflict has been resolved. For example, couples, families, coworkers, and union and management all have to interact after the negotiations are completed.

List all the possible steps you might take to help develop a close, respectful, and trusting working relationship among the negotiating parties. The following are some representative strategies:

1. Build into the process initial personal introductions that reveal important data about who is at the table, including hobbies, their families, personal work histories, favorite movies, and so on.
2. Plan meals, side trips, and recreational events together.
3. Agree that there a core group of negotiators from all parties will attend all sessions and be involved throughout the process—with no absences, substitutes, or alternates.
4. Have the people who will live with the agreement negotiate it. Don't depend on attorneys and professional negotiators.
5. If negotiations take place away from home, arrange to stay in the same hotel and have all meals together so that members of the teams can develop informal relationships with each other.

Think of relationship building as depositing goodwill into a trust account to be drawn upon during difficult moments in the negotiation. With enough goodwill built up, there will be a greater willingness to give each other the benefit of doubt and some slack when the parties need it most. The focus will more likely be on solving the problem at hand rather than questioning the other side's motives or intentions.

Recap: The Six Stages of the Negotiation Process

Below are presented, in outline form, six stages through which negotiators and collaborative problem solvers typically work to reach a final agreement. This applies to both interpersonal and interorganizational negotiations.

Keep in mind that these six stages could be organized into more or fewer than six stages. The important point is to follow the inherent logic of the sequence that is spelled out. It resembles the same general steps that anyone trying to solve a problem would follow: gathering background information, getting those working together to agree on the process, generating options on how the problem(s) might be resolved, putting these in the form of proposals, agreeing on what seems most sensible and satisfying to those involved, and finishing up with a detailed written agreement.

Having a staged sequence of steps to follow (as presented below) should give practitioners comfort that they have logical guidelines to fall back on, and that they have a way to know where they are in the sequence at all times. This order can be helpful to negotiators who otherwise might be distracted in the middle of a very divisive and lengthy confrontation with the other party.

Stage 1—Plan and Prepare

- Conduct an assessment of the causes, costs, and benefits of the conflict.
- Research the other side's motivation, underlying interests, contacts and allies, and so forth.
- Develop an understanding regarding your side's interests and expectations.
- Identify Best Alternatives to a Negotiated Agreement (BATNA) that are available to you.
- Assemble your negotiation team, assign roles, and arrange for training in negotiation and relationship building among team members.
- List procedural issues that you would want addressed and resolved within your negotiation team.
- Develop an internal team consensus on negotiation objectives and negotiation strategy.
- Present the objectives and strategy to your organization's leaders for their formal approval.

- Set up a communication process between the team and your hierarchy and constituents, and schedule periodic meetings to update them, negotiate next steps, and obtain guidance.
- Get in touch with the other side and explore their commitment to entering negotiations.
- Discuss with the other side—not in person—some preliminary agreements regarding the setting (where and when), some ground rules for the negotiation, and the agenda items (problems) they want to discuss and resolve.
- Arrange the first meeting with the other side.

Stage 2—Begin Face-to-Face Negotiations

- At the first formal meeting with the other side, both negotiation teams should introduce themselves and provide a little personal information about themselves and their relationship to the conflict.
- Introduce the team leaders and their roles, and provide contact information.
- Discuss and resolve procedural issues, for example, use of alternates and observers.
- Agree on a negotiation schedule, including locations, dates, times, and names of participants for subsequent sessions.
- Negotiate a procedural agreement that establishes ground rules for subsequent discussions—rules of decorum, use of caucus, steps to protect the confidentiality of the process, and rules for releasing information to the public.
- Identify any additional steps that are necessary to reach final approval of the agreement from your organization's ultimate decision makers once it has been agreed upon by the negotiators.

Stage 3—Each Side Shares Its Perspective by Providing an Opening Statement

- Each side presents its opening statement without interruption, describing its perspective on the conflict, its causes, the perceived problems (agenda items) that need to be resolved, its interests, and preferred outcomes.

- Each side listens attentively for the other side's underlying interests, problems they want resolved, potential common ground, proposals, conciliatory gestures, and more.
- After each side makes its initial presentations, parties work together to create an agenda and the order in which these items are to be discussed.

Stage 4—Generate and Explore Options

- Parties take up each agenda item in the agreed-upon order.
- Parties develop a better understanding of the other side's interests and proposals by exchanging information and actively listening (asking questions, reframing, rephrasing, clarifying, validating, summarizing, etc.).
- Parties offer proposals and counterproposals to resolve the identified problems—addressing and resolving them one agenda item at a time.
- Parties identify any additional data requirements before an agreement can be consummated, and concur on the sources of that information and the process to be followed (what, by whom, and by when). Also, parties agree on who will secure funds needed and how for obtaining these additional data.

Stage 5—Reach a Verbal Agreement

- Discuss and resolve each agenda item in the agreed-upon order.
- Make general agreements in principle, if needed, that promise to satisfy the interests of both parties.
- Offer concessions in exchange for concessions from the other side (quid pro quo).
- Do not ignore the other side's proposals. Send a modified version back that meets your interests as well.
- Make additional agreements, even at this stage, that may be very detailed and specific (who, what, when, where, how, and how much). Alternatively, agreements may be only tentative until all issues are resolved and a complete package is agreed upon.

Stage 6—Negotiate a Detailed Written Agreement

- Negotiate specific language for the final agreement. Be behaviorally specific in writing the agreements—what, when, where, how much, and by whom—to prevent future disagreements.
- Use a flip chart, whiteboard, or projector to post the evolving agreement on the board in front of the negotiators. In this way, everyone can track the progress and begin to collaborate in problem solving by working together on the language and addressing the omissions in the verbal agreement.
- Avoid writing vague language; spend the needed time to be more specific and clear about the intent of the provisions and thus avoid future misunderstandings.
- Create a balanced agreement that specifies and distributes responsibility among the parties.
- Include a future dispute resolution provision describing an agreed-upon process for resolving any future disagreements encountered during and after the implementation of the agreement.
- Acknowledge that the agreement reached at the table is only a recommendation to each team's final decision makers until it receives their formal review and approval.
- After the parties have met with their final decision makers and identified any remaining issues, return to the table and work with the other team to further refine the written agreement to incorporate needed clarifications and close identified loopholes. Further negotiations may be necessary before the final version can be ratified.
- Affix signatures of those with the authority to give final approvals, make copies for all participants, and retain an official copy for the records.

5

MEETING THE STRUCTURAL CHALLENGES OF NEGOTIATING WITH GOVERNMENTS

Before discussing the ins and outs of the intergovernmental negotiation process, and the skills and strategies that can be used to increase a tribe's effectiveness, we need to start with some background on the importance that Native nations place on their ancestral land and on natural resource management issues. It is at the top of most of their agendas and the issue for which many negotiations will likely take place in the years to come.

Tribal Protection of Natural Resources and Ancestral Lands

Since American Indian tribes were overrun by European immigrants, they have lost most of the land they once regarded as their own. Treaties were negotiated in which Native Nations ceded vast areas of their former ancestral lands in exchange for certain promises from the federal government. Tribes were guaranteed permanent reservations and perpetual financial support for specific programs and services (e.g., education, health, and resource management). As their legal trustee, the federal government also promised to protect their rights and resources and advance their interests in judicial and political forums.

Treaty Land Survey Errors

Over time Indian tribes repeatedly discovered that these government guarantees were not sacrosanct. To begin with, a pattern emerged of government land surveyors "inadvertently" leaving out huge sections of the land that the federal government had previously promised to the tribes during the treaty negotiations. For example, the Umatilla in northeastern Oregon, the Klamath Tribes in southern Oregon, and the

Colville Confederated Tribes in north central Washington all lost close to half of the treaty lands they had been promised, allegedly because the federal government land surveyors were "confused" and made "mistakes."[1] Other Native nations likely suffered the same fate.

The Dawes Allotment Act (1887)

In addition to these so-called survey errors, federal legislation whittled away tribes' land bases even more. Over the years it became abundantly clear that the federal government and non-Indian pressure groups followed an agenda of trying to take away tribes' lands and resources, while simultaneously assimilating them into mainstream society. Most famous was the Dawes Allotment Act (1887). It provided for "allotment" of the reservation to individual tribal members as part of an official policy to destroy tribalism (i.e., holding land communally).[2] Before the 1850s almost all Indian land had been held communally by the tribes, but the Allotment Act was intended to change that by breaking ownership down among individuals and reducing the overall amount by selling off "surplus" lands that were not allotted to the members. These surplus tribal lands were made available for non-Indian settlement, resulting today in a checkerboard land tenure pattern on many reservations. Some forty-one million acres of former tribal land were allotted.[3]

Termination

Decades later, in 1953, the U.S. House of Representatives passed Concurrent Resolution 108 (commonly, if inaccurately, referred to as the Termination Act), which called for the liquidation of assets belonging to many Indian tribes, followed by the cancellation of their federal trust status. As a result, huge tracts of tribal land promised in treaties were taken away (with minimal compensation), along with Native people's natural resources and other forms of support that they had been promised in perpetuity. Between 1953 and 1964, the government terminated recognition of more than 109 tribes and bands as sovereign dependent nations. More than two thousand Native Americans, or 3 percent of their population, were affected.

Similar to other land grabs by the federal government, "economic ambitions on the part of outsiders and the acquisition and use of tribal assets by non-Indians were key motivations behind termination legislation. Most of the targeted tribes and their reservations had timber, minerals, agricultural lands, and other natural resources coveted by non-Indians." This congressional act was later rescinded, but the damage was already done. Rarely was any land returned to the terminated tribes as part of their "restoration."[4]

Other Strategies for Seizing Native Lands

The federal government also permanently seized Indian lands for national parks, national forests, monuments, and wildlife refuges and to meet national "emergencies" (e.g., the Badlands in South Dakota were taken for bombing ranges and landing strips during wartime).[5]

To this day, the loss of their lands is a continuing source of grievance for tribes. Their sense of loss goes beyond having simply forfeited a piece of real estate. Tribes are inextricably connected to their ancestral lands and resources. Often, they were home for thousands of years: where their families lived, died, and were buried; where their sacred sites are located; where they practiced their religious ceremonies; and where their customs and traditions originated. Indian people still sing their songs, hunt, fish, trap, and gather their subsistence foods and medicinal plants on these lands. It is also where they historically assumed the responsibility for stewardship, that is, continually protecting, restoring, and enhancing the natural environment and wildlife.

Times have changed since tribes were just unsuspecting victims of outsiders' decisions. With stronger, more developed, and independent political institutions, tribes are more organized nationally. Moreover, in many cases, greater financial self-sufficiency due to owning casinos and other profitable businesses means that certain tribes now have surplus revenues to buy back land parcels within their ancestral land base. In addition, a few Native nations have been able to establish cooperative relationships with federal agencies (e.g., the Bureau of Land Management [BLM], national forests, the National Park Service [NPS]) and to negotiate the return of sections of their former lands. Other Native peoples have gained access to their lands without gaining ownership rights. Some have been granted these concessions through litigation. Others have entered negotiated agreements that have helped them advance their interest in getting back on their lands to practice religious ceremonies, protect their culture, and proactively steward and restore the health of the forests and other natural resources.[6]

Some of these federal agencies may have a growing interest in cooperating with the tribes in the future. It would seem logical that federal government decision makers would become increasingly concerned with larger and larger federal deficits. Huge costs in connection with federal land management are also an increasing problem. Natural resource agencies such as the U.S. Forest Service spend a major portion of their funds, billions of dollars each year, for fire suppression activities to contain a growing number of catastrophic wildfires in the West. As a result, the agencies have even fewer resources available for proper fire prevention, forest restoration, and other responsible natural resource management practices. They need to pool resources, expertise, and staff with other agencies, nonprofit organizations, and tribes to get the job done.

More cooperation would be good news for tribes. However, this will not occur overnight and certainly not on its own. Native nations have to approach the agencies with persistence and resolve, and adopt effective intergovernmental negotiation skills and strategies.

Other Intergovernmental Negotiations

The lessons that Indian Dispute Resolution Services (IDRS) and its partner tribes have learned in natural resource–related negotiations clearly have broader application in Indian Country today. Tribes are involved in a growing number of government-to-government negotiations largely because they are sponsoring community and economic development projects whose impacts extend beyond their reservation boundaries. Projects that include destination tourist sites, construction of entertainment centers (gaming halls, hotels, spas, and resorts), new education and health centers, infrastructure improvements (utilities, internal and external access roads, etc.), new business incubators, and so forth inevitably impact outside jurisdictions and require coordination and compliance with their regulations. On the one hand, these tribal development activities may put additional financial pressure on local county services (e.g., law enforcement, fire protection, road maintenance, etc.). At the same time, however, these tribal activities also help to enrich surrounding areas with new opportunities for the increased purchase of local goods and services, the development of new ancillary small businesses, and the employment and training of local non-Indian residents. In any case, each of these new projects brings with it the need to sit down and discuss and resolve with local government entities a significant number of issues.

Potentially hundreds of other conflicts do not pertain to natural resources or the impact of tribes' economic development projects. These can also be resolved through government-to-government negotiations.

Types of disputes could include that of a tribe's Social Service Department with its local county welfare department regarding the need for stricter compliance with the federal Indian Child Welfare Act (1978). It could be a dispute with a state or federal agency over gaining regular access to the tribe's ancestral lands to conduct traditional religious ceremonies. Or an ongoing dispute may be taking place between a tribe and its local public school district over the quality of education services and the equity of its disciplinary program as these affect local Indian youth and children. These are just a few real examples of the need for greater coordination and negotiation with external entities.

Establishing Relationships with Agency Officials

Many Indian tribes still have relatively little regular contact with federal, state, and local agencies, even though in some cases they may have been physical neighbors and have shared borders with some of them for several hundred years. What are the underlying reasons for this limited contact?

Public agencies have a mandate to serve everyone in their jurisdictions equally. However, some groups are commonly favored, enjoying easier access and influence, while others are effectively excluded. With few exceptions, Indian tribes are still viewed as "outsiders." To this day, there is a residue of fear, ignorance, and prejudice toward Indian tribes. In addition to being influenced by these negative attitudes, government officials who hold positions of local power can be expected to try to protect the status quo and resist sharing their influence with "outsiders."

In some areas where tribes have been successful in recent years in implementing economic and employment development projects, such as casinos, there often is palpable resentment among non-Native locals, especially among people who grew up and still live in their vicinity. They remember when the same tribe was impoverished and struggling, and they have difficulty adjusting to the change in the tribe's increased prosperity and status.

Despite having certain interests in common, tribal leaders also have been reluctant to initiate relationships with public agencies and outside communities. Preoccupied with survival issues and the challenges facing their own communities, historically they have been primarily inward-looking. Lacking the financial resources and personal relationships to successfully engage in external political processes, tribal leaders adopted what appeared to them to be the more practical strategy of maintaining low visibility and non-engagement.

Structural Challenges of Government-to-Government Negotiations

Negotiation is a process, not an event. Tribes that embark on negotiations with a government agency have to realize that negotiation is a process that very likely will have to be managed over an extended period of time. All the issues are not normally resolved in one sit-down meeting. The tribe will have to commit and allocate the time of elected leaders and staff, budget financial resources for travel and travel-related costs, possibly hire consultants and other experts, engage in research and prepare documents that support the tribe's case, and possibly support litigation. A tribe that currently lacks these funds has to mobilize them from government programs and private foundations to be in a position to stay engaged for as long as it will take.

Many tribes and government agencies alike have had limited or no experience structuring and managing a government-to-government negotiation. Because there still is a certain amount of mystery associated with this subject, we attempt in this chapter to break down this challenge into a series of manageable parts. We also identify some best practices that tribes should follow to maximize their chances for success.

Tribal negotiations with governments and other large organizations are structurally more complex than negotiations between single individuals who have the authority to make final decisions regarding an agreement. They are more complex because those who make the final decision for the entity (e.g., top leaders in the agency and the tribe's elected leaders and sometimes all their enrolled members) are usually not involved in the negotiation process itself on a full-time basis. Many of these leaders are not able to devote the required time or they lack the specific technical skills and negotiation expertise that are needed. And obviously, in the case of the tribe, too many decision makers would be sitting around the negotiating table.

In the absence of those final decision makers at the table, the organization's leadership needs to appoint a negotiation team to steer and undertake the work of the negotiations. It will be composed of persons who in effect will act as spokespersons for the primary constituencies and for the general interests of the organization during their deliberations.

The negotiation team is actually involved in three different negotiations simultaneously during the entire process: (1) across the table with the other party ("horizontal negotiations"), (2) with members of their own team who have different perspectives and interests ("internal team negotiations"), and (3) periodically with the final decision makers in the organization who ultimately have to approve the final agreement ("vertical negotiations"). Here we examine all three dimensions and how each factors into the process.[7]

Vertical Negotiations

Agree on a Negotiation Strategy

In preparing for a government-to-government negotiation, the tribal government needs to reach internal agreement on its underlying concerns and interests and what outcome(s) it wants to achieve in the negotiations with the agency or agencies. One of its first tasks is to appoint a negotiation team with the responsibility of proposing to the tribal leadership a coherent set of negotiation objectives and a negotiation strategy for its consideration and approval.

Because all major decisions are usually made collectively within tribes,[8] the team should begin this process by meeting and consulting with a number of different people and groups within the tribe to get their perspectives and input. At the very least, this includes the elected leaders, the executive staff and management team, the various administrative departments, and other tribal groups (e.g. tribal elders) that may have a strong interest in the subject matter and outcome.

This outreach effort takes time, but reaching out to the various parts of the organization and community is time well spent in building awareness and support from people who have a stake in the outcome. By giving these constituents the procedural satisfaction of being consulted, the team helps to build its own credibility and people's confidence that it will be responsive to this group's interests. The negotiation team will also be alerted to the range of internal concerns as well as to specific groups and individuals within the organization who may be problematic if not brought along.

Once the tribe's negotiation team has solicited information from the membership and formulated a negotiation plan, it needs to sit down in a structured meeting and get general buy-in from the tribal leaders who ultimately will be signing off on any agreement.

In these negotiations with the leaders, the negotiation team faces two challenges. First, it needs to find a way to keep in the loop the leaders who will not be at the negotiation table. This includes getting them to agree to meet periodically during the negotiations to stay up to date on its progress. It is important to bring the decision makers along during the entire process rather than surprising them at the end with news that does not conform to their earlier expectations.

Second, the team should already start to manage exaggerated expectations by injecting some reality into the discussions about what may or may not be possible.[9] The team can prepare the decision makers to anticipate the dynamic nature of the upcoming negotiations by letting them know that subsequent meetings with them will be needed to discuss strategic adjustments that the tribe may have to make in view of new and unanticipated information that it learns from the other side as the negotiations progress. These decision makers should also be alerted about the importance of confidentiality and the fact that the team will only disclose the negotiation's internal proceedings at the scheduled formal meetings, and that these communications must be circumspect.

Even though the team has to defer to the top leaders whose role is to give ongoing direction and to ultimately approve the negotiated agreement, the relationship has to be more collegial than the typical top-down command structure. The negotiation team and the tribal leaders are interdependent and depend on each other to share their expertise. To do its job effectively, the tribe's negotiation team cannot afford to be caught simply in an obedient-messenger role that does everything its leaders ask it to do. During its interactions with the other side, the team acquires insights into what is possible, and needs to share this information with its own leaders and use it to persuade them to modify their expectations and their proposals, if necessary. Of course, they may also find that they can get a better agreement than originally thought. In that case, lowering expectations of their ratifiers provides the team members an opportunity to come back as heroes rather than as scoundrels who got less than expected.

The Team's Authority to Consummate an Agreement

Since the negotiators at the table are representing people who are not at the table, the negotiation team is not given the authority to make a final decision until the ratifiers have reviewed and approved the tentative agreement reached by the negotiation teams. Until that point, both parties' representatives at the table are expected to work together to come up with an "agreement to recommend" that they are reasonably sure will be approved by the leaders they are representing. In the case of the government agency, officials at the top levels of its hierarchy, often including those in the local, regional, and national offices, will be the ones giving the final approval.

The Dangers of Not Communicating with Top Decision Makers

Before leaving the discussion about vertical negotiations, we should avoid glossing over an all-too-common problem in tribal government-to-government negotiations. Agency negotiation teams often fail to communicate with their top decision makers during negotiations. Tribal negotiation teams must understand the dangers here and ensure that this does not occur. Unfortunately, tribes often discover the problem late in the game, unless the matter is explicitly addressed at the outset during procedural negotiations.

Sometimes negotiation teams think that minimal or no contact with their top leaders during the negotiations serves them because it gives them more flexibility to respond to the other team, but this approach often backfires. Teams that attempt to negotiate without direct and periodic contact with their ultimate decision makers (ratifiers) will be unable to answer the other team's questions about the agency's interests and what they will ultimately accept and not accept in the final agreement. The agency negotiators will be unable to give clear answers because they didn't have any occasion to ask. Then when the time comes to get their bosses to approve the final agreement the agency team will not be able to deliver. The team will likely have moved far ahead of their leaders' original expectations. Without periodic communication and necessary adjustments in strategy and expectations, the negotiation will be fatally flawed. It is perhaps the most critical aspect of the process design.

Consultation versus Negotiation

A big source of misunderstanding during tribes' government-to-government negotiations is the lack of distinction between "consultation" and "negotiation." Why is this problem so prevalent among agencies? It boils down to the fact that agencies and tribes have very different understandings and expectations when they enter a government-to-government relationship. One reason for this confusion was that when President Bill Clinton issued his Executive Order 12875 in 1994, which became Executive Order 13175 two years later, prescribing a government-to-government relationship, it failed to distinguish between a consultation process and a negotiation process, and to state a preference as to how this order should be operationalized.

In reality, consultation and negotiation are distinctly different processes. Consultation is top-down and unilateral rather than a process in which the parties are on an equal level and negotiate to reach a mutually acceptable agreement. In consultations, the agency speaks to the tribe to gather information, which the agency officials then take back to their office to evaluate. Then the agency decision makers typically reach an independent decision without further input from the tribe.

When the agency sees itself engaged in consultation rather than negotiation, its decision makers have no motivation to maintain ongoing communication with their team during negotiations. Chances are, at this point, the agency has not even identified its interests and what it will and will not agree to. These agency decision makers believe that they are responsible for making the decision by themselves unilaterally. The so-called negotiations will be truncated, essentially limited to sitting with the tribal representatives asking them what they want with little or no discussion or feedback. The government agency typically does not indicate to the tribe what the agency wants—what its interests are—in meeting with the tribe.

Unless persuaded otherwise, agencies prefer to think that they are fulfilling the government-to-government relationship called for by President Clinton's Executive Order through consultations. In stark contrast, tribal leaders prefer bilateral negotiations in which the parties are committed to work toward developing an agreement that serves both of them and that they both accept. Many tribal leaders, when the federal government asks them only for an opinion that does not involve a discussion and an agreement, believe that consultation is insulting. They feel that they were not taken seriously, just used by the agency to fulfill the requirement of the agency's consultation policy, and were simply checked off the agency's list of invitees after they testified. They are usually not even apprised of the results after the consultation process has been completed; as such, this process rarely improves the agency's relationship with the tribe.[10]

Some agency officials contend that they cannot negotiate with a tribe because the government has the ultimate responsibility—the legislative mandate—to make the final decisions. They maintain that they would be giving up their sovereign authority by letting the tribe make the decisions. Regrettably, that position reveals a complete lack of understanding about the negotiation process. The correct stance to take is that negotiations involve parties making decisions together, and that neither party needs to agree to anything that is contrary to its interests. It can be a win-win process in which both parties work together to reach an agreement that meets both of their underlying interests, and where the agreement does not require either party to sacrifice its sovereign authority.

The second point is that federal agencies already have a track record in government-to-government negotiations. It should not be a foreign concept to them. Many agencies have engaged in negotiations with groups of their constituents through what is known as "negotiated rule making." In this process, the agency that is promulgating new regulations to implement a new law invites the groups that will be affected to enter face-to-face negotiations with the agency. They meet until they reach mutual agreement about what these regulations should consist of before they are published in the *Federal Register*.

Some agencies readily agree that the negotiated-regulations process can be cheaper and quicker than when the agency formulates the rules in isolation, and then has to resolve challenges in court before they can be implemented. Another result has been greater compliance once the regulations are in effect because those affected by the regulations had a part to play in formulating them.

When Native nations sit down to negotiate with agencies, the leaders should ask two questions at the beginning of the process: Is the agency ready to engage in a negotiation and not a consultation? Also, will the agency team be meeting regularly with their ratifiers during the negotiations? These fundamental process issues should be clarified in the beginning when the procedural agreement is being negotiated.

Reluctance to Tell Bosses What to Do

There is another reason why agency officials participating in negotiations with tribes may not be involved in ongoing conversations with their agency's primary decision makers. Communication is typically from the top down in bureaucratic agencies, which makes it particularly awkward for people lower in the chain of command to request involvement or advise those higher up the chain about how to be involved in the intergovernmental negotiation process.

Someone who is not buried in the agency hierarchy might have to request that this communication link be built into the negotiation process. This can be done in one of three different ways:

1. *The leader of the tribe's negotiation team, in the course of procedural negotiations, can ask his counterpart on the other side of the table the two questions posed above.*

In the Timbisha Shoshone Negotiations (described in chapter 7), it took over seven months before face-to-face negotiations began to get the agency to agree that it was willing to negotiate (rather than consult) with the tribe. That was communicated only on the first day of the face-to-face meeting. However, it was an explicit understanding from that point forward.

Since the Timbisha Shoshone Tribe was dealing with a team of representatives drawn from four federal agencies, the tribe's negotiation team secured a commitment that the directors of these four agencies back in Washington, D.C., would form an Agency Working Group that would track progress and negotiate among themselves on how to respond in a timely manner to questions raised by their federal team leader. The tribal negotiation team adopted the practice of holding short, informal talks with the federal team leader in the evening before the next session and informing him about what it was prepared to propose the next day. This allowed him to discuss it with his Agency Working Group in the morning in Washington, D.C. (three hours difference in time), and to prepare his response before meeting with the tribe that day.

2. *The tribal chair and the tribe's negotiation team leader can agree to go above the head of the agency's team leader.*

If the agency's negotiation team leader is reluctant to ask his agency's top leaders to keep in contact with their negotiation team, then the tribal leaders can reach out to the agency leaders and confirm that the agency's intention is to (a) negotiate and (b) be involved in periodic communication with the agency's team to give direction and track the progress of the discussions. Remember that the tribe is not part of the agency's hierarchy and should be able to have direct access to the agency's directors within the context of its government-to-government relationship.

IDRS has been involved in negotiations with agency negotiators who have tried to inhibit the tribe's team from talking to people higher up the chain or to people outside the agency. This may have been motivated by a desire to keep total control over the process, or based on the belief that the issues were not important enough to warrant the attention of the agency directors. In any case, tribes should not agree to that kind of limitation on their freedom of movement. The tribe is a sovereign government and should be able to talk to anyone.

3. *The mediator or facilitator can meet with the agency directors to discuss process design if the services of an outside mediator or facilitator are being used to assist in the negotiations.*

The mediator or facilitator is hired to work with both parties and move them toward a negotiated agreement. This action may include educating the top leaders of the agency and the tribe about the difference between negotiation and consultation, and the importance of maintaining internal communications throughout the negotiations.

Talking to Tribal Ratifiers during Negotiations

As suggested above, Native nations' negotiation teams also need to keep in communication with their ultimate decision makers. There are too many examples of tribal teams spending a lot of time, energy, and resources negotiating an agreement only to have the tribe's ratifiers ultimately reject it.

As one example, a tribe in eastern California some years ago negotiated a novel partnership agreement with some shopping center developers who were interested in partnering with the tribe on tribal land. This agreement promised to produce substantial tribal revenues and lead to the transfer of full ownership and management to the tribe after five to seven years of operation. The draft agreement provided that the developers would train tribal members alongside experienced managers working in their other shopping centers to prepare for the transition.

When it was brought to a vote by the tribe's general council, the proposed agreement was vigorously opposed and ultimately defeated by a vocal elders group. It objected to the site chosen for the development, to the financial incentives paid to specific families that would have to give up their land assignments to make space for the shopping center, and to the concept of the tribe leasing scarce tribal lands for business purposes. These constituents had not been consulted or informed about the content of the agreement during the entire two years of negotiations, and the negotiators did not foresee what would be unacceptable to the members at a time when they still might have been able to make suitable adjustments.[11]

Internal Team Negotiations

As mentioned above, one of the first decisions a Native nation makes to prepare for a government-to-government negotiation is to appoint a competent and well-balanced tribal negotiation team to represent it. The tribal council, the governing body in charge of day-to-day matters, will likely be responsible for selecting the members of the tribe's negotiating team.

But who should it appoint? Certain misconceptions surround this question, the most common being that it should automatically select the elected tribal leaders. The other misconception is that selecting lawyers to represent the tribe is the ideal strategy.

Whom Should the Tribe Appoint to Its Negotiation Team?

The most successful negotiation teams comprise members who represent a broad spectrum of the community and consist of people with the full range of perspectives, knowledge, skills, and credibility that are needed to address the specific issues with which the negotiation is concerned. Consider whether the problems concern cultural resources; fish, wildlife, and land management; economic development; the intricacies of water rights; or other matters dealing with tribe's legal rights and history; education, housing, and health services; and so on.

The tribal council should appoint people who can talk about these issues competently and hold their own in discussions with their counterparts on the agency's negotiation team. Also, the council should ensure that the team consists of people who understand the negotiation process, have good language and communication skills, and can negotiate the tribe's interests rather than bringing solely their pent-up emotions of anger, suspicion, frustration, and hurt.

Perhaps none of the elected tribal council members meet these criteria. Nor may they have the time or interest needed to serve, and therefore should not be burdened with this responsibility. On the other hand, at a minimum, one elected leader should be included on the team for at least one reason: it helps to consistently remind the agency that it is engaged in a negotiation between two sovereign governments, and that the negotiation is in fulfillment of the government-to-government relationship.

The Role of Lawyers

Historically, many tribes have relied on their lawyers to represent them in negotiations, largely because lawyers are perceived to speak the language of the dominant class, and they are professionals who know how to put up a good fight. There should be no doubt that a lawyer can be helpful as a member of the team to answer legal questions and provide a legal perspective. Nonetheless, tribal members are the best ones to present the tribe's point of view. It will be more authentic and compelling, and after all, when all is said and done, these leaders remain in the community and have to live with the agreement. Moreover, it will be a learning experience for the tribal members when they do not depend exclusively on their lawyers. It will empower and increase these leaders' capacity to move their members to self-determination, which should always be a major objective for the tribe as it enters the negotiation process.[12]

What's more, not all lawyers are good negotiators. Lawyers who specialize in litigation can be aggressive and adversarial, and can miss opportunities for deal making, which is the essence of the negotiation process. Some lawyers, regrettably, can be problematic for another reason. On some occasions they actively and covertly have tried to discourage tribal leaders from engaging in direct negotiations with external government entities. The lawyers preferred to initiate litigation and resolve the matter in the courts, or alternatively, they wanted the tribe to rely on lawyers to negotiate on its behalf. Whether motivated by their lack of confidence in the negotiation process or in the tribal leaders managing the negotiation themselves—or maybe they preferred to seize the opportunity to capture additional billable hours—it is a troubling interference with the tribe's fulfillment of self-determination and the positive exercise of its sovereignty. It is also a lost opportunity for tribal leaders to gain experience and expand their leadership skills.

The Role of Other Technical Professionals

Many of the considerations applicable to lawyers are also valid with respect to the limitations of other professionals working for tribes. In some cases they have preferred that the tribe let them fix things with their counterparts in the agency rather than have the tribal leaders initiate higher-level government-to-government negotiations with the agency's leaders. The problem is that, without tribal government involvement, the professional staff is only able to influence agency operations at the program level on a case-by-case basis. They try to influence the agency on the basis of their personal relationships and on their personal skills of persuasion, not on the strength of their affiliation with a sovereign tribal entity nor their ability to call on a government-to-government relationship with the agency.

In the meantime, the tribal government may need to address larger questions with the agency than case-by-case adjustments in the agency's programs and procedures. To get the results it wants, the tribe may have to change the nature of its relationship with the agency so that it is regularly informed and consulted about plans, policies, and operational changes that are made affecting the interests of the Native American client community before they are implemented. It also may want to convey to the agency that it prefers getting a heads-up beforehand rather than have to appeal such decisions in the courts or at higher administrative levels.

In these negotiations with the agency, the tribal negotiators may also want to justify being involved with the agency at this higher level by comparing it to the negotiated rule making that occurs at the federal level. The state or local government would be bringing in its Native constituency to jointly negotiate the policies, rules, programs, and so on that will affect it *before they go into effect* to ensure that they meet local needs and are resolved before being challenged in court or elsewhere.

To accomplish these changes, the tribal government needs to ratchet up the conversations with the agency's top management and initiate a structured government-to-government negotiation with the agency. Bringing the discussion up to this level means disturbing the status quo. Not only is it possible that agency staff will become antagonistic, but another concern emerges: tribal staff members who are conflicted. Some may fear losing their personal access and ability to take care of individual problems through their established personal relationships. Here, too, instances have taken place in which tribal staff members have overtly or covertly stood in the way of the tribe's effort to assert its sovereignty and initiate a government-to-government relationship. When this is the case, tribal staff members are pre-empting the tribal government from negotiating a change in the relationship and possibly losing the opportunity to introduce new policies that can, in one fell swoop, resolve many issues that previously were settled on a case-by-case basis.

Apart from these considerations about the merits of involving technical staff members on the tribal negotiation team, in some ways they can play a very important role. For example, they can serve as technical advisers to the tribe's negotiation team while it is planning and implementing its strategy. The tribal government may also want to put certain members of its technical staff on the negotiation team if their special expertise is required. However, staff members should not be appointed unless the tribal government is confident that they have the needed expertise, a deep understanding of the tribe's perspective, and an unflinching loyalty to the tribe's exercise of its sovereignty and success.

What Is the Negotiation Team's Job?

The first job of the negotiation team is to identify and agree on the tribe's interests and objectives, and to design and implement the tribe's negotiation strategy. Once it secures the top leaders' buy-in, the team can begin to negotiate and try to reach an agreement with the other side.

Differences of opinion among the tribal negotiation team's members are a given. They will differ regarding the substance of the negotiation as well as the degree to which they trust the motives and actions of the agency's team. Some members may be suspicious and cautious about reaching agreement, while others may be more positive and hopeful that good agreements can be achieved. Team members may also differ on what to ask for, how to justify the tribe's proposals, and how to respond to new information coming from the agency negotiation team.[13]

While these different perspectives on the team are inevitable, they are not necessarily bad. A diversity of perspectives on the tribe's negotiation team helps ensure that team members consider the full range of points of view and potential objections, refine their thinking, and find ways to resolve internal differences. These internal team deliberations may take extra time, but better that the differences are worked out at this early stage. If a particular point of view is present in the community but the team excludes or ignores it, the tribe will likely have to deal with this oversight at a later stage when a proposed agreement is up for final approval by the community. If a significant interest group is left out of the loop, it may seek revenge by trying to quash the entire negotiated agreement. From the example cited earlier regarding a tribe's negotiations over a shopping center, we can see that such action is a real possibility.

The Team Leader

The negotiation team needs a leader who will be responsible for orchestrating the team's participation, building and maintaining internal team consensus, and coordinating with the tribal leaders and agency's team leader. In effect, the team leader will serve in the role of a quasi-mediator and needs to have strong relationship skills: to listen and speak well, relate to and involve each of its team members, and mediate among diverse interests and personalities. Moreover, the team leader serves as the public face for the team and should have sufficient charisma or gravitas to establish a strong presence, and the personality and skills to establish a good working relationship with the agency's team leader and team members. This is an important job. In contrast with a professional mediator who is impartial, a team leader or quasi-mediator is very much a partisan leading his group to a win.

The Team's Internal Procedural Ground Rules

Just as establishing procedural ground rules is an essential first step in successful negotiations with a government agency's representatives, the negotiation team members must agree on an internal process even before they try to define a negotiation strategy and deal with the substantive issues of the negotiation.

Among some of the internal procedural issues the team should resolve are the following:

- When, where, how often, and how long should the team members meet together?
- What rules should the members adopt for internal decision making—consensus, modified consensus, majority rule, or others?
- What will the rules be regarding regular attendance at the team's meetings?
- What type of record should be kept on internal agreements the team reaches?
- What different roles should there be for the team members during negotiations across the table: chief spokesperson, scribe/wordsmith, recorder, technical expert, process observer, and so on?
- What steps should be taken to keep confidentiality regarding internal team deliberations, communications with the agency team, and so forth?
- Will team members be able to call a caucus, and how will they call one at the table during horizontal negotiations?
- What ground rules should be observed when team members want to meet offline with members of the other team?

- What kind of discussions will be permitted with constituents outside the established formal process?
- How will the agenda be established for internal deliberations?
- Will a facilitator, mediator, or coach be brought in to assist in internal team decision making?
- How will absences, alternates, and observers be handled during preparation activities?
- What kind of formal negotiation training should the members receive?'

These procedural ground rules provide team members a greater sense of safety, control, equality, and predictability. They help guarantee that every team member's perspective will be treated as important and that each has an opportunity to make a contribution, hear, and be heard. These rules can also help prevent a small group of team members from gaining control over the team and reducing the role of other members.

Good rapport and trust enhance a team's effectiveness. In contrast, any unresolved internal disagreements that persist will find their way into the larger community, undermine the team's effectiveness, and increase divisiveness by encouraging people to take sides.

Relationship Building among Team Members

Negotiations are dynamic, and new information and unanticipated problems always arise that the team will need to address during negotiations. These developments can be internally divisive and destabilizing. Team members from the same tribe do not always know and trust each other.

The team leader should deliberately organize structured opportunities for team members to socialize, travel, and break bread together to help build the bonds of mutual respect and trust that are essential for a unified and smoothly functioning team. Better to do this during the preparation phases than to have to resolve personality clashes in the middle of intense negotiations with the other side. The payoff will be significant. The more comfortable team members are with one another, the easier they find it to deal with surprises and uncertainties, reach internal agreements, and bring to the effort their individual strengths, self-confidence, certainty, and authenticity. Empowered individuals empower the whole team, and those on the other side of the table can feel their presence and unified resolve.

Relationship Building within the Agency Team

Tribal negotiators should realize that the government agency also has to prepare for negotiations by appointing an agency negotiation team and a team leader, and by building and maintaining consensus among its own team members. Agencies are not monolithic, and their teams generally consist of people who represent different parts of the agency that also have different values, perspectives, and expectations. There also may be several different agencies represented on a federal team that have their own unique cultures and perspectives. The agency team needs to blend these differences to ensure that it speaks to the tribe with one voice. The tribal team should watch for internal disagreements among the federal team members that may represent opportunities to influence outcomes that are in the tribe's favor. In doing so, though, the tribal team should avoid destabilizing the federal team because that will clearly undermine its trust in the tribe.

Horizontal Negotiations

As the tribe is completing its internal preparations, it will be ready to contact the agency and schedule meetings with its representatives—"horizontal negotiations." During this stage, the tribe's negotiation team puts forward its best case, makes explicit its interests and expectations, makes proposals, and justifies why its proposals will advance its interests as well as the interests of the agency.

Enrolling the Agency in the Negotiation Process

Getting off on the right foot has an important bearing on the ultimate outcome of the negotiations. Once the tribe has begun its internal negotiations and agreed on its underlying interests and what it wants from the agency, the tribe should contact the agency and request a meeting. The local agency is most likely to be the first level to contact. If the agency has a person assigned to serve as an intergovernmental liaison this would be the first person to call to request a meeting with the local agency director.

Arranging a time for the first meeting should be followed very quickly with a letter addressed to the head of the local agency spelling out the tribe's purpose for the meeting, who will attend representing the tribe, and the general outlines of what the tribe is prepared to talk about. Some people might be reluctant to show the tribe's hand at the outset, but we have learned that this approach has certain compelling advantages.

If there is no response, and you are trying to get a meeting with a federal agency, take the next step and send a second copy of the letter, this time with copies to the regional and national offices. If you want to meet with a state agency, consider sending a copy of your letter to appropriate state legislators. If meeting with a local agency, copy the members of the county board of supervisors or members of the city council. It may also be important to include your tribal attorney. Such a letter is harder to ignore if other potentially interested people have been informed of the tribe's intent and the letter indicates that these people were copied. Informing more people also introduces more seriousness in the tribe's request for a meeting; moreover, such an approach communicates to the local agency that the matter can easily attract a larger audience and get out of its control if the agency continues to delay.

Negotiate with People in Authority

Regarding team composition, in government-to-government negotiations, the tribe wants to be dealing with an agency team that has substantial authority over determining agency policy. (On the flip side, the agency team also wants to know that the tribal team consists of people who enjoy credibility within their own hierarchy.) Remember that the higher the officials are in the agency's hierarchy, the more latitude these officials have to respond with flexibility and creativity. These people are not your strict rule enforcers; they are agency policy makers who have greater discretionary authority than the officials at the lower levels. They work at the level of decision making where they have the responsibility to respond to unusual or exceptional circumstances and can treat different situations appropriately. People at the top also have responsibility for protecting and advancing the interests of the agency itself, which should include developing positive relationships with Native nations in its jurisdiction.

The tribal negotiation team can formally request that specific agency directors and program managers whom they already know and have confidence in be assigned a spot on the agency's negotiation team. This proposal is not so preposterous when one considers the importance of having a team that the other side trusts.

But also realize that when it comes to involving those at the top of the agency, their time availability may be limited. As a result, they will likely prefer to designate other people who can give the negotiation the time and attention it deserves. This approach is workable as long as the agency negotiation team will be reporting to and conferring with the top agency leaders on an ongoing basis to keep them in the loop. But while the tribe can request that certain officials be placed on the agency team, ultimately the team's composition is up to the agency, as the tribe determines its own team makeup.

Just as it is important to make sure that the agency team has ongoing communications with its hierarchy, the tribal negotiation team should be aware of the need to educate the agency team about the tribe's internal process, especially that the tribe needs to have its recommendations ratified by the tribal membership. The team has to make clear well in advance how things work within the tribe to avoid the other side's misunderstanding and impatience.

No Surprises

Providing general information before a face-to-face meeting gives the agency's director or manager adequate time to review and consider the agenda items, which have been listed and submitted in writing, before he has to respond to the tribal representatives. When the principle of "no surprises" is honored, the responder has the opportunity to thoughtfully and creatively respond rather than react and thus avoid defaulting to negative or outdated attitudes, prejudices, and positions.

When approaching a multilayered bureaucracy, remember that the person you speak with is part of a hierarchy and has persons above and below her who may be directly or indirectly part of the decision-making process. This approach gives the director or manager the opportunity to do her homework and take the pulse of her entire staff of technical experts and policy personnel who work at the grassroots level. The director may also consult people at higher levels of authority—at the state, regional, and national levels, even at this early stage—to get a general sense of policies vis-à-vis coordinating with tribes, and to take a reading on agency policies that will either favor or discourage the agency from moving in the direction the tribe is proposing. Having something in writing from the tribe about what it wants to discuss is helpful, so that it can be shared with everyone who is involved.

People in general do best when they have had time to think things through so that they can *respond* rather than *react*. When people are surprised, they usually react with heightened emotions and are prone to be protective and resistant. When a relationship has already been contentious and volatile, officials may be apprehensive and experience considerable stress. Being surprised only exacerbates the situation.

First, the Procedural Agreement

Prior to any substantive discussions between the parties, the tribe and agency must negotiate a procedural agreement, designed to anticipate what the parties need in order to provide a sense of safety and predictability—an arrangement that is conducive to calm, creative, and productive deliberations.

We have discussed the importance of negotiation teams starting with procedural ground rules, but it bears mentioning again as it relates to intergovernmental negotiations. In general, the most important cause of unsuccessful negotiations is the parties' failure to spend the time and effort necessary to develop an explicit agreement about the process they will follow. The emphasis here is on those particular issues that are especially important in complex government-to-government negotiations. The tribe should enter their negotiations with proposals to the agency for dealing with a broad range of procedural issues. Questions that the two teams should address include the following:

- *What is the purpose?* Agree explicitly whether the stated purpose of the meetings is to develop a negotiated agreement in writing, as opposed to engaging in a consultation process.
- *Who will participate?* List the names and titles of the agency members and tribal negotiating teams who will be participating. Make this list available before the meetings to provide some predictability and avoid unnecessary surprises. It is up to each team whom it chooses to bring, but hearing that a particular person on the team will be regarded by the other team as "destructive" should be a reason for evaluating whether the drawbacks of that person's inclusion will outweigh the benefits.
- *Will there be a role for observers and alternates?* Members of the negotiating teams should consider proposing an agreement to have all team members of both teams attend all sessions (no alternates) to ensure continuity and have the opportunity to build personal relationships between the members of the two teams. Observers can inhibit the work of the negotiators, and alternates may not be necessary if the core members of the team are committed to attend all sessions.

- *What should be the size of the negotiation team? How many people from each of the parties should be seated at the table?* As a rule, the size of each team should ensure that it is large enough that each side's major constituents are represented while keeping each team small enough to avoid becoming unwieldy. Smaller teams more quickly and easily build relationships within the team and with members of the other side. Ultimately, the strength of these relationships gets the work done. About five to seven on each side is ideal.

  Determining who and how many will be on a team in government-to-government negotiations is not always easy. A number of years ago the governor of Alaska invited the Native villages in his state to negotiate with his cabinet on establishing a set of protocols for government-to-government negotiations. IDRS was asked to facilitate preliminary negotiations among the Native villages to prepare for these negotiations. Achieving internal agreement on who would represent the villages in these negotiations became an almost insuperable challenge. There were 227 villages, each of which considered itself as sovereign, and jealousy protected its right to speak for itself. But a negotiation team of 227 representatives would be unwieldy, impersonal, and inefficient.

  The villages were persuaded to winnow the number down but could not get below a negotiation team of fifty people—still too many. What evolved informally once the negotiations were underway was that about seven of the state's better-known Native leaders emerged to effectively act as the villages' spokespeople. Unfortunately, without a system for representation and communication in place that was formally agreed upon by the villages, there was growing internal resentment that reduced the potential impact that the Native communities could have had—but it was probably the best they could do, given the existing circumstances.

- *How will cultural differences be accommodated?* Answering this question is essential to balancing the sides and demonstrating a commitment to mutual recognition and respect for all the parties: How should people be addressed? What will be the role of elders? Will sessions start by offering a prayer? What will be the seating arrangements and the timing of meal breaks, and who should provide the meals? What language(s)

will be spoken? Will an interpreter be available? Will there be a facilitator or mediator? These questions are all procedural issues that should be resolved as the negotiators design the process that will be followed.
- *What negotiation schedule will be established?* Negotiate a schedule of the specific dates, times, and length of the sessions that will be agreeable to everyone on both of the negotiation teams. If the calendar is agreed to far in advance all core team members can build the dates into their personal calendars and will better be able to make themselves available for all the sessions.
- *Where will the sessions be held?* Agree on where the negotiation sessions will be convened—either in a neutral location or with some balance between having the agency coming to the tribal headquarters for some of the sessions and the tribe going to the agency's location for the other sessions. This setup implies that the parties enjoy equal status.
- *What type of record will be kept of the proceedings?* Consider recording only explicit substantive and procedural agreements that are written down, discussed, and approved by the entire group during the negotiation process. When little trust is present among the parties, they often want to catch every word and therefore tape record the entire session. However, a tape recording is not only very inhibiting but it is expensive to transcribe. Having one person take "official" minutes is also one-sided and problematic. Those minutes have to be written up after the session is adjourned and then sent out, and inevitably there are omissions and things that one side considers wrong. Suspicions will be raised, trust compromised, and arguments will result over relatively unimportant matters.

    The written agreement is ultimately the only document to which the parties have formally agreed and for which they can be held accountable. It states things succinctly and is briefer than any of the other listed options. Post the agreement on the wall as it is being developed.
- *Will a caucus be used?* Spell out how a private caucus can be managed to enable the parties to move away from the table to a confidential meeting intended for regrouping, decompressing and considering and responding to new information. Have a time limit on caucuses to minimize time away from the table, which helps keep the other party psychologically

and physically engaged during the other team's absence. We suggest fifteen minutes with the option of coming back to ask the other team for another fifteen minutes. If the time allotted is exceeded, consider postponing the caucus until lunchtime or a time after the scheduled session. By the way, the group caucusing should leave the negotiation room to preserve it as a special place where the agreed-upon rules are maintained, people are on their best behavior, and differences are honored and ultimately reconciled.

- *Will additional studies be conducted?* The parties should record and anticipate in the procedural agreement what, if any, additional questions or issues need to be researched during the negotiation process before an agreement can be reached. Agree on what additional data are needed, how and by whom they will be obtained, and when this process will be completed. Leaving the schedule open-ended may make the tribal negotiators feel that the agency is stringing them along with delaying tactics and not taking the tribe's representatives seriously.

- *Will the parties be held to confidentiality?* During the negotiation, teams have to be guarded in speaking about the content of the negotiations with their constituents, their hierarchy, and others, such as the media, who are not directly involved in the direct deliberations. They have to balance the need to provide some information with the need to protect confidentiality. Things change over time while negotiations are under way, and the teams do not want information leaked that may already be outdated, inaccurate, or taken out of context. Providing general information about where the parties are in the negotiation process, what agenda items are currently under discussion, a listing of problems anticipated, and so on, usually suffices without getting too specific.

Confidentiality is so important to success that most states have statutes protecting the confidentiality of the negotiation and mediation process. These statutes are based on the recognition that the absence of confidentiality inhibits creative problem solving. The privacy of these conversations bears heavily on whether the negotiators can feel comfortable exploring, speculating, brainstorming, thinking outside the box, and suggesting a variety of different strategies and solutions. These explorations can prove to be a liability if, in the end, specific

proposals were made but not agreed to and the negotiators are still held to account for them.
- *Should the agenda for the next session be set?* When each session comes to an end, there should be an agreement about what issues will be addressed at the following session so that the teams can come properly prepared.
- *What is the ratification process?* Define the additional steps to take to elicit final approval from each side's ratifiers once the parties at the table "agree to recommend" a final agreement. Reach consensus on what are these steps and how long each will take before it can become official and binding.

Benefits of Procedural Ground Rules

A certain attitude is typical among relatively inexperienced negotiators when they first sit down with representatives from the other side. They do not know what to expect as they enter uncharted territory, and they may be still influenced by the combative relationship that preceded their coming together to attempt resolution. They can feel wronged, suspicious, distrustful, hostile, and angry. They are much more likely to want to get even than to cooperate and make nice. If their more primitive fight-or-flight reactions are allowed to dominate, any attempts at negotiations are likely doomed.

At this point, the reader should refer back to the discussion about the functions and benefits of developing a procedural agreement, and general procedural issues that should be addressed and resolved at the outset of the negotiations (see chapter 4).

Teams as Quasi-mediators

In government-to-government negotiations, each team may find itself functioning as a "quasi-mediator," that is, acting in an intermediary or mediating role. Because of the unique architecture of the process, both teams are really functioning in the middle—between those who sent them to the table and those on the other side. This role is particularly apparent in the final stages of the negotiation, when the teams are making the last efforts to move both closer together. The tribal negotiation team at this point is going back to its ratifiers and explaining what the other side seems to still need before it is ready to sign an agreement. The team is also explaining to the agency team what its own ratifiers need modified in the proposed agreement before they will be willing to sign it. The agency team is also following the same process. Each team may have to make some small modifications in its proposal(s) to satisfy the other side's interests and expectations—before there is a document to which both sides feel comfortable agreeing. These adjustments should be minor at this point if each team was in communication with its ratifiers throughout the process and gained insight into what they needed in the final document.

The negotiation team logically is the one to assume this mediating role. Of all the people involved in the negotiation, the teams are in the best position to understand the remaining constraints and areas of flexibility of both their own ratifiers and the other team. The teams already have been sitting with both for significant periods of time, and are able to listen, observe, and ask a lot of questions. They therefore are in the best position to surmise what each party can and cannot realistically agree to do in a final agreement. The ratifiers are well advised to listen carefully to their negotiation team's assessments and advice. Thomas Colosi summed up this last stage of the process with this observation: "Negotiators mediate and mediators negotiate."[14]

6

LEVERAGING POWER

Before considering how tribes can increase the political resources at their disposal it is important to consider what they do not have that segments of mainstream society routinely use to leverage political influence and to increase their portion of system rewards. In the United States, a countless number of political interest groups with their lobbyists perpetually seek to gain access to and influence decision makers at all local, state, and national levels of the political and administrative systems. Interest groups typically establish a network of personal contacts with legislators and government officials, making inroads into the political process by using these contacts and relationships. Having previously cultivated a level of familiarity, they are able to approach decision makers informally and often quietly through the doors of their private offices.

These groups can work from the inside because they are part of the dominant mainstream culture. Their lifestyles, backgrounds, values, and aspirations in many respects resemble those of the political class—that is, politicians and government officials in positions of authority who wield influence. In fact, many have held office before they returned to the private sector as lobbyists and influence peddlers to cash in on the political contacts they have already established.

In addition to these similarities, their lives may overlap regarding their work, leisure, and social lives. They may be members of the same civic and professional associations, attend the same churches, use the same exercise facilities, belong to the same social networks, support the same professional ball teams, be graduates of the same colleges and universities, and so on. They may live in the same neighborhoods and their children may attend the same schools, carpool and ride public transportation together, and be members of the same sports teams. Their spouses also may travel in the same circles. Because of these overlapping contacts and ongoing social interactions, they will be familiar and comfortable with one another and politically more approachable and successful in gaining influence.

In contrast, Indian leaders usually lack the resources to access and cultivate relationships with members of the inner circle: the political class. There is little overlap in their lives, and as a result there may be little commonality, familiarity, and natural informality. Moreover, they often lack sufficient resources to sustain a reciprocal mutual assistance relationship. Typically, in exchange for the support that the politician or agency official provides, the petitioner is expected to reciprocate in a variety of ways.

In general, Indian leaders lack the currency petitioners typically have to exchange for political favors. What currencies are generally available? Petitioners can offer in exchange electoral support (e.g., campaign donations, votes, endorsements, additional constituents who can be counted on) and access to greater influence and upward social mobility (e.g., new strategic alliances with prominent people and organizations; personal introductions to new networks of people who can be "helpful"; and their own credibility, visibility, and social status, which they can bestow by virtue of their own support and prominence).

In addition to lacking the currencies usually traded for political influence, tribal leaders may face significant structural barriers to having closer political relationships. In the first place, they may lack the financial resources it takes to sustain communication and ongoing involvement at critical access points. Moreover, tribal leaders often live outside a metropolitan area, often in remote areas, and may not have access to reliable and modern transportation and telecommunications systems. The distance prevents them from dropping in frequently to do lunch or chat with politicians and strategically placed officials.

There are also other barriers. Coming from very different cultures, historical experiences, and upbringings; different educational experiences and achievement; and different native languages may hinder informality and understanding of typical cultural cues and idioms. In addition, tribal representatives may not fully understand how the system works and how to work the system. Finally, they usually do not have associates or a group of regular contacts who enjoy political influence and credibility themselves, and therefore are not able to bring them into play to increase their own influence.[1]

Yet it is not impossible for Indian leaders to gain access and exert influence through the informal route. Today, we have only to look at successful tribes that have casinos in California and elsewhere that deliberately and strategically use their money to engage in public relations, financially support public projects in the surrounding communities, and help finance politicians' campaigns at the federal, state, and local levels. Many leaders from these tribes have been quite effective in getting the ear of politicians, and these contacts have been parlayed into getting legislation they want, as well as access and favorable treatment from administrative agencies that were unresponsive to their requests prior to some Native nations' business success.

Alternative Political Resources for Tribes

The gaming tribes, however, are still the exception. Most other tribes lack the resources to be able to rely on informal and personal networks to influence outcomes. Remote from the inner circle of power, these tribes have to work from the outside to compensate for their tribe's relative powerlessness to gain the necessary access and influence.

Leveraging the Tribe's Rights and Status

Tribal leaders no longer have to approach their discussions with external governments and agencies with trepidation and from a servile position. Today, tribal governments have significantly more leverage than they did in the past by virtue of their more developed administrative and political systems, and the increased capacity of leaders who have been educated and experienced in the non-Indian world. They have a greater understanding of potential power resources—and just have to become more comfortable using them.

One obvious place to start to leverage a tribe's influence in negotiations with the federal government is to use the historical and legal rights of their Native nation. Over the years, tribes' rights and leverage in relation to the federal government have become increasingly clarified pursuant to treaties, statutes, Executive Orders, judicial decisions, and other legal instruments.

The federal government maintains a special trust relationship with Indian tribes. This relationship is unique, as the federal government does not owe any other entity—state or private—a trust responsibility. Inherent in this relationship is an enforceable fiduciary responsibility to an Indian tribe to protect its lands and resources, which are held in trust status. In addition, the federal government is the tribe's legal trustee, obliged to protect and enhance tribal interests and rights. In coordination with the tribe, the U.S. government must advocate on its behalf in administrative transactions (i.e., negotiations) in which the tribe has an interest, and the government also must lend its support by supporting the tribe in litigation either as a co-defendant or by filing amicus curiae (friend of the court) brief.

President Clinton's Executive Order 13175

One of the best-known clarifications of tribal rights in Indian country is Executive Order 13084 issued by President Bill Clinton in 1994 (and later recast as Executive Order 13175).[2] It explicitly required the federal government to recognize tribal governments as the governments of separate sovereign nations. Federal agencies must accord sovereign Indian nations a government-to-government relationship. Before taking any action that affects federally recognized tribes, these agencies "shall consult the tribe and thereby address the specific and unique needs of tribal communities."[3]

Today, each federal agency should have a tribal consultation policy that spells out explicitly the tribes' rights and the agencies' obligation to enter into dialogue with them over decisions that will affect their interests and rights. Some state governments, including Alaska and Oregon, have formally recognized this government-to-government relationship as well.

In brief, recognized as separate sovereign governments, Native nations today should expect to be treated respectfully as equals, as would any state, county, municipal, or foreign government. They enjoy a higher status than political interest groups that also may want to weigh in on public policy decisions. Tribes can insist on having first priority as a government, and can step to the front of the line.

Quasi–Property Rights to Ancestral Lands

When it comes to entering dialogues with federal and state resource management agencies, tribes typically have additional leverage by virtue of retaining quasi–property rights that were defined in their treaties with the federal government. Most tribes, for example, are entitled to engage in a range of fishing, hunting, trapping, and gathering activities on their traditional lands to meet their subsistence needs. Moreover, they can insist that the federal agency, as their trustee, has an obligation to properly protect and enhance these resources on which tribes depend for their sustenance and livelihood.

The Endangered Species Act (ESA) and Native Nations

A modified federal Endangered Species Act (ESA) provides tribes with additional opportunities to exert control over management of their own trust lands. In the early 1990s, a coalition of Native nations came together and protested to the federal government that their special rights had not been fully taken into account and accommodated in 1973 when this legislation was initially enacted. The government was nearly silent on its potential application in Indian Country and did not anticipate the inherent tension between tribes' recognized right to economic self-sufficiency and the United States' power to preserve dwindling species and their habitat under federal law. In particular, the Indian coalition argued that their historic rights to hunt, fish, and gather to feed, clothe, and shelter their members were being infringed upon, either directly or indirectly, by federal conservation statutes.

In 1994, officials from the U.S. Fish and Wildlife Service and the National Marine Conservation Service sat down with a coalition of Native representatives from a cross-section of the country to negotiate an agreement that would address and resolve the tensions that arose in implementing the ESA in Indian Country. Following these negotiations, Secretarial Order 3206 was issued by the U.S. secretary of the interior and the U.S. secretary of commerce pursuant to the Endangered Species Act of 1973.

The Secretarial Order established that the departments would do the following:

- Work together directly with tribes on a government-to-government basis to promote healthy ecosystems.
- Consult with and seek the participation of the affected tribes "to the maximum extent practicable."
- Obtain permission from tribes before knowingly entering Indian reservations for purposes of ESA-related activities by communicating with appropriate elected tribal officials.
- Recognize that Indian lands are not subject to the same controls as federal public lands.
- Recognize that Indian tribes manage Indian lands in accordance with their own tribal goals and objectives.

- Take proactive steps to help Indian tribes develop and expand their own tribal programs to promote enlightened stewardship and ensure that conservation restrictions are unnecessary.
- Pledged that the departments will be sensitive to Indian culture, religion, and spirituality.

This Secretarial Order clearly recognizes the sovereignty of tribes and their rights to self-determination, offers to partner with them, and invites and supports them to create and implement their own habitat management plans as alternatives to designation of critical habitat on Indian lands.

Tribes' Water Rights

Another source of leverage that tribes have available to them in relation to external entities is their retention of reserved water rights on their ancestral lands. In a 1908 Supreme Court decision, *Winters v. United States*, the court clarified water rights in order to satisfy the future as well as the present water needs of American Indian reservations: it is known as the Winters Doctrine. By dint of their long presence on the lands, Indian tribes often have "senior water rights" and enjoy precedence over all other water users who moved into their area more recently. In many instances, the tribes have been successful in asserting that they have occupied the area "since time immemorial," which no other water user can assert.

As a case in point, the Klamath Tribes in southern Oregon have lived in the Klamath Basin along the Klamath River and its tributaries for centuries. During the last one hundred years, non-Indian farmers and cattle ranchers moved into the area and diverted huge volumes of water for irrigation. These activities decreased the in-stream water flow and increased the water temperature, resulting in the loss of salmon and other fisheries that had been abundant and a major source of tribal members' sustenance and survival. The government also erected dams along the river that inhibited salmon and other fish species from swimming upstream. After lengthy litigation that began in 1975, the courts established that the Klamath Tribes had occupied the area "since time immemorial" and possessed "senior water rights." The effect of that language is that the first person to obtain a water right is the last to be shut off when there is not enough to go around.

Tension between the tribes and the irrigators over water flows and water usage came to a head in the early 2000s. The federal government, in an effort to settle the conflict in a multiparty negotiation, brought together four tribes, the irrigators, and twenty-five other stakeholders, which included counties, cities, and federal and local county agencies. Armed with their newly acquired legal designation as the "senior water user," the Klamath Tribes were able to assert extensive influence over the river's in-stream water flow and water quality, the protection and enhancement of fisheries, and maintenance of the integrity of riverbanks and riparian corridors.

Other Legislative Sources of Leverage and Control

Some other important federal statutes explicitly recognize tribes' continuing legal rights and interests in what transpires on their ancestral and Indian treaty lands. Tribes can also use these statutes to address their concerns and leverage their influence with the agencies.

Native American Graves Protection and Repatriation Act

A case in point is the Native American Graves Protection and Repatriation Act (NAGPRA), passed in November 1990 to protect Native cultural resources. The act outlines the procedure to follow in returning skeletal remains, funerary items, sacred objects, and objects of cultural patrimony to Native peoples. It pertains both to returning these items when found in the possession of federal agencies, museums, and academic institutions, and when these items are discovered or uncovered on federal and tribal lands because of construction and mining activities, excavations, logging, flooding, forest fires, and so on.

Native nations have long been opposed to these items being in the possession of non-Indians, with particular concern over skeletal remains that have been in museum basement drawers for decades without being buried properly according to Native spiritual practices. American Indians have been frustrated by those institutions that have maintained they have a proprietary interest that should take precedence over the disposition by Native people, and that these items have been in these institutions' possession and on display without the permission of Indian people already for a very long time.

For the first time, this legislation acknowledges that human remains and other cultural items removed from federal or tribal lands belong, in the first instance, to lineal descendants, Indian tribes, and Native communities. Finally, the act allows the living to exercise their traditional responsibilities toward their deceased.[4]

NAGPRA further extends tribal rights by obligating agencies to work out with the tribes' plans to protect and restore these sites and preserve the skeletal remains and cultural objects that are present. Many states have comparable statutes that pertain to state lands and state-recognized tribes.

While implementing NAGPRA has attracted much interest among tribes, and a significant number of items have been returned within the purview of the legislation over the past thirty years, the process of repatriation has not always been smooth. Although "thousands of government, museum and agency offices have been able to arrive at acceptable resolutions to hundreds of NAGPRA cases with thousands of Native Americans,"[5] considerable pushback from the scientific and museum communities has taken place. A significant number of these people still hold the belief that they have certain proprietary rights over the items. Often they have argued that further study is necessary to advance scientific inquiry and therefore the items in question must remain in their custody. The museums' curators, together with the scientific community (e.g., anthropologists and archaeologists), have challenged Native people who want the items returned, raising questions about the following:

- Whether the Native's efforts to establish lineal descent are valid
- Whether the tribe making a claim on thousand-year-old items can truly prove that they are culturally affiliated
- Whether the tribes or lineal descendants have satisfactorily resolved competing demands from other parties claiming lineal descent
- Whether the tribe requesting return has sufficient resources and facilities to house the items or rebury them

Court cases and oversight hearings held by the Senate Committee on Indian Affairs (July 2005) have tried to further clarify the statute and associated government regulations and have provided language in the transcripts that tribes might be able to use for additional leverage. The law itself provides penalties for noncompliance and set up a review committee to monitor the various processes and to assist in dispute resolution involving repatriation issues. However, despite finding language that might give Native people greater leverage, there is evidence that certain museums and scientific communities still believe they have a proprietary interest superior to those petitioning for their return. Moreover, the petitioners still appear to have the burden of proof rather than those in possession of the items having the burden to justify retaining control over their disposition.[6]

In conclusion, Native nations that approach the return of their cultural heritage through NAGPRA generally find a receptive audience among most institutions. Nevertheless, some exceptions put up strenuous resistance that will not be overcome by litigation alone, since things are still murky under the law. We believe, however, that these and other controversies are suitable for resolution through properly leveraged negotiations, ones in which Native nations prepare well, marshal their political resources (including allies in the National Park Service and other federal agencies), and consider taking the disagreement to the public sphere.

National Historic Preservation Act

The National Historic Preservation Act (NHPA), passed in 1966 and amended in 1992, is another federal statute that gives Native nations additional legal standing and leverage to protect and preserve their historic and cultural heritage sites on tribal and public lands. It requires each lead federal agency involved in a federal undertaking to consult with Indian tribes or Native Hawaiian organizations whenever historic properties are affected to which tribes attach religious or cultural significance. This pertains to any lands located on or off tribal lands. The approach should be consistent with Section 106 of the NHPA.[7]

In 1998 the Advisory Council on Historic Preservation (ACHP) "recognized and increased the role of Indian Tribes and Native Hawaiians in its implementation of the Section 106 review process."[8] It established a separate Native American program within ACHP. In November 2000 the council prepared and issued "A Policy Statement Regarding Its Relationships with Indian Tribes," which defined a closer working relationship with Native nations by explicitly addressing issues of tribal sovereignty, government-to-government consultation, trust responsibilities, tribal participation in historic preservation, sympathetic construction, and respect for tribal religious and cultural values.

Importantly, the National Historic Preservation Act called for the establishment by tribes of their own Tribal Historic Preservation Offices (THPOs) to enable them to retain jurisdiction over their own cultural, historic, and sacred places, and to enable these tribes the opportunity to consult on projects that impact any area on which they place religious and cultural significance, regardless of location. It further acknowledged that the federal government has a legal and financial responsibility to comply with the NHPA requirements, to consult directly with the designated tribal representative (generally the tribe's THPO), and to actively assist tribes in preserving cultural and spiritually significant sites and lands within the context of a government-to-government relationship. The act also authorized grants to "federally recognized" Indian tribes for cultural and historic preservation projects, including the protection of Native language, oral history, plant and animal species important in traditions, and sacred and historic places, and funds for the establishment of THPOs.[9]

American Indian Religious Freedom Act

The American Indian Religious Freedom Act (AIRFA; 1978) protects the rights of Native Americans to exercise their traditional religions by ensuring access to sites, the use and possession of sacred objects, and the freedom to worship through ceremonials and traditional rites. It permits tribes to continue to perform their traditional religious practices on their ancestral lands and eliminates government interference with the free exercise of Native religions.

Tribes Should Champion Their Cause in the Public Sphere

The preceding sections suggest that Native nations typically lack the access they need to influence decision making by the political elite and therefore need to implement special strategies to maximize their effectiveness in intergovernmental negotiations. The first strategy suggested was for Native nations to be fully conversant with their unique separate nation status and their distinctive legal and historical rights, and to use these rights where and whenever possible to leverage the treatment they are entitled to by the federal government. These rights and their special status are spelled out in statutes, regulations, court decisions, and executive orders, some of which were described in the narrative above.

An additional and complementary negotiation strategy that Native Nations can use to compensate for their general lack of access to the inner circle consists of getting out from under control of the agency or institution that the tribe is appealing to, bringing the issue out into the public sphere, and enlarging the range of individuals and interest groups involved in resolving the issues.

To do so, the tribes have to tell a compelling story and demonstrate to the agencies and political jurisdictions with which they are negotiating that they can marshal significant, influential, and numerous constituencies to support their tribe's proposals. When this show of support becomes public it will help to persuade and convince agency and political decision makers that they risk becoming unpopular and appearing insensitive to the popular will if they remain intransigent. Few agencies and politicians can afford to risk having this negative public image for long.

People who are effective in influencing public opinion in the public sphere design and implement comprehensive strategies that do not rely on any one tactic. Rarely can they convince the other side to change its ways in one fell swoop. Instead, they have to educate the public in a multitude of compelling ways using a variety of forms of messaging. Simultaneously, they need to organize and orchestrate the involvement of a broad base of support if they are to get the attention and enjoy the credibility of the party on the other side.

Of course, in order to project a positive image the tribe has to be careful not to hand the media cause to ignore the real issues and focus on behavior to discredit the tribe's cause. Best to leave at home the flame throwers and others who would behave in ways that violate local social norms.

Ways to affect public opinion include the following:

- Filing strategic public interest lawsuits
- Letter writing campaigns in the local and regional newspapers
- Using social media
- Publishing news and feature articles in newspapers
- Persuading periodicals to run feature articles
- Holding press conferences
- Calling for and participating in special government investigations
- Staging street demonstrations
- Picketing
- Making appearances and interviews on talk shows
- Giving public testimony before legislative bodies
- Lodging formal complaints with agencies
- Filing formal Freedom of Information Act (FOIA) requests

These activities raise public awareness of the issues and should concern the agencies that are responsible.

A Comprehensive Organizing Strategy

An example of this approach occurred a number of years ago during the winter months in a rural county in California in which there was a serious shortage of decent housing, and massive unemployment, hunger, and hardship. This case did not involve American Indian tribes. Instead, it involved a grassroots organization that had mobilized supporters throughout the county, consisting of a combination of Mexican American, African American, and low-income white American residents. The latter were descendants of families that came out of the Midwest to escape the famine during the Dust Bowl era in the 1930s.

The organization that initiated the effort called itself the Stanislaus County Tenants Rights Association. It began its organizing campaign by spending many months assembling a slideshow presentation of over three hundred photographs that vividly pictured dilapidated, poorly maintained, and substandard houses and apartments that were being rented in the county. They documented the housing and health code violations, the inflated rental rates that were being charged, specific complaints that had been lodged with the landlords and their lack of response, and the names of the slumlords. They then arranged meetings in which the slideshow and the data were presented. The organization contacted and visited with a cross-section of dozens of local organizations (e.g., the local Council of Churches, the County Labor Council, Senior Citizens Council, the Office of Economic Opportunity (OEO)–funded Community Action Agency, the local Realtors and Apartment Owners Association, and the County Welfare Association).

The tenants' rights organization also worked closely with attorneys from a local California Rural Legal Assistance office. Each week or two they sued some of the bigger landlords over numerous new transgressions. They also addressed the larger issues. In an attempt to describe the underlying causes of the housing crisis, the tenants' organization began to point to housing and food shortages, local unemployment data, the growing welfare rolls, health conditions, and more.

Handicapping the County Welfare Department from responding more aggressively to the emergency need was a federal U.S. Department of Agriculture (USDA) regulation that prohibited it from distributing surplus food commodities if it was already giving cash grants and food stamps to welfare recipients. Attorneys from the legal assistance office filed a class-action lawsuit in federal court in San Francisco. They asked the court to strike down this regulation and requested the federal judge to order the state of California to release federal surplus commodities it had stored in a Sacramento warehouse, located a hundred miles away. They asked the federal judge, as a temporary measure since it was approaching Christmas Eve, to at the very least make an exception to the regulation by releasing some of these commodities.

Part of the organizers' strategy was to take the issue to the public and beyond the exclusive control of the local county government. In a public media event intended to help to highlight the issues, while the attorneys were in court arguing their case in San Francisco, members of the tenants' rights organization backed three empty flatbed trucks up to the warehouse loading docks in the state capital (Sacramento) "to wait" for the release of the surplus food. Ultimately, before the end of the day the federal judge ordered twenty thousand pounds of these surplus foods to be released. That evening, approximately twenty-five hundred low-income people were waiting in line in Modesto to receive the surplus food along with other food donations solicited all day long over the radio by church leaders and volunteers under the auspices of the local Council of Churches. This was also covered by the broadcast and print media, adding to the urgency of the day's events.

An integral part of the evolving strategy over the preceding months had been establishing a close working relationship with a local newspaper reporter assigned to the poverty beat who wrote about many aspects of the developing story. He covered the lawsuits against selected landlords, the organizing activities of the tenants, and the drama that unfolded in federal court in San Francisco. It addition, he interviewed and photographed homeless families living along the Sacramento River, under bridges, and in their cars and documented the overall housing shortage and an unemployment rate of more than 20 percent.

Simultaneously, the tenants' rights organization made efforts to build a county-wide low-income multiethnic coalition. It enlisted widespread support by joining forces with a welfare rights organization to present documents prepared by the County Welfare Department's Emergency Assistance Program that showed that it was spending down the annual budget six months prematurely. The tenants' rights group also drew support from an influential Mexican American Farmworkers' Cooperative Association that was supported by farmworkers in the rural areas of the county. Several neighborhood organizations from the large African American neighborhoods participated, as they were interested in addressing their food, housing, and employment needs. The campaign also appealed to mainly middle-class social action organizations in the county, including the Council of Churches, a county labor council, local chapters of the League of Women Voters, the Association of University Women, and the large governing board of directors of the OEO Community Action Agency.

Then with over two hundred supporters, many of whom were from organizations that had hosted the photo presentation, the tenants' rights organization along with other organizations' representatives made a presentation to the local county board of supervisors. They requested stricter housing code enforcement, a county initiative to apply for federal and state funds to build two thousand new units of new low-income housing, and a new revolving loan fund that would offer below-market rates to eligible borrowers to upgrade their substandard rentals. The organizations also requested that the county supplement the budget of the Emergency Food Program operated by the local Community Action Agency and waive the federal restriction against simultaneously issuing food stamps and commodities. At the end of that meeting, at the request of those packed in the supervisor's chambers, the board of supervisors declared a local "Hunger Disaster" that made the *NBC Evening News*, which sent out a film crew on Christmas evening. After the supervisor's declaration, members of the tenants' organization contacted the media in Los Angeles and San Francisco to share the news and get maximum coverage.

Within the next six months everything the people requested had been either done or was in process. The federal, state, and local government agencies were responsive after having seen the data uncovered by the coalition of concerned citizens and the visible political support it had garnered among the local population.

Understandably, and to be expected, not everyone in the county was happy with the negative publicity the county received nationwide. After the dust settled, a county grand jury was assembled to investigate. It focused on whether the federal property—the surplus foods—had been properly distributed. Fortunately, all activities were carefully documented and each recipient was determined to be eligible under poverty guidelines to receive surplus food. No problem was discovered.

USING ORGANIZING STRATEGIES TO OVERCOME AGENCY RESISTANCE

While not involving Native nations, this example is nonetheless relevant to how disenfranchised groups in society can increase their negotiating power in the public sphere. It largely consists of direct actions that we described in the first chapter as strategies some organizations use to influence public opinion in support of their policy initiatives. These strategies are available to Native nations as well. They are spelled out in the following section with specific examples of how they have been used in government-to-government negotiations.

Tribes should not be surprised if initially government agencies resist their initiatives. Sometimes the agency personnel have to overcome old ways of thinking and uncharitable images they may have of the tribe and tribal members before they are willing to pay attention and cooperate. This is especially true for local officials who have lived in an area for many years and have been conditioned to think of tribes in a negative way. The agency may also fear being attacked or sued if there is a history of antagonism and conflict.

IDRS worked for a number of years with the Klamath Tribe in southern Oregon through its government-to-government negotiations with the Fremont-Winema National Forest located in Klamath, Oregon. In an early meeting with the National Forest supervisor, tribal representatives indicated that they had an interest in obtaining forest restoration and other types of contracts in the National Forest to increase the forest's health and resilience. They requested a list of upcoming agency contracting opportunities they might bid for. The representatives cited their members' very high unemployment rates, a general interest among the members in working outdoors in forestry, and the fact that the National Forest being discussed was within the tribe's former reservation boundaries before the tribe was terminated by Congress in 1954.

The National Forest supervisor rebuffed the tribe by responding that the tribe's separate-nation status, the rights associated, and its historical ties to the National Forest would have nothing to do with a "business relationship." The supervisor indicated that the tribe would have to compete with other contractors, that no special treatment would be accorded, and that its chances of obtaining contracts would be small given the lack of tribal capacity and the absence of a documented track record in forest-related work. The supervisor further claimed the agency "did not have any responsibility for providing the tribe with opportunities to build tribal capacity" to gain the experience that was required.

The tribe was invited to prepare and submit a white paper indicating why it wanted to establish a closer working relationship with the agency and what it wanted to accomplish. Several weeks later it submitted the paper but did not hear back from the agency for the next four months. When the agency finally responded it ignored most of the white paper's content. Instead, it zeroed in on the tribe's interests in transforming biomass feedstock (left on the forest's floor after thinning and fuel load reduction activities) into energy production and focused on the problems with the technology the tribe was considering using to convert the biomass.

The agency's posture did not change for the next year until the supervisor retired and was replaced by someone who was clearly interested in establishing a more cooperative relationship with the tribe. There was good reason to suspect that the tribe's political organizing activities made a significant difference, persuaded the supervisor to retire, and was responsible for the regional office appointing a more hospitable supervisor to replace her.

HOW DID THE TRIBE EVENTUALLY LEVERAGE INFLUENCE OVER THE LOCAL NATIONAL FOREST SERVICE?

The Klamath Tribe had to persuade the local agency to sit down and negotiate. To do so, it had to appeal to the agency's interests. The tribe had to convince the agency that it would suffer negative consequences if it chose not to sit down and engage in good-faith negotiations, and persuade it that the benefits would exceed the costs if it chose to be more cooperative.

It is common for an agency not to immediately understand the potential costs and benefits, and it may take some time and activities by the tribe to do the convincing. When Moses negotiated with Pharaoh in ancient Egypt to let his people go, he adopted a similar negotiation strategy. When Pharaoh was not immediately convinced that he had to do anything to accommodate Moses and his people, ten plagues were the result, each one more devastating than the last, until the Pharaoh finally relented.

Agreed, a tribe cannot rely exclusively on divine intervention. Its negotiation team has to know what its interests are and what the agency's interests are. The agency also may take some persuading to understand that the tribe could either jeopardize or enhance the agency's interests; specific actions might be needed first.

Typical Agency Interests

We start by focusing on what we know to be the interests of most public agencies and where they are particularly vulnerable:

- Public agencies do not want to be exposed and publicly criticized. There are not many ways they can fight back against negative publicity without appearing defensive and partisan. Moreover, today most of them usually do not want to be known as unfair to American Indian people and to appear to shun some groups and favor others. This is particularly true for agencies that have regular transactions with Native nations. They want to appear to adhere to standards of equal protection.

- Agency officials usually do not want to do any extra work, such as having to spend time and their already limited funds and staff to defend themselves in court, or to participate in depositions or answering endless interrogatories during the discovery period of a lawsuit. Moreover, having to spend literally months gathering information to respond to a tribe's inquiries under the FOIA is particularly onerous but a potential tool in tribes' repertoire.
- Agencies do not want members of Congress initiating inquiries into their activities, sending official letters, asking questions, and expecting written responses within a specified time. Agencies work hard to ensure that these elected leaders do not withdraw their support during hearings when budget appropriations are up for a vote.
- In some situations, an agency may be in competition with other agencies for status and funding, and each will want to retain the upper hand without being played against the others.
- Bureaucratic agencies are very conservative and prefer to be safe rather than sorry. Agency bureaucrats do not want to make mistakes and be called on the carpet for an alleged transgression. Often, they'd rather do nothing than something that may get them in trouble. When trying to get the agency to do something it has not done before, tribes have to show how risk will be minimized, and preferably eliminated.

Agencies Internally Pluralistic, Not Monolithic

Avoid thinking of agencies as monolithic entities that enjoy total internal agreement about the agency's purpose, values, perspectives, and commitments. On the contrary, within each agency there is diversity among individuals, roles, functions, departments, and levels in the organizational hierarchy. In these circumstances, it is often possible to get helpful information, assistance, and support from within the agency itself—sometimes from people who do not even realize how helpful they are being.

In addition, when negotiating with a team of agencies, there may be significantly different perspectives, some of which might be closer to the interests of the tribe. In the case of the Timbisha Shoshone negotiation discussed in the next section, the tribe's negotiation team specifically asked that the Bureau of Reclamation (BOR) be included on the federal negotiation team. As they described it, BOR was in the business of finding and using water while the National Park Service (NPS) was focused on saving and not using it. They wanted to offset the NPS narrative that the Death Valley National Park did not have sufficient water resources to support the tribe establishing residential communities in the park. During the actual negotiations BOR brought out its water drilling rigs and identified where there was water to sustain tribal villages.

With respect to the example cited above concerning the U.S. Forest Service, the Klamath Tribe had to deal with an intransigent local supervisor. She was confident that her office enjoyed total control over what happened in her forest and assumed that the tribe would be left with no room for independent maneuver. But this was true only as long as the tribe dealt with the local agency exclusively within the agency's local organizational framework. To get different results, the tribe had to enlist other parties with potential influence that were not under the control of this local office. This included appealing to the regional and national offices and to organizations outside the agency.

Appealing to the Agency's Regional and National Leaders

Tribes can legitimately use their government-to-government relationship with the federal government to arrange appointments and get direct access to the top of the chain of command in the same agency. They can meet directly with agencies' top directors, bypassing levels of the agency hierarchy and conveying directly the grievances they have against them.

In the case of the Klamath Tribe and the National Forest Service, the first step the tribe took consisted of traveling to Oregon's capital to meet with the regional director of the U.S. Forest Service. Afterward the tribe traveled to Washington, D.C., to discuss the problem with the top directors of the agency. By moving vertically from local to regional to national levels, the tribe was able to access agency decision makers who were less rooted in negative local attitudes toward the tribe, and who were, because of their position in the agency, more conscious of the possible harm that could come from continued agency resistance to an important tribe in its jurisdiction. Part of the top officials' job is to promote good public relations and establish and maintain favorable external relationships. They are expected to better understand that the tribe could have direct access to its congressional representatives and other entities who could have negative influence over congressional decisions regarding the agency's annual budget allocation.

During their time in Washington, D.C., members of the Klamath Tribe's negotiation team met with top leaders of the U.S. Forest Service and with various department and program directors. This included meeting with its Native American Liaison Office, and also with the agency's planning office that was exploring how its national forests could profitably convert feedstock off the forest floor into biomass fuels. It also met with several members of the agency's Executive Policy Group, which was considering such issues as comanagement, and the implementation of a new law, the Tribal Forest Protection Act (TFPA-1994). TFPA gave tribes more leverage on federal lands that are administered by the U.S. Forest Service and the Bureau of Land Management when these are contiguous to and potentially endangering tribes' forestlands and the lives of their members. TFPA gives tribes the right to initiate proposals to undertake forest restoration projects on government lands that are contiguous to the reservation. It no longer is solely up to the agency's discretion: the agency has to comply unless it can make a persuasive argument that the tribe's proposal is inappropriate.

Clearly, a strategy tribes often use to influence public policy is to meet with their congressional representatives. They also may meet with members of Congress who serve on key congressional committees that have jurisdiction over the substantive matter and agencies being targeted. They can also sit down with the staff members of these congressional representatives, for they typically serve as their gatekeepers, carrying the messages and often writing the elected leaders' scripts and legislative initiatives. Congressional representatives may be quite receptive to their Native constituents because they increasingly want tribal members' support at election time. They maintain local offices with staff back in the tribes' district to cultivate that support of voters back home.

While in Washington, D.C., members of the Klamath Tribal Negotiation Team made contact with and requested assistance from their congressional representatives, and members of the staff of the Senate Committee on Indian Affairs and the House Natural Resources Committee.

Appealing to NGOs

Another strategy to get out from under the dominance of a specific local agency is to broaden the lateral front. With the support of local, state, and federal organizations that are independent of the agency and that enjoy local credibility and leverage of their own, tribes can change the local balance of power more to their advantage.

This device to amass and leverage greater political influence is well known. It is the inspiration behind coalition building. By bringing together a diverse group of like-minded organizations pressing for the same solutions, the tribe, or any other entity seeking greater influence, is able to bring to bear additional constituencies that have their own networks of contacts and influence. Other tribes, environmental and civic groups, academic institutions, prominent scholars and experts with relevant expertise, local politicians, and others who are potentially supportive of the tribe's proposals can be invited to weigh in behind the tribe and help offset the influence of a hostile agency. Those outside organizations that are organized regionally and nationally can potentially bring the leverage of the entire organization to bear locally.

In this particular case, members of the tribe's negotiation team also met with numerous national environmental organizations that were interested in more enlightened management of the country's National Forests, specifically with the Nature Conservancy, the Trust for Public Lands, and the Conservation Fund seeking their political support with the Agency. The tribe also met with several other organizations to identify public and private sources of financial support to purchase former tribal forestlands that were then in the hands of private owners.

The tribe also sought support at a more local level. The tribe's own Department of Natural Resources had established a close, long-standing relationship with two nationally recognized forest experts at two Oregon universities. The tribe commissioned them to help it develop its own forest management plan and to help persuade the U.S. Forest Service to manage the National Forest differently. The Forest Service had a degree of professional pride and ultimately sought approbation from these national experts in the field. Eventually, at the tribe's urging, the local Forest Service Agency contracted with these outside experts to train the agency staff in a new approach to forest restoration and management, and it incorporated relevant sections of the tribe's forest management plan into its own revised forest plan. It is doubtful whether the tribe could have persuaded the Forest Service to accommodate it without this alliance with credible forestry experts and their university departments.

Another example demonstrates how mobilizing allies can improve the power position of a tribe. The same tribe tried for several years to persuade the same National Forest Service office to enter forest restoration agreements with it. Unsuccessful in its bid, the tribe created a partnership with the local and regional offices of the Nature Conservancy and the Lomakatski Project, a local nonprofit that had a fifteen-year history managing forest restoration projects in several other National Forests in the area. Both were dedicated to the same principles of natural resource protection and forest restoration as the tribe. Where the tribe failed on its own to persuade the agency, these two organizations added an enormous amount of credibility, expertise, and political leverage.

When the members of the tribe's negotiation team spent a week in Washington, D.C., they explored how the tribe could initiate a comanagement agreement with the National Forest back home. For some people in agency headquarters, "comanagement" was still regarded as a dirty word. But these tribal members discovered that the agency had legal authority to create a master stewardship agreement (MSA), which permits National Forests to enlist local cities, counties, NGOs, and Indian tribes to partner with it in managing its forest. This was a new way for the Forest Service to increase local involvement and mobilize additional financial resources and technical expertise in forestry, as well as to organize local political support for agency policies and activities with the local public. Presumably, the MSA was also motivated by persons interested in creating a countervailing strategy against persistent opposition from environmental organizations. These organizations were repeatedly suing the agency whenever it launched initiatives to thin the forest and remove trees and underbrush as part of their fuel's reduction efforts.

Together with their new partners, the Nature Conservancy and Lomakatski, the Klamath Tribe was able to negotiate a ten-year MSA that covered up to 1.5 million acres of the local National Forest. The Agreement spelled out how they would work with the Forest Service to restore the health of the Winema National Forest. In effect, this MSA enabled the tribe to play a central role in managing and stewarding 1.5 million acres of forestlands that had been part of its reservation before the tribe was terminated by Congress in the 1950s when its land was transferred to create this National Forest. This MSA was a major victory and went a long way to satisfy the tribe's long-held desire to get back to performing its historical stewardship role on its ancestral lands. It also provided employment opportunities for the tribe's forest restoration team and potential contracts for ancillary forest enterprises that belonged to tribal members.

The Timbisha Shoshone Tribe (discussed in the next chapter) used a similar negotiating strategy to leverage power in its dispute with the federal government in the 1990s to establish a homeland for the tribe in the Death Valley National Park. The tribe created a national coalition of like-minded Native Nations that they named the National Alliance to Protect Native Rights in National Parks. These other tribes were fighting similar battles with the National Park Service in other parts of the country. Through one of its members, the Miccosukee Tribe in the Everglades, the alliance had access to its own PR firm and law firm in Washington, D.C. The alliance held press conferences and meetings with national Indian organizations to publicize their grievances with the National Park Service. Among other actions, the alliance called for congressional oversight hearings "concerning the National Park Service's 'discriminatory' policies toward Indian Tribes." What seemed ultimately to motivate the National Park Service to reconsider its recalcitrant position was its attachment to the belief that it was a friend of the Indians, a notion that the alliance was publicly questioning. This proved to be a powerful wake-up call for the NPS.

Currying Local Public Opinion

Up until now we have emphasized the importance of influencing public opinion by taking the tribe's issue into the public arena and telling its story to garner the support of the public. Additionally, a tribe should not overlook the importance of cultivating favorable local public opinion on an ongoing basis by generating and disseminating positive information. Public opinion is in effect an additional party in the negotiation that each of the primary parties wants on its side.

A tribe can either take the initiative to define itself or be defined by others. Establishing personal relationships with members of the media and placing positive stories in the media (feature articles in periodicals, op-ed pieces, editorials, publicized interviews with important people, etc.) about the tribe's local accomplishments can increase the public's receptivity to the tribe's narrative. Seeing it in print lends credibility in the public arena.

Tribal governments or agencies, civic groups, voluntary organizations, and nonprofits can qualify to run public service announcements (PSAs), usually for free, to reach a wide and diverse audience, making them an effective marketing tool for your tribe and organization. PSAs can convey information, promote a point of view, create awareness, and encourage a change in behavior with the public. In most rural areas there is not much happening, and radio and television stations might welcome public interest programs as filler in their programming schedules. Services are available to help you develop the narrative and graphics as you prepare your PSA. Editorials and personal interviews with radio and TV hosts might also be a way the tribes can promote their narrative—for free.

A well-orchestrated PR campaign can in effect build a tribe's goodwill account and give government decision makers the confidence that association with and support of the tribe will not be risky and instead will ultimately reflect well on them. This can positively impact an agency's willingness to fund projects and to negotiate important agreements with a tribe. It can also serve to give the tribe the "benefit of the doubt" when negative publicity occurs.

Tribes are also well advised to use PR to counter antagonistic narratives that hostile agencies, organizations, and private individuals promote. Effective political warfare requires immediate and well-conceived responses to nip negative publicity in the bud. Be aware that shedding public light on issues usually can work to the tribe's advantage. However, it can also activate the opposition, so it is a calculated risk that has to be handled carefully. Tribes that have purposely maintained a posture of low visibility may initially be nervous and uncomfortable being this proactive. However, with careful planning, good public relations can be a new and bold way for the tribe to present itself.

One approach to consider when moving in this direction is as follows. Some nonprofit organizations have contacted SCORE, a volunteer organization of retired professionals, and requested the assistance of a longtime expert in developing media campaigns and public relations. A consultant can come to your community on a pro bono basis and help arrange meetings with prominent members of local media organizations, personally introduce tribal leaders and some members of the tribal staff, and facilitate a joint discussion of steps the tribe and people from the media could take to establish a closer working relationship.

Developing Internal Capacity to Maximize Leverage

There is one last subject to discuss regarding a tribe's potential power. Up until now we discussed some things that a tribe can do in its external environment to increase its political negotiating leverage. In addition, a tribe's power to influence government agency's decisions is a function of the quality of its internal organizational and leadership capacity. All tribes do not have the same ability to mobilize influence in their external relations because their levels of political, economic, and cultural development vary. The more developed the tribe is in this respect, the more political resources it will have, and the more persuasive and formidable it will be in its external relations.

This internal capacity has three components that contribute to the tribe's potential influence and leverage:

1. The size and quality of the tribe's resources, expertise, and other assets will determine the degree of its economic and political self-sufficiency and hence its ability to act independently and decisively with respect to outside agencies and communities. Such resources include the following:

   - The size and reliability of its material resources—for example, natural resources (land, natural resources, water, minerals, and so on), monetary/business income, savings and investments, and so forth
   - A good track record in raising substantial amounts of public and private development funds
   - Reliable political support from and good relationships among the tribe's leaders from a cross-section of the tribal community (e.g., youth, emerging leaders, traditional and nontraditional people, elders, etc.)
   - Elected leaders who have extensive experience and expertise leading the tribal community
   - Ability of tribal leaders to think outside the box and come up with innovative solutions (i.e., resilience and adaptability to new and changing conditions)
   - Continuity of leadership over significant periods of time (current leaders' accumulated and retained wisdom and knowledge)
   - Widespread internal agreement among the nation's citizens on their tribe's priorities, values, and commitments
   - A political culture that values internal cooperation and the ability to put the collective interests of the Native nation above factionalism based on family, clans, ego needs and personal feuds, and so on
   - Leaders with past experience engaging in and successively managing major government-to-government negotiations.

- Leaders with good verbal cross-cultural communication skills, a tolerance for diversity and ambiguity, and patience and vision
- Leaders who have knowledge of the tribes' history and special legal rights due to their treaties, separate nation status, government-to-government relationships, the federal government's trust responsibilities, and other statutes such as the Religious Freedom Act and NAGPRA

2. The size, quality, efficiency, and professionalism of a tribe's administrative organization, and the ability of the tribe's elected leaders to rely on it, also affect the tribe's capacity to influence agency decision making. The following assets are important:

    - Tribal staff and consultants who have lengthy quality time serving the tribe
    - Decisive staff managers with appropriate expertise and authority to do their jobs
    - Good internal communication between managers and staff exchanging reliable up-to-date information
    - Close coordination, responsiveness, and trust between staff and elected leaders
    - Existence of a tribal newsletter and periodic information sharing with council and staff (e.g., a good rumor-control system)
    - Ability to deliver a message effectively by using social media and other modern electronic technologies

3. The extent of the tribe's external network of relationships, its past interactions, and its capacity and commitment to maintain contacts and sustain this involvement will also determine its ability to effectively engage and succeed in transactions with outside agencies. The following assets are essential:

    - Tribal leaders, staff, and consultants who enjoy credibility in the external community
    - Experience in building and managing coalitions and strategic partnerships with other tribes, intertribal organizations, NGOs, agencies, and so on
    - History of tribal cooperation and coordination with federal, state, and local agency programs and activities

- Previous successful efforts to establish and maintain close personal relationships with agency officials at all levels
- Knowledge of agencies' internal differences and the departments and individuals who may be sympathetic with the tribe's interests
- Existence of a tribal public relations and intergovernmental relations office within its administration
- Established relations with persons in the media (e.g., newspapers, periodicals, TV, social media influencers).
- Existence of a grant development office that tracks and captures external funding opportunities
- Good relationships with academic institutions, experts, and research organizations, and with legislatures, congressional representatives and committees, and their staffs.

In the following chapter we offer a detailed case study of the very successful win/win negotiations between the Timbisha-Shoshone Tribe in Death Valley, California, and four federal agencies (1994–2000). It describes the process by which the tribe was able to secure an acceptable agreement by using specific negotiation strategies that were instrumental in creating a more favorable balance of power between it and the federal government.

7

HOW THE TIMBISHA SHOSHONE TRIBE GOT ITS LAND BACK

A Case Study in Government-to-Government Negotiations

In September 1998 the Timbisha Shoshone Tribe in Death Valley, California, reached a comprehensive agreement with four federal agencies in the U.S. Department of the Interior, which was later incorporated into congressional legislation that established the Timbisha Homeland Act. A major grievance was thereby resolved that the government had ignored since 1933 when President Herbert Hoover seized the tribe's ancestral lands and created the Death Valley National Monument.

At that time, the federal government made no provision for the tribe, which had occupied these lands for hundreds and perhaps thousands of years. Government officials hoped the tribal members would pack up their meager belongings and disappear quietly. To their surprise and frustration, 50 of some 275 people refused to go. For the next sixty-five years, the members who remained were under almost continuous pressure to clear out and lived as virtual squatters on the outskirts of the national park headquarters in Furnace Creek. They clung stubbornly to the hope that they would live to see the day when the federal government would acknowledge the injustice done and restore their tribal homeland.

Despite repeated attempts over the years to attract the federal government's attention, all the tribe's efforts were unsuccessful until October 1994, when Congress passed the California Desert Protection Act. This act added roughly 1.3 million acres of land to a newly established Death

---

This case study is a revised and pared-down version of my "Government-to-Government Negotiations: How the Timbisha Shoshone Got Its Land Back," *American Indian Natural and Cultural Research Journal* 24, no. 4 (January 2000): 127–65.

Valley National Park, but it still did not provide the tribe with any land. However, the tribe was able, with the help of California Indian Legal Services and Hawaii senator Daniel Inouye, to get a special provision, Section 705(b), inserted into the bill. It required the Department of the Interior to study the tribe's ancestral lands within and outside Death Valley National Park, with the purpose of identifying lands "suitable for a reservation." The department was given one year to conduct the study and prepare and submit a report to Congress. It was instructed to do so "in consultation with the tribe."

Department of the Interior officials were not pleased with Congress's directive. They delayed action for a full seven months after the bill passed, arguing that Congress had not appropriated funds for the study process. Finally, in May 1995, four agencies—the National Park Service (NPS), the Bureau of Land Management (BLM), the Bureau of Indian Affairs (BIA) from the Department of the Interior, and the United States Forest Service (USFS) from the Department of Agriculture (which later dropped out)—assembled in Death Valley National Park and began to meet with members of the Timbisha Shoshone Tribe.

Unfortunately, these talks between federal representatives and the tribe produced little other than the tribal members' disappointment and anger. Initially the government and the tribe agreed to come up with a recommendation together. But by March 1996, the NPS had taken full control over the study process and made no pretense at collaboration. After nine months of so-called study, at least five major meetings between the tribe and a host of government officials, and three drafts of the study report, the federal government agencies maintained that no lands within its 3.5-million-acre park were suitable for a reservation.

The Tribe reacted strongly. It called the NPS decision an "act of bad faith" and a repudiation of congressional instructions to consider lands both within and outside the park. Instead of having what it regarded as additional futile talks, the tribe chose to follow a different strategy. It launched a national political organizing campaign designed to publicly expose the NPS's alleged anti-Indian policy, and to put pressure on the Park Service to come to the negotiating table in good faith.

No further face-to-face contact between the tribe and the federal government took place for the next two years. However, by the end of 1997, the tribe had implemented a political strategy that proved effective in changing the balance of power and moving its cause closer to the top of the interior secretary's priority list. In January 1998, in a new political context and with some new federal representatives at the table, a second, more balanced and successful round of negotiations began.

After more than nine months of intense discussions, the federal agencies and the tribe produced a comprehensive and precedent-setting agreement. It provided the tribe with a permanent land base. Almost ten thousand acres of desert land were to be set aside in trust status for tribal residences, community and government services, and economic development. Three hundred of these acres were to be in the heart of the national park. Almost another million acres were designated as a special Timbisha Shoshone Natural and Cultural Preservation Area. A wide range of opportunities for the tribe, the NPS, and the BLM were identified for cooperative management of natural and cultural resources within this new preservation area.

What was done to finally initiate, structure, and manage a successful government-to-government negotiation process after so many years of neglect and enmity? What was done differently during the second round of talks that had not been done originally to account for the dramatic shift in the outcomes? How was a small tribe of roughly three hundred members able to persuade an enormously powerful federal government to sit down with it as an equal, negotiate in good faith, and reach a win-win agreement? How was the huge cultural gap bridged between a very traditional Indian tribe—wedded to its unique perspective and attached to its ancestral land—and federal land management agencies, which had very different perspectives on land, land use, and land ownership? Finally, how was the National Park Service persuaded to allow for the almost unprecedented establishment of an Indian reservation in the middle of one of its parks?

The purpose of this case study is to address all these questions in the course of describing the process by which the Timbisha Shoshone Tribe and the federal government reached a negotiated agreement. Apart from the story being an interesting account of one small tribe's experience, it provides a number of important general lessons about the negotiation process itself. The case offers a unique opportunity to look in depth into a multiparty dispute involving a sovereign Indian tribe and multilevel bureaucratic government agencies, and to observe what negotiation strategies may and may not work in this context, and why.

This case study also addresses the ever-popular concept of win-win negotiations in a context in which huge power disparities existed between the parties. We have the unusual opportunity to compare the first round of talks—dominated by the federal government and ending in a complete breakdown in the talks—with a second round, in which the formerly weaker party (the tribe) had been able to reposition itself to enjoy more leverage and change its political relationship with the federal government.

Finally, this transaction between the Timbisha Shoshone Tribe and the federal government has significant public policy implications. In April 1994, President Bill Clinton issued Executive Order 12875 in which he made a public commitment to institute a government-to-government relationship between all federal agencies and sovereign Indian nations. However, most of these agencies have not been altogether clear about how to put this order into practice.[1] Should they initiate a consultation process, which is still top-down and allows them to retain unilateral control, or should they initiate a negotiation process in which the relationship is more equal and problems are resolved by mutual agreement? The successful experience in Death Valley demonstrates how two sovereign governments can come together as equals in bilateral negotiations and reach agreement without either party having to abdicate its sovereignty and sacrifice its vital interests.

Historical Background

There never was any question that Death Valley was the tribe's ancestral homeland. Tribal lands in Death Valley were taken away through external conquest by a more powerful entity. The federal government itself acknowledged the tribe's legitimate claim to the area when it granted formal federal recognition in 1983. The government relied on solid data that the Timbisha Shoshone people lived as a distinct and self-governing tribe in the Death Valley area for hundreds of years.

Before Euro-American contact, the Timbisha Shoshone people were hunters and gatherers engaged in limited farming activities. They were seminomadic, living in extended family clusters within an eleven-million-acre area. Every year, they moved their camps from the lower elevations (over two hundred feet below sea level) to higher, cooler, more mountainous areas during the extremely hot and dry summer months when the temperature is commonly over 125 degrees Fahrenheit.

In the late 1800s, the tribe's traditional way of life was interrupted by westward expansion and by prospectors moving into their area looking for gold and silver. A large deposit of borax was discovered in Furnace Creek, and the mine's owners quickly consumed available timber and scarce water to fuel their fires and extract and process the natural resources. From the perspective of these outsiders, the Indians were in their way. Their settlements were repeatedly pushed further and further to the periphery of Furnace Creek.

The harassment by private interests was followed by the federal government's decision to establish the Death Valley Monument in 1933. From this point on, the National Park Service explicitly prohibited tribal members from moving freely to their cultural and spiritual sites and to those areas that provided their sources of sustenance, including mesquite beans, pinion nuts, wildlife, and springwater. They were no longer permitted to make their seasonal rounds from the lower elevations to the high country.

For the next sixty-five years, the National Park Service engaged in repeated efforts to run off the remaining tribal members who refused to leave. After moving these members three different times, those who remained were restricted to a small, barren, windswept forty-acre parcel of land on the outskirts of Furnace Creek and were prohibited from building any permanent structures. According to the tribal chairperson, Pauline Esteves, "Over the years, there were countless incidents in which we were intimidated and arbitrarily arrested by National Park Rangers. They shut off our utilities and water supply and destroyed some of our adobe houses by hosing them down when members left for work or to serve in the armed services. They did other things as well."[2]

The tribe felt it had no one to whom it could appeal during this period. No one in the nation's capital—either in the executive branch or in Congress—was willing to talk to the tribe about restoring its land base, despite repeated efforts by tribal leaders to raise the issue.

The California Desert Protection Act

The turning point for the tribe did not come until October 8, 1994, when Congress passed the California Desert Protection Act. It added roughly 1.3 million acres of multiple-use land, previously managed by the Bureau of Land Management (BLM), to what had been the Death Valley National Monument. The legislation raised the status of the monument to a national park and put all of the lands under more restricted use by designating them as "wilderness areas."

The Desert Protection Act was passed as a result of a hard-fought political struggle led by California senator Dianne Feinstein, who sponsored the bill, and a broad coalition of environmental groups and organizations that supported it. Other user groups, such as hunters, cattle ranchers, prospectors and miners, off-road-vehicle owners, local counties, Friends of the West, and others were opposed to vast areas of western land being controlled and restricted by the federal government. California congressman Jerry Lewis, who reflected the bitterness of these constituencies over their defeat, was part of a group of congresspersons who made sure that only one dollar was appropriated for its implementation.

Members of the Timbisha Shoshone Tribe, becoming aware of the impending passage of the Desert Protection Bill, were unhappy that it provided no lands for the tribe even though all the BLM land being transferred to the NPS in Death Valley was part of the tribe's ancestral homeland. The tribe launched a last-ditch effort and managed to get Section 705(b) included, instructing "the Secretary of the Interior . . . to identify lands suitable for a reservation within and outside the boundaries of Death Valley National Park." It prevailed even though the secretary's Office of the Department of the Interior, the leadership in the National Park Service, and Senator Feinstein were opposed to having an Indian reservation in the national park.

In retrospect, the tribe's ability to insert itself in the political process may have been the single most significant breakthrough in the tribe's sixty-five-year-long struggle for a land base. While no land was restored, the issue was finally on Congress's radar screen.

Round One of the Talks

The tribe and the federal government began their formal talks in May 1995. From the beginning of this process, the tribe saw itself as a full negotiating partner. In its effort to show up at the table in the strongest possible position, it applied for funds from the Administration of Native Americans (ANA) to help it form and train a negotiation team, and to hire historians, anthropologists, archaeologists, and economic planners to produce data. These consultants assisted the tribe's negotiation team in presenting data documenting the boundaries of the tribe's ancestral homeland and supporting the tribe's proposals for land transfers, housing and economic development, and natural resource management opportunities presented to the federal agency representatives.

The First Meeting with Federal Representatives

Approximately thirty people attended the first meeting in May 1995 in Death Valley. A negotiation team of five persons represented the tribe.

The team consisted of the tribal chair, the tribal administrator, two elders of the tribe, its attorney from California Indian Legal Services, and its negotiation consultant, the executive director of the Indian Dispute Resolution Services (and author of this book). The federal government team consisted of staff people from local, state, and regional offices of four federal agencies (the NPS, BLM, USFS, and BIA). Two local counties were represented as well.

At the first meeting a study process was outlined, including a meeting schedule for the next five months and the designation of specific persons to serve as chairs and members of four working groups. They agreed to produce the study report together, and to refrain from releasing information to the media or outside groups unless both parties first agreed.

Subsequent Meetings between the Parties

In subsequent meetings during the following months the tribe made its case for acquiring trust land and participating in the management and preservation of natural and cultural resources in Death Valley. It presented its historical and anthropological data to describe the boundaries of its ancestral homelands as well as its traditional land uses and cultural practices. There was no serious disagreement about this information.

The government asked the tribe to make its proposals, specifying location, size, and the intended use of parcels both inside and outside the park boundaries. At the top of the tribe's priorities were five thousand acres in the Furnace Creek area that it wanted taken into federal trust status for residential and community economic development. Furnace Creek is an oasis that the tribe always regarded as its central location. Most tribal members lived there prior to Euro-American contact. The Death Valley National Park Service headquarters, a major visitor center, NPS offices, and personnel housing are also located there. The Furnace Creek Inn and a large motel complex, both owned by the AM-FAC Corporation, provide today over 1.5 million park visitors each year with overnight hotel accommodations, several restaurants, and a mini-mart and gas station. The land on which these facilities are located, along with permanent water rights, had been in private ownership even before the 1933 establishment of the Death Valley National Monument.

The Tribe requested another 750,000 acres in the western part of the park. These were under the jurisdiction of the BLM before being transferred to the NPS by the California Desert Protection Act. This region is of special historical and spiritual significance to the tribe, encompassing seven sacred areas as well as major watershed lands and resources (wildlife, medicinal plants, springs, pinions, mesquite, and other food staples) that the tribal members historically had used and cultivated. These lands form one large, integrated ecosystem.

The Tribe's third area of interest comprised four smaller parcels, located at the periphery of the ancestral homelands and outside of the park on land the BLM had designated for disposal. These lay along main entrance routes into the park. Together they amounted to about another 11,000 acres. The tribe wanted these parcels for their future economic and residential development potential. Each of these parcels is in an area in which groups of tribal members had lived in small family clusters on a subsistence basis before contact with Euro-Americans.

The tribe received very little direct feedback from the federal representatives during the meetings in 1995. However, the tenor of the questions they raised revealed the general sentiment that the tribe was asking for too much land within the national park. A few federal representatives shared their belief that certain members of Congress would be reluctant to transfer ownership of any substantial parcel of land in the park, especially after the heated political battle that led to the passage of the California Desert Protection Act. According to their logic, Senator Feinstein and environmental groups would fear that their winning coalition would unravel if there were any tinkering with the land that had just been brought into a new national park. It was suggested that Congress would not want to give these protected wilderness areas to the tribe, and that, even if it did, the tribe would be unable do anything with that land under these restrictive conditions.

A few members of the federal team also questioned how the tribe would be able to manage 750,000 acres, "given its lack of previous experience or training." To this, the tribe pointed out that these lands had been "managed" with only the most minimal BLM staffing in the past, and that tribal members were "trainable." The Tribe's team also pointed out that one could assume that since no additional funds were allocated to the NPS for managing the additional million-plus acres, no one in government anticipated that the additional management responsibilities would be onerous or costly.

The federal representatives also expressed concern that there would not be sufficient amounts of water available in response to tribal representatives who described their need for home sites and the development of business enterprises to provide employment and income opportunities.

The federal representatives never provided any counterproposals or suggestions about how the tribe might restructure its proposals to accommodate the federal government's constraints and underlying concerns. For the most part, the two sides were very far apart, and the conversation was one-sided.

The Federal Government's Study Report

In October 1995, the first draft of a report was prepared by the San Francisco Regional NPS office with the assistance of BLM officials. The NPS asked the tribe to write sections pertaining to its historical presence and traditional uses of the area. It was also asked to respond in writing to the federal agencies' recommendations.

The federal government called for transferring into trust status only the forty-acre "tribal village" in the national park plus roughly eleven thousand acres of disposable BLM lands outside the park. The NPS suggested that the tribe could negotiate agreements in the future with the NPS and BLM to cooperatively manage lands and resources that were of interest to it.

Over the next three months the tribal team submitted increasingly hostile critiques and suggested revisions to the NPS's San Francisco office. Despite the original procedural agreement that preparation of the report would be a joint effort, the NPS gradually took on the sole responsibility of preparing the study report. It relegated the tribe and the other agencies to a role of reviewing and submitting comments that the park service at its sole discretion revised, included or excluded.

The tribe was not pleased with the decision by the federal government to transfer only forty acres of land in the park, arguing that roughly half of the proposed forty-acre parcel was unusable and that there would be no room for the tribe to build housing and tribal offices, engage in economic development, or create a viable tribal community. Moreover, the BLM lands being recommended outside the park boundaries provided limited economic development opportunities—even at that, only far into the future. Lastly, these BLM parcels were desert lands without existing infrastructure, and water was too limited to support significant residential development.

By December 1995, the tribe had seen no improvement in the NPS's second draft of the study report. It was convinced that the NPS regional office in San Francisco had not listened to anything that the tribe had proposed. It made the decision to go to Washington, D.C., to try to persuade people at a higher level to intervene. In the capital, the team members also conferred with staff working with the Senate Committee on Indian Affairs and several other House committees. They also made a presentation at a meeting chaired by the assistant secretary of Indian affairs, and to at least fifteen directors, deputy directors, and staff from the NPS, BLM, BIA, the Bureau of Reclamation (BOR), the Office of Indian Trust, and other departments.

The tribe left Washington with the assurance that in the next few weeks an interagency working group would be formed in the Department of the Interior that would schedule high-level meetings with the tribe. However, despite the good intentions of the persons who conveyed this impression to the tribe, there was an internal agency conflict between the national and San Francisco regional offices of the NPS that the people in D.C. could not overcome.[3]

No high-level interagency group in Washington was ever formed, nor were any additional meetings scheduled in Washington with the tribe. In fact, there was no further dialogue between the park service and the tribe from December 1995 until March 1996, when the San Francisco regional office presented a third draft of the study report it had written. In a meeting arranged by an NPS planner that took place in the corner of the NPS fire station in Furnace Creek, he informed the tribal representatives that the forty-acre Indian village in Furnace Creek was no longer being recommended for transfer into trust status, and that no lands within the national park would be considered suitable for a reservation. At the same time, he asked the tribe to endorse the third draft of the study report so that it could be approved by the secretary of the interior and finally submitted to Congress.

The tribal representatives were in complete shock. Reacting to the indignity of having to sit on turned-over buckets and on a very hot day tolerate the absence of any air conditioning during the meeting, and then being asked to sign off on the report, they reached the conclusion that the intention of the National Park Service all along had been to continue its policy of forcing the tribe out of the Park.

The tribe refused to endorse the third draft of the study report and to have any further discussions with the NPS. In a long letter to Interior Department secretary Bruce Babbitt, the tribe warned him against submitting the third draft of the report to Congress. It maintained that no study had been conducted, no lands within the national park boundaries had been seriously considered, and no consultation had been undertaken with the tribe.[4]

The First Round of Talks Assessed

In retrospect, the breakdown of the study process was predictable. From the beginning, the federal agencies and the tribe had very different notions about the intended nature and outcome of the talks between them. The tribe perceived the process to be a negotiation between two sovereign entities with the purpose of ultimately agreeing upon recommendations that would be submitted to Congress in a final study report. It looked to the meetings with the federal representatives as a forum in which the two sides could exchange information, spell out their concerns, generate options, and ultimately work out their differences. The tribe anticipated that once an agreement was reached between the tribe and the federal agencies, the agreement would be embodied in the report to Congress. The tribal team believed that the parties were expected to come to Congress with essentially "one voice." It believed that Congress would not want to find itself in the middle of a controversy between the tribe and the Department of the Interior, and then either have to sift through the debate and take sides, or ultimately do nothing to resolve the conflict.

In marked contrast to the tribe, the federal agencies saw their task as being the completion of the study Congress mandated. The agencies viewed this responsibility as consisting of research, data analysis, mapmaking, and report writing—a task that should and could be undertaken by staff technicians in the NPS's Pacific West Regional Office in San Francisco, with a little help from the BLM.

These federal agencies did not see the study as a government-to-government negotiation between two sovereign entities. They never felt that they had to come to any agreement with the tribe. Their understanding was that the study was to be conducted, in the words of Section 705(b), in "consultation with the tribe." In government parlance, "consultation" is not synonymous with "negotiation." The federal representatives' expectation was that they would engage in consultation much like they do with any other constituent group. They would sit and listen to the tribe's presentations, review its data, and consider its proposals. Then the agencies would submit a report on their findings and their recommendations.

The Secretary of the Interior's office did not initially see the resolution of the Timbisha Shoshone Tribe's land claim as a high-priority matter that required attention from the secretary or his immediate staff. The few persons involved at the level of the secretary's office did not take seriously an issue that concerned only some three hundred Indians out in the desert. They therefore made no attempt to resolve policy questions at the top and to spell out negotiating parameters for the lower-level people representing the agencies at the table. The upper-level decision makers were operating with a different model in mind.

The Tribe's National Political Organizing Strategy

The Timbisha Shoshone Tribe knew, after the March 1996 meeting in the park's firehouse, something would have to change in its relationship with the Department of the Interior if it was to have any hope of satisfying its interests in obtaining a land base. The tribe would have to establish its credibility as a party that had to be reckoned with, one powerful enough to cost the Department of the Interior more than it was willing to pay for not sitting down and negotiating in good faith.

The tribe also recognized that it would have to get out from under the National Park Service, which had long dominated and controlled its destiny. While Section 705(b) looked like it would finally provide the tribe a national forum to highlight its issue and advance its cause, the NPS had been effective in ratcheting down the study process to a local forum over which the agency again had the final word.

The tribal team recognized that it would have to broaden the battlefront beyond the NPS bureaucracy and increase the external pressure on the Department of the Interior. In other words, the tribe had to expand its own political base before it could create the "social space" in which to successfully advance its case.

Moments after the fateful March 1996 firehouse meeting with the NPS, the tribe launched a national political organizing campaign designed to generate political support from other tribes, national Indian organizations, congressional leaders and committees, environmental groups, the courts, the media, public opinion, and park visitors from the United States and abroad.

The tribe began with a scathing press release and followed up with a national letter-writing campaign, including news releases periodically faxed to all U.S. representatives and senators. Long letters were sent to the secretary of the interior and to the White House. In addition, the tribe opened a new front: it sued the BLM for having permitted gold mining in the tribe's backyard without the legally required consultation. It also submitted to both the NPS and BLM extensive requests for data under the Freedom of Information Act as it began to prepare a major lawsuit against the Department of the Interior.

National Alliance to Protect Native Rights in National Parks

The tribe identified and contacted other Native nations with reservations adjoining national parks that also were frustrated with the NPS's attitudes toward Indians and with its implicit policy to refuse tribes the use of national park lands. All these tribes were aware that their adjoining national parks had all been carved away from Indians' ancestral lands after their treaties had already been negotiated.

The Timbisha Shoshone led the way to establish a National Alliance to Protect Native Rights in National Parks. It recruited as members the Navajo, Hualapai, Five Sandoval, and Miccosukee Tribes as well as a coalition of Native Hawaiian communities and environmental groups. Many more Native nations, including the Blackfeet, the Oglala Sioux, and the Yurok Tribes, were contacted and in varying stages of joining as well.

The alliance secured the support of national Indian organizations, including the National Congress of American Indians (NCAI), California Indian Legal Services, Native American Rights Fund (NARF), Indian Dispute Resolution Service, and others. Members of the Alliance attended the NCAI convention in Washington, D.C., that year and asked all tribal delegates to pass two formal resolutions that criticized the NPS and asked the secretary of the interior to rectify the problems. They called for congressional oversight hearings to look into NPS's anti-Indian policies. The NCAI then joined the alliance in holding press conferences in Washington, where they called for the NPS to establish a national Indian policy in negotiations with a cross-section of tribes.

Public demonstrations and information marches were organized in Death Valley National Park. Information was written in English, Japanese, Italian, and German and was passed out to park visitors who came from all over the world. Many of the visitors indicated that they were appalled by the plight of the tribe and the NPS's apparent policy of excluding them from park lands. Visitors also questioned why there was no mention, at the park's Visitor Center and Museum in Furnace Creek, of the Timbisha Shoshone Tribe's continued historical presence in and contribution to life in Death Valley. Many of these visitors sent letters and faxes to NPS officials, congressional leaders in Washington, D.C., and to President Clinton himself.

New Windows of Opportunity

What made the federal government eventually willing to negotiate with the tribe? What accounted for the shift in the government's position by January 1998? In brief, the Timbisha Shoshone Tribe was eventually successful in mounting enough political pressure on the NPS and the Interior Department to persuade them to come to the table and once there to work with the tribe in good faith. While it did not have the political leverage to compel the department to do anything in one fell swoop, it seems to have pounded away on enough different fronts simultaneously to have a cumulative impact on swaying opinion against the department's initial position. At the very least, it managed to become a "nuisance" that would not go away until the Department of the Interior adopted a different approach.

By taking the offensive, the tribe put the federal agencies on the defensive. The Tribe was effective in defining the issue and trying to delegitimize the department on both moral and legal grounds. It targeted the NPS for denying the tribe any land in Death Valley National Park and for effectively forcing the tribe out of the park. It maintained that the NPS and the Office of the Secretary of the Interior were committing an American version of ethnic cleansing by still trying to throw the tribe off its homelands in Death Valley and for refusing to settle its age-old land claim. The tribe maintained that the federal government was still implementing the anti-Indian policies of the 1800s in the mid-1990s. The tribe cited numerous examples in Indian Country and among Native Hawaiians, where the NPS was discounting Native people's rights in the national parks.

In addition, the Timbisha Shoshone Tribe maintained that the NPS refusal to consider lands within Death Valley National Park as potentially suitable for a reservation was contrary to the intent of Congress and therefore illegal. The tribe was preparing a lawsuit with this as one cause of action.

The tribe was able to generate negative publicity against the Park Service and managed to keep the unresolved issue in the public eye for an extended period of time. The NPS was criticized in public. An increasing number of important people inside and outside government began to privately ask the secretary of the interior why his department could not settle the matter more amicably. These questions came from many different sources, including members of the California congressional delegation, national environmental groups (Greenpeace, the National Parks and Conservation Association), members and staff of the Senate Committee on Indian Affairs and other House and Senate committees, and park visitors who cared enough to communicate with the White House and other branches of the federal government.

A key factor in the mounting pressure on the NPS was the National Alliance to Protect Native Rights in National Parks. It had broad support in Indian Country and included politically significant tribes that were all aggressively pursuing their own agendas and were in their own right thorns in the NPS's side. Nowhere was this truer than in the case of the Miccosukee Tribe, which was engaged in a raging battle with the Park Service over land and jurisdictional issues in the Everglades National Park. This tribe was challenging the NPS in court, in Congress, and in the media. The Miccosukee Tribe was a mover and shaker in the National Alliance. The Timbisha Shoshone Tribe was in close contact with its leadership and its legal and public relations staff. At least in the Senate Committee on Indian Affairs, the NPS was acquiring the reputation of being insensitive and ineffective in dealing with Indian tribes.[5]

Also, there were important changes in personnel in the NPS leadership and in the interior secretary's cabinet that had a direct bearing on negotiations with the Timbisha Shoshone Tribe. The past director of the San Francisco Regional Office of NPS retired, and his replacement, John Reynolds, proved to be comfortable with the negotiation process and better able to relate to Indian people.

The other major change in personnel was Secretary Babbitt's appointment of Donald Barry as assistant secretary of Fish, Wildlife, and Parks. Barry had become a believer in the negotiation process as the proper basis for a government-to-government relationship with tribes. He had been involved in representing the government in negotiating a comprehensive agreement between a national coalition of tribes and the Departments of the Interior and Commerce regarding how the Endangered Species Act should be implemented in Indian Country.

There was yet a third factor. Around the time the second round of negotiations began, in the winter of 1998, there was a significant development in the Everglades National Park that gave the NPS an added incentive to come to the negotiation table. Because the NPS leadership had chosen to be intransigent in its dealings with the Miccosukee

Tribe, Congress and Secretary Babbitt's office eventually took the matter out of NPS hands and settled it themselves. The NPS did not want to risk being frozen out of the negotiations with the Timbisha Shoshone also. At this point the NPS believed that both the Senate Committee on Indian Affairs and Secretary Babbitt wanted the Timbisha Shoshone matter resolved expeditiously.[6]

Secretary Babbitt gave Donald Barry the responsibility and authority to resolve the matter with the Timbisha Shoshone Tribe. Barry organized an interagency working group and asked John Reynolds, the NPS's new director of the Pacific Region in San Francisco, to lead the federal team.

Changes in the composition of the tribe's negotiation team also may have made a little difference in the receptivity of the federal government. Both the former CILS attorney and the tribe's administrator had resigned after the conclusion of the first round of talks. Both were very protective of the tribe's interests and became angry and cynical, as reflected in their subsequent correspondence and public pronouncements. The NPS may have been buoyed by the prospect of no longer having to deal with these two strong advocates.

The Second Round

The first round of transactions ended in polarizing the sides and creating more bitterness and distrust between them than had existed before. The second round, beginning in January 1998, was very successful. What had changed? In the remaining sections of this chapter, we analyze the negotiation process itself and identify a number of key negotiating principles that were adopted and account for the success enjoyed by both sides. The fact that both sides were now motivated to come to the negotiation table, and to stay there through difficult moments during the process, was extremely important. But so were a variety of other items that are worth noting.

The assessment that follows is offered within a particular framework. Negotiators must enjoy, as well as direct their efforts to producing, satisfaction on three different dimensions. The three dimensions are (1) satisfaction with the negotiation process itself (with how we talk about what we talk about), (2) satisfaction with the substantive results (with the solutions to the problems that brought the parties to the table in the first place), and (3) satisfaction with the relationship established between the parties (with the degree of the trust and respect developed between them).

Creating Process Satisfaction

During the first round of talks between the tribe and the federal government, process agreements were reached that were not kept. This undermined trust. For example, there was an agreement that the study report would be drafted and submitted as a joint document. With each successive draft, less collaboration took place. Moreover, certain agreements were omitted. There was no explicit understanding about whether the process was a "consultation" or a bilateral "negotiation," or about its intended outcome. Was it to be an agreement on recommendations to create a reservation or a report on a government study with a possible dissenting opinion included from the tribe?

Procedural Negotiations Preceding Substantive Discussions

Seven months of process negotiations were held before the first face-to-face meeting between the parties. The tribe identified a series of procedural issues that would have to be addressed and resolved before the tribe was willing to try again.[7] These were discussed on the telephone and sometime later by a letter from the NPS. Among the procedural agreements made were the following:

- The parties agreed on who specifically would represent the government and the tribe at the table at the first meeting. Being intent on raising its land issue to a place high on the interior secretary's list of priorities, the tribe requested that persons in the secretariat also be directly involved in the talks. Secretary Barry included his special counsel, a member of a midwestern tribe.

    The Tribe also requested that the Bureau of Reclamation (BOR) be part of the federal team since it anticipated that the availability of water in Death Valley might be used again to undermine the tribe's land acquisition and land use proposals. The tribe hoped the BOR would be a good counterweight to the NPS, and it wanted an agency that was independent from the NPS and the BLM to inform the process. Ultimately, the federal team included the BOR as a gesture of goodwill to the tribe.
- The Tribe proposed in its letter that the federal government explicitly agree to enter government-to-government negotiations, and to work for a written agreement on what lands to recommend to Congress for a permanent home for the tribe.

As late as December 22, 1997, NPS's official answer was negative. It responded, "It is important that all parties understand that the study process *is not a negotiated agreement.*" NPS wrote that the "statute authorizes the Secretary to conduct a study in consultation with the Timbisha Shoshone Tribe and the study process will reflect that direction from Congress. We very much want to reach agreement with the Tribe on a collaborative process for completing the study in consultation with the Tribe.... It is our hope an 'interest-based consultation' will assist us in clarifying what both sides need to have addressed in the process of completing the Study."

Only at the first face-to-face meeting did the federal government agree to negotiate a bilateral agreement on what specifically would be recommended to Congress, not just an agreement on how the study was to be completed.

- The parties agreed to jointly identify any additional studies that would be needed, and to define beforehand the specific research questions, the scope of the research, what data would be gathered, the projected costs, the sources of information, and the length of time needed. The tribe did not want the government to use a study as a delaying tactic.
- The parties also finally agreed to engage in interest-based negotiations (IBN). However, the government resisted the idea of interest-based negotiations until the first face-to-face meeting in Death Valley. The tribe, in a letter to the NPS, laid out its nine interests and asked the federal government to be "forthcoming with respect to its interests or underlying concerns." In its letter the tribe wrote,

> The Tribe understands that the federal government will have concerns [interests] regarding the location, size, and legal status of the Tribe's presence, and regarding the scope, nature, aesthetics, and coordination [with NPS] of the Tribe's activities. However, it hopes that this time the government can make these concerns explicit so that there can be a full discussion of the perceived obstacles and the possible modifications, re-configurations and alternatives in an effort to accommodate mutual interests. A true win-win solution will depend on the full exploration of how the interests of both parties can be satisfied to an acceptable level.

In the government's formal reply to the tribe's November 18 letter, it agreed that there should be "a full discussion of underlying concerns and interests . . . but these must be discussed as part of the study process and this will not be possible to discuss all of these matters at the first meeting."[8]

This question was left open until the first meeting when the tribe's negotiators asked John Reynolds directly whether his team was prepared to address and respond to the tribe's list of nine interests. His answer was, "Yes," and he proceeded to discuss them one by one. The tribe listed the following interests:

a. Coexistence with the NPS in Death Valley.
b. Establishment of a permanent homeland in traditional ancestral land areas falling within today's national park boundaries.
c. Establishment of housing clusters close to schools, services, and physical infrastructure (roads, electricity, water and sewage, etc.), in locations in and near Furnace Creek.
d. Use of its traditional summer camping areas for seasonal residence, harvesting, stewarding land and natural resources, and so on.
e. Location of its government headquarters and community and human service programs in and near Furnace Creek.
f. Preservation and development of its own dynamic culture by living as a community on its ancestral lands.
g. Economic and employment development activities, particularly in low-impact eco-tourist development.
h. Active involvement in the protection and preservation of the environmental (water, vegetation, wildlife) and cultural resources of the Death Valley area.
i. Being an integral part of the Death Valley National Park's landscape and program by presenting and interpreting its own history and culture to park visitors.

- The parties agreed to invite an impartial third party to facilitate the negotiations. Charles Wilkinson, a prominent law professor from the University of Colorado Law School in Boulder, was selected as the facilitator. He had been involved in the negotiations between Indian tribes and the Departments of the Interior and Commerce over the application of the Endangered Species Act (ESA) in Indian Country. He knew Secretary

Babbitt and Assistant Secretary Barry personally and enjoyed their confidence as well as that of others in the Department of the Interior. Moreover, he was regarded as one of the foremost experts in Indian law and other matters of great importance in the West—including water. Wilkinson also had previously worked on the staff of the Native American Rights Fund (NARF), a highly regarded and effective national public-interest law firm working on behalf of Indian tribes.

The tribe was also persuaded to have Wilkinson serve as the facilitator by its observation that his reputation as a fair-minded person dedicated to the principle of the government-to-government relationship would be on the line. The tribe believed he would help protect the integrity of the negotiation process and be witness to any effort by the federal representatives to undermine or thwart it.

- The tribe sought to clarify two additional issues before the face-to-face negotiation sessions began in Death Valley. It asked the Department of the Interior to declare explicitly whether land within the Death Valley National Park would be considered as possibly suitable for a reservation. The tribe wanted an explicit yes or no at the outset and was intent on limiting the number of surprises and maximizing predictability. John Reynolds replied to it in his opening statement at the January 15 and January 16 meetings in Death Valley.
- The tribe also asked the federal team to agree to have an ongoing dialogue between the negotiation teams and their ultimate decision makers during the negotiations. The Park Service did not address this request in writing. However, the interagency working group assembled by Assistant Secretary Berry to coordinate the effort had already been very active.

Meeting with Assistant Secretary Donald J. Barry

The first meeting between the tribe and the federal agency representatives in Death Valley, first scheduled for December 10 and 11, 1997, was postponed to January 15 and 16. With little more than a week left before this meeting, the tribe was notified that Deputy Assistant Secretary Barry wanted to first meet with tribal representatives in Washington. He indicated he had been asked by Bruce Babbitt, secretary of the interior, to "coordinate a renewed effort by the Department of the Interior to complete the study authorized by Section 705(b) of the California Desert Protection Act."

The assistant secretary assured the tribe he would track the progress directly and that he expected negotiations between the U.S. government and the tribe to be conducted on a government-to-government level. He also indicated that he expected negotiations to produce an agreement to take to Congress regarding lands suitable for a reservation. From the perspective of the tribal negotiators, it appeared that Barry's decision to kick off the process meant finally that the secretary's office was committed to a collaborative process to resolve its dispute with the Timbisha Shoshone, and that Barry, not the NPS, would call the shots during the second round.[9]

Procedural Agreements Formalized at the First Session

The first face-to-face meetings took place January 15 and 16, 1998, in the tribal offices in Death Valley. The first day was devoted to developing and agreeing on a framework within which to proceed for the remainder of the negotiations. The parties agreed on the following:

- That they had a "special political relationship, including a trust relationship, between the Timbisha Shoshone Nation and the United States."
- To engage in "bilateral government–to-government negotiations between the two sovereigns."
- To participate in negotiations that would "lead to a specific, formal proposal for achieving a Timbisha Shoshone Homeland."
- That they would serve as the "core group" of negotiators from the federal team and the tribe's team who would use their best efforts to attend all of the meetings. Subsequent meetings would be scheduled around their availability to maximize continuity and solidarity.
- To engage in ongoing consultations with their hierarchies for the duration of the negotiations. They agreed that they "had the responsibility to follow up and get answers promptly" when matters discussed required ratification at a higher level. Moreover, if a recommendation was rejected, they agreed to explain why.
- That all agendas for future sessions were to be jointly developed.

- That any party could call a caucus at any time to facilitate internal team negotiations and agreement.
- To maintain "confidentiality" and that information shared with external persons, including the press, would be limited to a report on the issues under discussion and the status of the process. The substance of the discussions would not be shared "except through written statements agreed upon or as required by law."
- That summaries of the discussions, including all understandings reached, would be kept for each meeting.
- To complete four studies (corresponding to four areas in which the tribe was interested) by "working jointly as governments and in full cooperation." The parties agreed not only to reach agreement on the type of study and the process for completing it, but on the substantive recommendations.
- That they work to fulfill a list of thirteen "interests" or principles. They included the nine interests the tribe spelled out above, and the NPS offered four of its own.[10]

Creating Substantive Satisfaction

Over the next nine months, the two teams met a total of six times for two to three days at a time. During the time between the end of Round 1 and the beginning of Round 2, both sides' original expectations of what might be possible had been lowered by the actions of the other side and the political context in which they were operating.

Reevaluating Interests and Negotiation Strategies

In the summer and fall of 1997, the tribe met to prepare for renewed negotiations with the federal government. The focus was on conducting a reality check and revising expectations, if that seemed warranted. The central question was whether, and how, it could satisfy its interests without having all the land it previously requested be transferred to trust status.[11]

Tribal representatives decided that asking again for large parcels of trust land in the national park (5,000 acres in Furnace Creek and some 750,000 acres in the western part of the park) would have limited success. Political realities dictated more restraint.

The tribe expected that Senator Feinstein would play a pivotal role in passing any legislation needed to put a negotiated agreement into effect.

The team believed that if Congress was asked again to make major changes in land tenure in Death Valley, Senator Feinstein and others in her coalition would resist.

The tribe's team also expected the NPS to resist the transfer of large amounts of park land to the tribe because other tribes with ancestral claims on national parks would use the Timbisha Shoshone example as a precedent.

The tribe had requested land during the first round of talks with the federal government for two primary reasons. First, it had an interest in establishing a viable, self-sustaining tribal community in perpetuity. To meet these interests, the tribe needed enough land on which to build permanent homes, deliver health and social services, house and operate its government, and engage in business development.

The second reason the tribe had initially requested land was that it had a deep and abiding interest in getting back on the land to actively steward the resources. The Timbisha Shoshone do not see land as simply a piece of real estate, separate from themselves, that can be acquired and transferred, bought and sold. The people are an integral part of the landscape and life of the desert; they have an intimate relationship with the mountains, valleys, plant life and wildlife, springs and streams. Moreover, they believe that they are not passive participants in this organic whole but rather have a historical and spiritual responsibility to protect and cultivate life in all its forms and to help maintain the ecological balance.

The tribal negotiation team members were willing to consider legal alternatives to trust land, as long as the federal government could convince them that certain basic conditions would be met. The land area would have to be within its ancestral homeland; large enough to accommodate its residential, service, governmental, and economic development activities; and be located near adequate physical infrastructure and social amenities. The Tribe would have to be guaranteed the right to occupy this land in perpetuity, and able to exercise sovereign authority over the activities on this land. The Tribe also recognized that having lands in trust would be a prerequisite for successfully obtaining any grants or loans from the government or private foundations to build housing, tribal government offices, and community facilities, and to start and operate business enterprises.

In the final analysis, the tribe's negotiation team did not give up seeing the entire area (approximately eight million acres) as its homeland—whether the federal government recognized this or not, or whether NPS occupied it or not. Chairperson Pauline Esteves made it clear that even though by agreeing to only a small section of land to be transferred to tribal ownership, the tribe had no less a connection to the remaining areas and no less a sense of responsibility for being present and actively involved in stewarding them.

The Park Service's interests also became clearer. The NPS had an overriding interest in promoting and protecting a certain ambience and aesthetic in Death Valley National Park, which is consistent with providing visitors a "desert experience." Toward this end, NPS had an interest in limiting the number and size of any new physical improvement. In fact, it is today an official National Park System policy to encourage all future commercial development designed to meet visitor needs to locate outside park boundaries.

With this strong interest it is not surprising that the NPS would be apprehensive about having an Indian reservation within park boundaries. It would be an area over which the Park Service would not have complete authority, and it consequently would be limited in its ability to protect the park.

The NPS's expectations also had been modified significantly from what they had been in 1995 and 1996. The Timbisha Shoshone Tribe had to be given a sense of predictable permanency and could not be removed from the park. While it might have been easier to manage the park without having to deal with an outside entity like an Indian reservation within its boundaries, it was no longer politically feasible. Once the tribe's continued presence was accepted as inevitable, the NPS's interests were reordered: complete autonomy and control by the NPS within the park's boundaries gave way to its concerns for maximizing predictability and containment.

It was in the interest of both the tribe and the NPS to avoid having the tribe living in substandard conditions without the opportunity to become economically self-sufficient. An impoverished tribal community inside the park could ultimately threaten the park's aesthetic and might also reflect badly on the Park Service's reputation.

On the other hand, the NPS wanted to define, and thus predetermine, the parameters (size, type, location, aesthetic, etc.) of this development as much as possible in the negotiated agreement. The NPS was also interested in identifying other lands outside the park because these parcels could eventually serve as sites for viable residential and economic development once the site in the park's Furnace Creek area reached an agreed-to maximum capacity. In this way, the NPS could protect itself against future demands for more space and tribal activity within the park, many decades in the future.

Emergence of Substantive Agreements

The federal team began the substantive negotiations by indicating that it was prepared to consider the tribe's village area in Furnace Creek as the permanent location for the tribe's major activities, including residences, a tribal government center, community and recreational services, and modest visitor-related business development. It recognized that Furnace Creek was not only historically important to the tribe but the only location within the tribe's homeland that currently offered the tribe the preconditions for developing a viable community: for example, access to sufficient water, physical and social infrastructure, and a reliable tourist market for local economic development activities.

The NPS and the tribe went on to informally agree to begin negotiations without taking a position on trust land status in the park. The major stumbling block during the first round of talks—trust lands or no trust lands—was thereby sidestepped. The two teams agreed that trust status would not be ruled out, but other legal arrangements would be explored first. In the end, however, there were no such legal arrangements identified, and trust status was agreed to.

The ensuing negotiations further highlighted the virtues of interest-based negotiations and the need to avoid what are considered positional negotiations. Instead of the parties arguing about the size of the Furnace Creek parcel by each arbitrarily reaching for a number and then vigorously defending it, the parties agreed that it had to be of a size sufficient to enable the tribe to create a "viable" community with adequate space for housing, services, and economic development.

John Reynolds suggested a way to address still-unanswered questions about the size of the parcel in Furnace Creek. He offered the tribe the services of landscape architects and community planners from the National Park Denver Service Center. Working with tribal representatives, they would prepare drawings of their concepts of a tribal village that contained all the anticipated physical facilities. It was ultimately agreed that the tribe's forty-acre village would be enlarged to three hundred acres. The parties also agreed to low-impact visitor-related service businesses, including a tribal museum and cultural center, a retail gift and Indian crafts shop, and a "small to modest-sized, desert inn," owned and operated by the tribe.

Interest-based negotiations once again helped to avoid a major confrontation when trying to define the concept of a "small to modest-sized" desert inn. The park and tribal negotiators began to argue about the number of rooms that could be built. The Tribe proposed one hundred rooms while the Park proposed twenty-five. The question was resolved when the tribe suggested that the inn's financial viability ultimately be the criterion for determining the size. At a minimum, the tribe wanted the inn to be large enough to generate net income that was consistent with industry standards. This made sense also from the perspective of NPS's interests. The NPS did not want the inn to be a financial failure, lest it close down, remain as an unoccupied building, and undermine the image of the national park. The parties agreed that it was premature to decide on the maximum number of rooms until the tribe was ready to launch the enterprise and the needed financial information was available.

The two negotiation teams also agreed that they would jointly develop building standards that would apply to all new physical developments in the park. Standards were an additional way to ensure that the inn's size would be something both the tribe and the Park Service could agree to when the time came for development review and implementation.

The three-hundred-acre parcel was significantly larger than the former forty-acre village site on which the tribe has squatted for almost sixty-five years. However, it is also much smaller than the five thousand acres in Furnace Creek the tribe had proposed be transferred to trust during the first round of talks several years before. On the surface, it appears that the tribe gave up an enormous amount. However, other provisions in the agreement that pertain to this area in Furnace Creek help again to illustrate the merits of interest-based negotiations.

In addition to the three hundred acres of trust land reserved for tribal development activities, the parties agreed to a contiguous buffer zone of about five thousand acres that would separate the tribe from the main road and the Park visitor area and would protect known archaeological sites. They also agreed to set aside three thousand acres adjoining the three hundred acres on the other side as a special-use area for the tribe with limited access allowed to park visitors. This large parcel contains one of the largest mesquite groves in the park and provides mesquite beans that have long been the primary food staple of tribal members. The tribe would once again be free to engage in traditional cultivation and harvesting practices to sustain the yield. Neither the buffer nor the mesquite areas would be transferred to trust status, yet the tribe's interests regarding these areas and resources would be satisfied.

In later negotiation sessions, discussions shifted to the western area of the park, which was of special importance to the tribe because of its spiritual sites and its historical and traditional uses. The Tribe longed to return to the area for gatherings, summer camping, and bringing the springs, wildlife, and vegetation (pinions, etc.) back to life.

In lieu of proposing to bring this area into trust status (it is now almost all under the wilderness designation), the parties agreed to designate approximately one million acres as the "Timbisha Shoshone Natural and Cultural Preservation Area." While it would remain part of the Death Valley National Park under the same legal status as before, it was agreed that official park maps would reflect the new designation and thereby inform park visitors of the area's special connection to the Timbisha Shoshone Tribe. It would also be a priority area for developing new cultural and natural resource comanagement projects between NPS, the BLM, and the tribe.

While no trust land was designated, the promise of having guaranteed access and a very active role in stewarding this vast area satisfied the tribe's interest in the area. In addition, the special designation that would become part of the congressional legislation was of enormous symbolic importance. After sixty-five years of having no legitimate standing in the park and no official recognition by the Park Service that the tribe was anything more than part of Death Valley's ancient history, the tribe was pleased to literally find itself on the map and finally accorded the respect it is due.

The parties also reached an agreement that four additional parcels of historical significance would be taken into trust. One of these was in the park, and the other three were lying outside the park and managed by the BLM. The major constraint on each of these parcels is limited water resources. These four parcels consist of approximately 7,240 additional acres.[12]

Creating Relational Satisfaction

Negotiations are more than a mechanical exercise of setting up a process and exchanging proposals until an agreement is reached. They are a human interaction between people with different feelings, attitudes, values, perspectives, memories, and personalities. What happens among the people at or away from the table during negotiations will have a direct bearing on how successfully the issues are resolved and how the parties will be able to work together and resolve differences in the future.

The human factor, the relationships that developed between the parties over a period of nine months, played an important role in creating a sense of trust, respect, and safety. People at the table developed some close personal connections with certain members of the other team. This provided the glue that not only held the process together but seemed to lubricate it as well.

One can speculate about the reasons that strong relationships developed during the second round and not during the first. Clearly, one process decision reached at the outset of the second round was particularly helpful. The parties agreed to limit the number of people who would sit at the table and to identify a core group of people who would consistently represent their organization and attend all the sessions without sending alternates. The continuity in group membership gave the participants an opportunity to get to know each other well over time.

Over the nine months of intense negotiations, the negotiators met for two to three days at a time, sometimes until midnight. They stayed at the same hotel and usually ate meals together. This concentrated time together, time that was not always devoted to business, gave people an opportunity to experience each other as more than two-dimensional figures across the table from them. They learned about one another's personal histories, values, opinions, and commitments. They started to develop a sense about whether they could trust one another as human beings, outside and beyond the roles they were serving in representing an agency or the tribe.

In addition to the structure of the negotiation being conducive to relationship building, there just happened to be, due to sheer luck, good chemistry between some key individuals who participated in the process. Their good humor and occasional lightheartedness, their shared optimism, and their mutual respect created a momentum and positive spirit that energized the negotiations.

These emerging personal relationships became the basis of an informal communication network that operated on a track parallel with the formal negotiations. The large number of representatives at the table, often seventeen or eighteen people, made it cumbersome at times to clarify understandings in any great depth. Some of the negotiators compensated by working through their own personal contacts on the other team. These informal contacts all helped to eliminate the element of surprise—the natural enemy of successful negotiations.

The facilitator was also of significant help. Charles Wilkinson is bright, has vast experience, is easy with people, and has a huge heart that everyone appreciated. He maintained close relationships with and was trusted by members of both teams. He was clearly always present and helped to clarify questions and provide his own observations to help make things understandable to everyone when that was needed. He provided written summaries of meetings and helped wordsmith agreements being reached.

The Timbisha story provides important insights into the conflict resolution process, what works and what doesn't. It sheds particular light on the role of power in negotiations, and on certain underlying assumptions commonly made about the merits of win-win approaches to problem solving.

The win-win approach is increasingly seen as the preferred way to resolve conflicts. However, it does not work when a significant power imbalance exists between the parties. The transactions between the Timbisha Shoshone Tribe and the federal agencies over the years reveal an important limitation of the win-win approach. For over sixty-five years the tribe was unable to get the federal government to seriously consider its grievance and establish a land base. Moreover, during the first round of talks, the tribe was still regarded as an insignificant threat to the interests of the federal government. The federal government persisted in making decisions unilaterally and refused to negotiate with the tribe.

This changed only after the tribe pulled out of the talks and launched a national political organizing campaign that successfully embarrassed and put public pressure on the NPS and the Department of the Interior. Only then did the federal agencies gradually perceive that they would pay a heavy price for continued intransigence. Once the agencies acknowledged the new power dynamics, they began to approach the tribe as an equal and chose to negotiate in good faith. Only then could the win-win model be implemented.

When all was said and done, the Timbisha Shoshone Tribe was the one to reshape the government-to-government relationship, which makes this case study all the more remarkable. Nothing in federal law or the congressional instructions to the Department of the Interior in the California Desert Protection Act required the federal agencies to approach the Timbisha Shoshone Tribe as an equal and commit to negotiate a win-win agreement. President Clinton's Executive Order that called for a government-to-government relationship holds out hope to tribes that this could be a standard that agencies might aspire to, but it still is just advisory.

After the disappointing first round of talks, the tribe had to assert its sovereignty and persuade the NPS in particular that it was in its interest to come to the table and engage in bilateral negotiations. The tribe had to demonstrate that it had the power to threaten the Department of the Interior's interest in maintaining its reputation and national image as being fair to American Indians. The Timbisha Shoshone Tribe had to demonstrate that it could threaten the agencies' positive relationship with and widespread support from members of Congress, environmental groups, other Indian tribes, national Indian organizations, user groups (park visitors) from the United States and abroad, and the national media. These groups reached a point where they began to question NPS and BLM policies vis-à-vis the Timbisha Shoshone Tribe and Indian people in general.

What impact might the Timbisha Shoshone experience have on future government-tribal relationships? This case created new opportunities for tribes and government agencies both to go beyond what is familiar to them, and to go beyond the consultation process. What the Timbisha case proves beyond a reasonable doubt is that the federal government can successfully enter negotiations that are committed to mutual gain—interest-based negotiations—without abdicating its congressionally mandated authority or giving up its sovereignty. Both parties can promote and protect their vital interests while ensuring that the other side is accorded the same opportunity. In the process, neither side has to give up anything that is vitally important to it.

In the final analysis, the negotiated agreement between the Department of the Interior and the Timbisha Shoshone Tribe satisfied the mutual interests of the parties and was perceived by both as a win-win. It is a fine tribute to every person around the negotiating table who had the courage to explore unfamiliar ground. What transpired is truly a prototype government-to-government negotiation. To the extent that more people involved in Indian Affairs in this nation follow this example, the cumulative effect could well transform the relationship between the federal government and American Indian tribes forever.

APPENDIXES

Improving Negotiation Outcomes with Better Communication Skills

An additional facet of the negotiation process not yet addressed is how negotiators speak and listen to one another. These behaviors determine how successful they will be in collaborating and reaching mutually satisfying agreements.

The appendixes to this volume provide learning exercises and self-administered questionnaires that highlight ways people can become more constructive communicators and contribute to the success of the negotiation process. We can all use these lessons to improve our personal interactions at home and in negotiations in the workplace, in government, and in the community. If this book is used in a class on conflict resolution, these exercises can be assigned by the instructor as homework.

These exercises have been sorted into three groups and geared to different chapters in the book. Of course, readers can decide for themselves when they choose to do any of the exercises.

APPENDIX A

Exercises for Chapter 1: Negotiation as a Strategy for Conflict Resolution

Exercise 1. Common Misconceptions about Negotiations

Below, is a list of common misconceptions about negotiations. Write a brief response correcting each of the following misconceptions. If the book is assigned as reading material for a class, the list of misconceptions can be topics for the students to discuss in small groups or as a full group.

  a. Everything can be negotiated.
  b. Negotiation is the art of compromise.
  c. Agreeing to negotiate is already a major concession and sign of weakness.
  d. The concept of win-win is new.
  e. Government agencies are not permitted to negotiate.
  f. Win-win agreements only exist when all parties acquire what they initially wanted, expected, or needed.
  g. Negotiators should conceal their interests from the opposing side(s).
  h. Consensus within a team or among teams is synonymous with unanimous agreement.
  i. Collaborative interest-based negotiation is a soft form of negotiation and the equivalent of accommodation.
  j. Collaborative negotiation is motivated by the attitude of peace at any price, and brings with the process a guarantee of settlement, high satisfaction for all parties, and amicability.
  k. In collaborative negotiation there is no competition.
  l. Assertiveness and cooperation in negotiations cannot be accomplished at the same time by a given party.
  m. Expressing emotions has no place in the negotiation process.

n. Substantive satisfaction in negotiation is more important than procedural and relational satisfaction.
o. The initial negotiation proposal should be an unsubstantiated, unjustifiable, and exaggerated version of what the negotiator really believes or expects in order to create a broad bargaining range.
p. Concessions are a sign of weakness.
q. The ultimate authority and decision makers must be at the table.

Exercise 2. "You" and "I" Statements

When we work with other people, our objective should be to enlist them in a cooperative effort. This is required if we are to be successful in achieving the purpose of our program or organization. People pulling in different directions are not effective in getting the job done.

Very often, even though our intention is to generate greater cooperation, we create the opposite effect. We turn people off. We push them away instead of drawing them closer. We throw them off course rather than bring them into greater alignment.

This exercise is designed to get us to look at the way we typically communicate, and to see how by simply making some minor changes, we might increase cooperation.

One common way we push people away is by using "You" statements.

"You" statements are statements made to other people that start with "You". They

1. Blame or accuse people for having done something wrong.
2. Put people on the spot.
3. Put people down.
4. Tell people what they should think, do, or feel.
5. Cause arguments about who is right and who is wrong.

For example:

"You are so inconsiderate."
"You always interrupt."

What is the impact of such statements on recipients?

a. Makes the accused want to immediately protect and defend himself or herself.

b. Gets the person angry and discourages any further listening.
c. Focuses on personalities rather than on solving a particular problem.

Converting "You" Statements into "I" Statements

When we carefully analyze each "You" statement we make, we can see that each is intended to get the listener to change a behavior and remove a problem that is vexing to us. But instead of focusing on the problem we use language that accuses and blames the person we are talking to. Instead of focusing on the problem, the "accused" focuses on playing defense.

"I" statements are statements to other people that start with "I" and provide information about you and your feelings, needs, values, or beliefs in a manner that demonstrates respect and concern for the other person. But instead of focusing on the person who is creating the problem, it describes the problem in general (e.g., talking too much) and impersonal terms. It thereby separates the "problem" from the "personality" we are addressing. It invites the listener to consider why the behavior is bothering the speaker and how it might change his or her behavior to eliminate the problem.

Use the magic formula:

I feel _____ when _____ because _____.
    (Feeling)   (Describe the problem)   (Reason)

Example:

"I feel angry when I am interrupted because what I have to say is important."

What is the impact of saying it this way?

1. The speaker's feelings are clearly expressed.
2. The problem situation is described.
3. The problem becomes the focal point—not the problem maker.
4. The listener is invited to consider the problem without having to be defensive.
5. The word "you" has been completely removed from the message.

Exercise: Converting "You" Statements into "I" Statements

Below are "You" statements that might come up in everyday conversations with adults and children. Your task is to convert them into "I" statements. Remember to use the three-part formula described above: "I FEEL (emotion) WHEN (describe behavior) BECAUSE (reason for the emotion).

1. You talk too much.
2. You always have big ideas for other people.
3. You don't listen and then you ask questions about what has already been covered.
4. You never do what you say you will do.
5. When I ask for a discussion, you all just sit there. (Supervisor to staff)
6. You never share the agenda. (Staff to supervisor)
7. You never back me up. (Supervisor to fellow supervisor)
8. You never seem to know how much money we have. (Supervisor to bookkeeper/accountant)
9. You always forget the minutes. (Manager to secretary)
10. You never think other people have good ideas.
11. You always give me jobs and then you won't give me any help.
12. You are always changing the subject.
13. You never participate in planning but you always complain about the results.
14. You always say "yes," but you never follow through.
15. You are not negotiating in good faith.
16. You and your group are always demanding more than what you give.

Exercise 3. Reasons Why Parties May Resist Entering the Negotiation Process

Negotiation and mediation are both voluntary processes. Parties have to decide to participate and can withdraw at any time on their own volition. The following list suggests a number of reasons why parties may hesitate to participate. Being aware of these reasons attunes us to how we might convince, persuade, and influence people to participate when there is resistance. Consider the possible reasons for their resistance:

1. Feels that there is no conflict.
2. Has justified all actions and believes that nothing wrong has occurred.
3. Believes other party has no merit in bringing the case to negotiation and does not deserve a remedy or relief.
4. Unable to provide remedy or relief.
5. Believes that "all is as it should be," and is convinced that there is no need to negotiate for rightness, equity, fairness, or justice.
6. Believes that negotiations would lend credibility to the other party and to the merits of their case.
7. Believes that negotiation means "compromise" and fears that the change in the status quo will be at their expense.
8. Does not have authority from constituents or superiors to enter substantive negotiations.
9. Believes that it would be a violation of policy or accepted practice.
10. Believes that it would be a violation of cultural values, beliefs, or behaviors.
11. Is not prepared to negotiate.
12. Wants more time to get his ducks in a row.
13. Does not understand or lacks the confidence in the negotiation process.
14. Feels that he is incompetent as a negotiator.
15. Doesn't speak English well enough.
16. Believes it is too time consuming.
17. Other people are telling him not to.
18. Believes another form of dispute resolution (e.g., litigation or arbitration) would be a more appropriate avenue than negotiation.
19. His attorneys are telling him not to.
20. Fears that she will not be understood.
21. Fears that sitting down with adversary will make things worse.
22. Refuses to be pressured into negotiations.
23. Fears that there will be a cultural imbalance in the negotiation process.
24. Feels that the other party may not participate seriously, fairly, sincerely, or honestly.
25. Fears that there will be a power imbalance in the negotiation process in the other party's favor.

26. Fears that he will be attacked and get hurt physically or emotionally by the other party (does not feel safe).
27. Thinks that there is no need to negotiate with anyone. Believes that he hold all the cards and everything is going his way.
28. Fears that negotiations will escalate or reopen conflict by calling attention to it.
29. Fears that most emotions are too strong and things would get worse rather than better.
30. Party has chosen a different method of dealing with the conflict.
31. Enjoys displaying conflict behavior (it is an emotional rush), and thinks that she currently is getting the better of her opponent.
32. Too disillusioned, hurt, angry, hungry, or tired to participate.
33. Lacks appropriate financial support/resources to engage in the process and to sustain long-term participation.
34. Lacks specific, necessary, or credible information to put forth as convincing evidence.
35. Believes own case is without merit and/or fears that his case will be regarded as meaningless or frivolous by others.
36. Wants to kick ass rather than talk about it.

APPENDIX B

Exercises for Chapters 2–4: Implementing the Negotiation Methodology

Exercise 1. Listening Proactively and Speaking Consciously and Deliberately

Negotiation is little more than communication between individuals who are trying to resolve their differences. This can sometimes be quite challenging, given the fact that we are often different from one another, with different perspectives, life experiences, genders, ages, personal histories and cultures, agendas, and so forth. In addition, we may use and understand words differently and attach different meanings to the same words and expressions. Finally, adding to these difficulties, when we are in conflict situations strong negative emotions are often at play that have to be acknowledged, addressed, and resolved before we can move on. All this will create disparities between what the message sender intended to communicate and how the message is ultimately received. This will make negotiations ripe for misunderstanding unless we are very careful and deliberate about what we say and how we say it.

Here we present a list of speaking and listening behaviors that negotiators and mediators can adopt to enhance understanding.

When Negotiators Talk, They Speak in Order to . . .

Create settings that are conducive to constructive problem solving.
Model good communication skills.
Help the other parties to relax and trust the process.
Establish and begin earning the other parties' trust.
Make sure that the negotiation (or mediation) process is understood.
Draw out the other parties' different perspectives on the conflict.

Demonstrate that they are listening.
Demonstrate respect.
Give evidence that the parties heard and understand what they heard.
Demonstrate that they care and take what they hear seriously.
Help their team members and the other team hear one another.
Manage tensions internally and between the parties.
Discover the nature of the relationship between the parties.
Manage (i.e., lower) the expectations of the other side and those of their own constituents and hierarchy.
Break the problem down into manageable parts (e.g., agenda items)
Facilitate fulfillment of expectations.
Manage (i.e., lower) exaggerated expectations.
Determine the underlying causes, costs, and benefits of the conflict.
Identify their own and the other parties' interests.
Help the parties create options for joint benefit and mutual gain.
Test the other parties' receptivity to various options.
Transform and share information.
Translate information (reframe statements positively).
Share positive accomplishments. Help the parties to explore various realities.
Explore and underscore the consequences of various options.
Keep the negotiations moving forward toward the resolution of their differences.
Help parties reach agreement and closure, and write explicit agreements.

When the Other Party Speaks, Negotiators Listen in Order to . . .

Communicate respect and interest.
Validate the speaker.
Model respectful listening.
Convey understanding and empathy.
Provide parties with an active listening posture.
Become educated about the parties' positions and issues.
Discover underlying causes of conflict.
Discover the parties' values, principles, and interests.
Hear the parties' expectations.
Learn the parties' responses to offers.

Uncover what "we and they" have in common.
Help the party understand what they have in common with you.
Help the party understand the differences that exist.
Identify the positives to share.
Emphasize that it is all right to have different perspectives.
Assist in creative ways to bridge the differences.
Find opportunities for breaking the impasse and creating momentum.
Discern a softening of attitudes.
Discern a readiness to settle.
Help the parties move from the past to the present and future.
Identify creative ways to accommodate the other side without sacrificing one's vital interests.

Exercise 2. Gathering Information

Gathering information for negotiation, clarifying and facilitating communication, and fact finding often pose problems for negotiators. The following questions and responses are designed to avoid being off-putting when asking questions and increasing effective communication.

1. *Self-disclosure*: simple statements of what one feels or thinks.

    Examples:

    "I'm a bit confused on this point, I need your help to understand."
    "I feel on the spot here. I'll need some time to sort this out."
    "I don't understand what you are saying."

2. *Self-assertion*: Stating one's position without excuses or justification.

    Examples:

    "I cannot do what you are asking."
    "I would like to tell the other person what you just told me."

3. *Empathetic assertion*: The listener recognizes the feelings or the position taken by the other party, and then describes his own position.

    Example: "I understand what you are saying. However, my situation is ___."

4. *Empathic acknowledgment*: The listener recognizes the position or feelings of another person without passing judgment, offering remedies, or stating her own position.

   Example: "I understand."

5. *The "I" inquiry*: The listener needs to obtain additional information to help the other party to clarify, determine, or identify his interests, issues, positions, and values.

   Example: "I wonder if you would mind telling me about ___."

6. *Workable options*: The listener floats trial balloons consisting of options or alternatives for the other person to consider. It is exploratory. It is important that the listener is not "married" to these "trial balloons."

   Example: "I am wondering what your thoughts might be about this as an alternative."

   Example: "That certainly is one interpretation. What might be some others?"

7. *Impartial statements*: Removing oneself from the conflict and restating or reframing the situation.

   Example: "I think that people could agree that the situation needs improving."

8. *Open questions*: This inquiry is designed to allow other persons to freely express themselves.

   Example: "Tell me all about it." "What are you thinking about?" "What is your perspective?"

9. *Closed questions*: Elicit a specific response (yes or no) or ask for specific information (e.g., How old are you? I am twelve years old.)

   Example: "Are we in agreement?" "If Xavier does this, then do you agree to do ___?"

10. *Indirect closed questions*: These questions have a strong interest statement. They are often less threatening and less confrontational to the person.

    Example: "I wonder what would happen if we went to court?"

11. *Probing questions*: Similar to the "I" inquiry, this question is used when there appears to be a need for additional self-disclosure from the person.

    Example: "What else?" "Would you say more about that?" (This is better than, "Is there anything else?")

12. *Leading questions*: These questions are closed and direct. As with other questioning they can cut two ways. In one sense, they are entrapment questions that may force the respondent to limit his options. In another sense, they may be necessary to use as a way to deal with denial or avoidance.

    Example: "Are you going to settle with Mr. Lau?"

13. *Multiple questions*: These questions often can confuse or limit the information-gathering process. Instead, ask one question at a time.

    Example: "Can we make this work by doing ___, William agreeing to do ___, and the both of you agreeing to do ___?"

Exercise 3. How Well Do You Listen to Others? A Self-Assessment

Your answers here will help you to become aware of some poor habits that keep you from being a good listener.

Instructions: Read each question. Do not try to second-guess the purpose. Answer with "yes" or "no," according to your customary behavior.

_____ 1. Science says you think four times faster than it takes you to talk. Do you use this excess time to turn your thoughts elsewhere while you are keeping general track of a conversation?

_____ 2. When somebody is talking to you, do you try to make that person think you are paying attention when you are not?

_____ 3. When you are listening to someone, are you easily distracted by outside sights and sounds?

_____ 4. When you are puzzled or annoyed by what someone says, do you try to get the questions straightened out immediately by interrupting the speaker?

178   APPENDIX B

_____   5. Do certain words, phrases, or ideas so prejudice you against the speaker that you cannot continue to listen objectively to what is being said?

_____   6. Do you listen primarily for facts, rather than ideas, when someone is speaking?

_____   7. If you feel that it would take too much time and effort to understand something, do you shut down and avoid hearing about it?

_____   8. If you want to remember what someone is saying, do you think it is a good idea to write it down as the person talks?

_____   9. Do you turn your thoughts to other subjects when you believe a speaker will have nothing particularly interesting to say?

_____   10. Do you decide from a person's demeanor and delivery that she will not have anything valuable or worthwhile to say?

_____   11. Do you use disapproving facial expressions to convey to speakers that you do not buy what they are saying while they are talking?

_____   12. Do you listen for underlying interests or get lost in the detail?

_____   13. Do you listen for common ground rather than for what might divide you?

Exercise 4. Improving Your Listening Skills: A Self-Assessment

The following questions are designed to provide you with additional insight into your listening skills. An effective communicator, mediator, or negotiator knows that understanding what is being communicated is directly tied to good listening skills.

The key to answering these questions is not simply to place a yes or no in front of each question. Ask yourself (and perhaps as importantly, other people) to what degree you practice these good listening skills. Using a scale of 1 to 5 with 5 being "excellent" and 1 being "not at all," rate your listening skills as you currently know them.

_____   Do I understand that when I am talking I am learning less than when I am listening?

_____ Do I consistently provide my listeners signs, signals, hints, or cues to know when to listen to what I am saying?

_____ Do I realize that nonverbal communication is the vast majority of each person's communication?

_____ Do I understand that I not only have the right to convince, persuade, and influence others but they have these same communication rights?

_____ Do I understand that being a good listener does not mean that I must agree with or believe what I am hearing, or subscribe to the values of the speaker?

_____ Am I aware of my biases and prejudices so that they do not filter out certain messages?

_____ Do I avoid responding to emotionally charged words and phrases?

_____ Do I wait until a person has finished speaking, or do I practice mind reading?

_____ Do I seek or request feedback to be assured that I am understood?

_____ Do I provide feedback when others request it?

_____ Do I know that a person who feels understood generally tends to be more open to listening and less aggressive and defensive?

_____ Am I aware of my biases and prejudices so that, when I speak, these biases and prejudices are limited or minimized?

_____ Do I know when I may be intimidating listeners through threatening behavior?

_____ When I disagree with something or find something exciting, do I still listen carefully?

_____ If I am having trouble being understood, do I fault myself or do I fault the listener?

_____ Can I tell when there is a contentious, emotionally charged atmosphere?

_____ When I listen, do I consider the person as well as the situation or context?

_____ Do I listen for what is not being said? Do I listen between the lines?

_____ Do I listen for tones and intent as well as the words the speaker is using?

_____ If I were the listener, would I be able to listen to and understand myself?
_____ Do I listen for similarities and potential common ground?

Exercise 5. Practicing Listening Skills

Find a partner to do this exercise with.

The first person should take three minutes telling the second person about a personal problem or situation.

The second person should listen attentively without saying anything for the three minutes.

After the three minutes are up, the second person should summarize what he heard.

Get in the habit of taking notes and listening carefully so that you can repeat what you've heard.

Take two minutes to summarize.

Now, reverse roles and do the exercise again.

After you have both completed the exercise, debrief by discussing with each other the following questions:

1. What did it feel like to be listened to so carefully?
2. What did it feel like to listen without interrupting or being distracted?

Exercise 6. Practicing "Empathic" Listening Skills

Instructions: Find a partner and decide who will speak first and who will listen.

The speaker should select an actual problem in which she is involved. Choose one that is limited in scope and that you do not mind discussing. Tell the listener about this problem and ask for his help in solving it.

The listener should facilitate the interaction in any way he can to aid the speaker in solving the problem. The listener's method is "empathic listening."

Ask questions and learn how the speaker feels about her problem, not how you feel about the problem.

1. The speaker begins by describing her problem. For the first three minutes, the listener should not say anything. Then the listener may begin to clarify and support the speaker.

Continue the exercise for another three minutes. The listener listens deeply by practicing the following listening skills:

   a. Listen attentively.
   b. Accept the speaker and the message.
   c. Clarify the speaker's problem if you do not understand.
   d. Paraphrase—repeat the problem back in your own words.
   e. Use perception checks—"It sounds like you feel. . . ."
   f. Remain non-evaluative, nonjudgmental, and open-minded.
   g. Help the sender see alternatives—"What would happen if . . . ?"
   h. Avoid talking about your own experiences.
   i. Empathize rather than sympathize.

2. Reverse your roles and do the exercise again. Complete the exercise and spend five minutes with your partner with these questions:

   a. What's the most difficult part of this exercise?
   b. Can you or your partner identify any personal listening weaknesses?

Exercise 7. Using Negotiation Terms

The following are general terms and concepts used in negotiation. In short sentences, describe the meaning of each and how it is used to move the other party closer to an agreement.

1. Agreements in principle
2. Arbitration
3. Caucus
4. Compromise
5. Concession
6. Confidence-building measures
7. Conflict aftermath
8. Consensus
9. Fallback position
10. General session
11. Horizontal negotiation
12. Impartial

13. Impasse
14. Initial position
15. Internal team negotiations
16. Interest-based negotiation (IBN)
17. Majority rule
18. Managing expectations
19. Mediation
20. Mediator
21. Neutral
22. Off-the-record
23. Parties
24. Position-based negotiation
25. Power imbalance
26. Principle-based negotiation
27. Proactive listening
28. Procedural, substantive, relational satisfaction
29. Quid pro quo
30. Ratification
31. Strategies
32. Table negotiation
33. Tactics
34. Tentative agreements
35. Traditional peacemaking principles and practices
36. Vertical negotiation
37. Zero-sum game

APPENDIX C

Exercises for Chapters 5 and 6: The Structural Challenges of Government-to-Government Negotiation

Exercise 1. Characteristics of an Effective Negotiator: A Self-Assessment

Instructions: Place a "yes" after those characteristics that you feel apply to you, and a "no" after each characteristic that does not apply to you. At the end, of the nineteen characteristics, how many did you answer with a "yes"? Did you gain any insight into where you can improve?

An effective negotiator is

> Able to take a thorough and honest inventory of self.
> Flexible, calm, and transparent.
> Able and willing to assume extra responsibility for understanding the situation and the other people involved.
> Not afraid to deal with the issues and can be decisive.
> Able to deal with ambiguity and the unexpected.
> Able to read between the lines.
> Able to keep cool in tough situations; responds and does not react.
> Is honest, steadfast, consistent, and dependable.
> Able to "educate others" to concepts, ideas, objectives, and goals.
> Has a good sense of humor.
> Is personable and generally comfortable with everyone.
> Demonstrates to others good faith and honest intent.
> Has good interpersonal/intercultural communication skills.
> Able to command respect without the need to be assertive.

Holds and fights for convictions.
Able to see interests of others and assist them in understanding.
Likes people.
Honors differences.
Is able to make a personal connection with a wide range of different types of people.

Exercise 2. Four Principles and Two Tools for Increasing Effectiveness in Intercultural Communication

We begin by elaborating on four communication principles that are relevant in the field of conflict resolution.

First Principle: One Cannot Not Communicate!

Roughly 80 percent of communication in Western cultures is said to be nonverbal. A nonverbal message is a form of communication without the utterance of any words. This includes what is commonly referred to as "body language": gestures with the body, hands, face, and arms; posture or movement; gait; tone and loudness of voice; eyes and other facial expressions; hairdo, attire, colors of clothing and accessories; exposure of the skin/modesty, and so on.

In conflict, people are often unaware of their nonverbal communication—at least it is easier to deny. People can be aggressive without saying anything, including: not speaking to someone, glaring, staring, scowling, making intimidating gestures, shaking one's head, peering down, standing uncomfortably close, just saying the absolute minimum, averting eye contact, not acknowledging the other person, "seeing through them," not holding the door, pushing, blocking access, slamming the door, walking ahead, and so on. People notice and interpret these nonverbal gestures as hostile, which is most likely how the gesture was intended. In a conflict situation these will be fodder that contributes to an escalation. During negotiations this nonverbal aggressive behavior will likely be among the issues that people identify and attempt to change in the interest of resolving the conflict.

Opposite messages can also be sent that communicate approval and affection, like smiling, winking, nodding the head, letting someone go ahead, hand motions to encourage others to approach, clapping, thumbs up, a pat on the shoulder, blowing kisses, whistling, and so on. These gestures normally do not provoke conflict.

Second Principle: Communication Is Reciprocal

For every action there is a response if the message sender is in the range of hearing, seeing, or feeling. Ron sees me on the street. I see Ron seeing me. He sees me seeing him. I see him seeing me seeing him. Actions and reactions are caused by one another's actions.

In conflict situations, it is common that what we do and say is responded to in kind. We set off a reaction or response. If we are disrespectful, rude, denigrating, dismissive, ignoring, unpredictable, abusive, or aggressive, then the other party is likely to respond similarly and we will have contributed to escalating and perpetuating the conflict. If we engage in the opposite type of behavior—for example, being calm, generous, quiet, centered, unflappable, understanding, accommodating, receptive, responsive, or listening on purpose—then it is possible that we can contribute to deescalating and defusing a conflict, and at the very least, not contributing to perpetuating the negativity.

Third Principle: We send and receive messages through our own filters or "prisms."

Our different prisms or filters are conditioned by our experiences, personality, cultural affiliations, language, and so on.

Because of this filtering system there will always be a gap between the intentions of the sender and the understanding of the receiver. Words may have different meanings for different people. Our past experiences with particular words have associations that may color the way we hear things and interfere with understanding. Being questioned, for example, may be regarded in one culture as aggressive behavior. So might interruptions and talking over someone, even though these behaviors are common and acceptable in other cultures and contexts. People have different reactions to direct eye contact. Some interpret it as aggressive behavior; others may regard it as a sign of sincerity and honesty. Today, expressing another opinion that is unpopular may be regarded as microaggression by younger generations and be a conversation stopper. Someone older, used to more lively debate, might regard it as perfectly acceptable.

A central form of communication is nonverbal. We refer to this aspect of communication as "body language." Body language occurs in all societies. In this respect, it is universal. But it does not always mean the same thing from culture to culture. As one example, nodding the head means "yes" in some societies and shaking the head means "no," while elsewhere it means the opposite. Some studies have shown that men and women communicate differently. Some observers have suggested that women are more likely to nod their heads to indicate that they understand while men more typically nod their heads to indicate they agree. We have to be careful not to assume that the same gesture means the same thing for everyone and everywhere.

Fourth Principle: Nearly all conversations are intercultural.

Our conversations involve people who are very different from one another. These differences emerge in conversation and are often the flashpoints in conflict. Important cultural differences can consist of a broad range of differences:

   a. Ethnicity
   b. Religious belief and observance
   c. Economic class and social status
   d. Gender
   e. Sexual preference
   f. Generation (seniors, "snowbirds," baby boomers, adults from the Depression, adults of the World War II era, Vietnam War veterans, adolescents, etc.).
   g. Region (South, East, North, Midwest, West, Alaska)
   h. Urban-rural life experience
   i. Historical experiences (e.g., trauma)
   j. Agency cultures (BLM, Forest Service, National Park Service, U.S. Bureau of Reclamation)
   k. Job roles (employer, manager, supervisor, employees)
   l. Union-management affiliation
   m. Professions (doctors, nurses, lawyers, accountants, stockbrokers, undertakers, detectives, uniformed police)
   n. Vocations (electricians, tile setters, drywall installers, roofers, dock workers)
   o. Disabilities or no disabilities
   p. Other subcultures (snowboarders, downhill and cross-country skiers, extreme athletes, NASCAR devotees, rodeo participants, carnies, and so on.

What are the implications of these observations? Is there anything we can do to ensure that we understand each other accurately in spite of the significant cultural differences among us?

First, we should realize that we create misunderstanding and perpetuate conflict more than we are aware of or acknowledge.

Second, while we have limited control over the behavior of others, we do have the potential to modify our own behavior.

Third, we can improve outcomes by being more fully aware of all the dimensions of our behavior, and by making sure that our behavior is designed to minimize, better manage, and resolve differences. This requires looking at and listening to ourselves—that is, being an observer at the same time we are an active participant in the interaction—which is not always easy.

Fourth, we should never assume that we have understood one another without using some proactive listening tools, such as repeating in their words, paraphrasing in our words, summarizing our understanding, repeating and verifying, asking questions and clarifying.

Two Useful Intercultural Communication Tools

Two tools that involve different behavior and ways of thinking, when applied, can create better results. These will help us keep our foot out of our mouths, take the time to think things through thoroughly, and stay nonjudgmental. The first are "the Precious Metal Rules" and the second is DIE

THE PRECIOUS METAL RULES

The Golden Rule. "Do unto others as you would have them do unto you." Treat people like you want to be treated. This rule or something similar appears in practically every culture and religious practice. It makes sense and is a good rule. However, it works best in homogeneous situations, where people are similar. It is based on the assumption of similarities and the presumed validity of one's own perspective, values, and experiences. We assume, *If it works for me, it should work for everyone else.* However, it is ethno- and ego-centered. This perspective is culture-bound and habitual, and is a function of one's own past conditioning. And it is not always appropriate or accurate, particularly where significant differences among people are present.

The Lead Rule. The Lead Rule kicks in when the Golden Rule breaks down, where there are significant differences among people. Then the common assumption becomes, *If they do not conform to our Golden Rule expectations, then we need to change these people.*

When people do not conform to what we expect, then we often assume they should change, and we should change them. They need to be realigned with the program. We reprimand, re-educate, re-socialize; get them into counseling or therapy; provide incentives; apply behavior modification, and so on. If the carrot does not work, we try the stick. We try to re-establish control by condemning, dismissing, ignoring the relevance of the other person's point of view, behavior, or opinion. We might punish, fire, remove, isolate, dismiss, relocate, banish, ostracize, or send them to therapy and "re-education" programs. We invoke the Lead Rule most when we are in stressful and conflict situations, where and when we have less patience and when ambiguity and unexpected "aberrant" behavior is least tolerated. These are not fertile grounds for successful collaborative negotiations.

Platinum Rule. "Do unto others as they would do unto themselves." This rule takes a cross-cultural or intercultural perspective. "Different strokes for different folks." Instead of defaulting to what is familiar and comfortable to us when dealing with someone who is different, we empathize, we get into their moccasins and explore how things may appear from their perspective. This rule is based on an understanding that there are multiple points of view, different vantage points, different ways of doing things—and that we all look through our own prisms that can have their own validity.

To apply the Platinum Rule, we need to gather more information than we have in our possession because the situation and conditions are unfamiliar to us, and understanding the present situation is beyond our own experience. We need to move from reacting to responding. Our context needs to become large enough to take into consideration both our own and the other person's perspectives and reality. Instead of trying to change the other person or change his opinion, values, positions, and priorities, we search for a solution that works for both of us. As pointed out earlier in the book, taking this posture is essential to being an effective win-win negotiator.

Applying the Platinum Rule is the more positive approach when dealing with cross-cultural differences. We allow others to define themselves, and their values, preferences, priorities, and interests. And we understand and value that there are different ways to do things. This is a powerful way to show people respect. Instead of trying to change or reject their ways, we listen.

DIE: DESCRIBE, INTERPRET, AND EVALUATE

This is a cross-cultural communication tool for slowing ourselves down to take the time to think things through thoroughly rather than immediately defaulting to immediate conclusions that reflect our ethnocentric or egocentric perceptions and limited experiences. We do this essentially by breaking the communication down into three parts and concentrating on doing each separately in sequence: *Describe* what you see. *Interpret* what you think you see. *Evaluate* what you think you see.

We can use this tool to open ourselves to differences and to people who may be different from what we are used to. We can use it to peel away our prejudices and immediate false impressions, and to seek more information before we reach conclusions. In effect, we can use this tool to ensure that we apply Platinum Rule thinking rather than Golden Rule thinking, assuming that people are different rather than all the same.

Break the process down into three steps:

1. *Describe.* Just describe the observable facts.
2. *Interpret.* List everything that you think you might have seen.
3. *Evaluate.* Indicate how you feel (and others might feel) about what you might have seen. When you evaluate, force yourself to identify both the positive (+) and negative (–) things people might feel about what you might have seen.

To illustrate the power of this communication tool, an exercise takes us through a step-by-step process:

a. Start with a demonstration of something ambiguous that might be interpreted in various ways (e.g., two men holding hands walking around the room).
b. Ask for a volunteer, take him to the side, and describe what you will ask him to do. Give him an opportunity to decline.
c. Walk around the room holding hands, not talking or looking at each other.
d. Next, ask participants to describe what they saw, staying with the observable facts. Write these down on the board in front of the room. Many people will not stay with the facts, but rather

immediately rush to make interpretations about what they thought they saw. Write all these down too as they come up.

e. Review the list with the participants and ask them to indicate whether each entry is a "D" (description) or an "I" (interpretation). The results will present a picture of how quickly people typically jump to conclusions without having any solid basis. Most groups will have a lot of "I's."

f. The next step is to generate more interpretations of what they thought they saw to get a fuller picture of the range of possibilities, going beyond the first ones they immediately defaulted to. Open their minds like an accordion and expand their range of understanding by generating many different interpretations. Write them all down, the more outrageous the better. People should develop the habit of opening their minds to new possibilities.

g. As part of the exercise, take several interpretations and explore how they would evaluate (feelings) them. They will have a dominant reaction to them, either negative or positive. The next step in the exercise is to go beyond their first evaluation and to list both negative and positive reactions. This step forces them to come up with what others might feel both positively and negatively—even if that is not the way they would feel. This part of the exercise once again encourages them to go beyond their comfort zones and to open their minds to other perspectives than they had initially.

Another exercise to use with DIE. Take the participants through another example to anchor the formula in their minds. For example, a candidate shows up for an interview for the position of executive director of an organization. In this hypothetical organization the entire staff interviews candidates and selects a person for the job. The group you are working with becomes the staff for purposes of the exercise. The candidate shows up in an open shirt, slacks, and less than formal shoes, wearing dark sunglasses. The trainer plays the role of the applicant as he sits with legs crossed, arms folded, and reclining somewhat in front of the group to simulate an interview. The trainer starts by prompting the group, "Describe what you see."

Take the group through the process of listing and then distinguishing between observable facts and interpretations. Then focus on one of the interpretations—for example, "arrogance"—and then ask them to separately list both positive and negative evaluations about the characteristic of a job candidate being arrogant.

Learning objectives:

1. Teach people how to sharpen their powers of observation and commit fewer errors in prejudging people and situations with which they are not familiar.
2. Teach people how to open up their minds and hearts to new understanding by breaking communication down into separate components: facts, interpretations, and evaluations.
3. Teach people a cross-cultural communication tool that they and others can use in conflict and stressful conditions to respond rather than react to new situations—a tool that allows them to take the time to think things through thoroughly and thoughtfully.
4. You can use this tool during a negotiation when a member of your team or the other team insists on one interpretation: for example, "They are lying to us." Suggest that that is just one interpretation and request that they generate some other interpretations as well.

Exercise 3. Reframing Aggressive and Provocative Remarks

Verbal and nonverbal communication is *reciprocal*, meaning that actions are followed by reactions. When people are aggressive, accusatory, and provocative with us, there is an almost immediate reaction to take the bait and respond in similar terms. That is how conflict can escalate quickly, get out of control, and undermine the negotiation. This possible aggressive behavior should not be a surprise to those working in the area of conflict resolution. The parties will likely be angry, and they might display this with snide remarks and negative characterizations.

But do not lose heart. Despite this bleak picture, there is a way out. Because of the reciprocal dynamic that exists among people, we can chose to de-escalate aggression rather than escalate it. It is up to us. After all, we have free will. The communication technique is commonly referred to as "reframing." This powerful tool is used by negotiators and mediators who are expert in communication and conflict resolution.

Below is a discussion of some things we can do to respond rather than automatically react to aggressive and provocative communication. For many of us, it takes practice.

1. Choose to shift the focus to the problem and away from the personality. Change an accusation against a particular person into an observation about an important problem.

   Example 1:

   Statement: Betty is lying through her teeth to protect her friend Henry.

   Response: From your perspective, it sounds like you may need more information before you can accept the previous statement as factual. Is that correct? What additional specific information would you like?

   Example 2:

   Statement: Ted stole the money from the cash register, plain and simple.

   Response: Money is missing from the cash register, and you would like to ask some people if they can shed some light on that.

   Another Response: Sounds like you might be interested in discussing some new security measures to protect the cash and prevent money from going missing in the future.

   Another Response: You would like to discuss implementing improved petty cash management strategies.

   Example 3:

   Statement: You can't take a joke. You overreact to everything. You are so damn sensitive, it is impossible to work with you.

   Response: There seems to be some misunderstanding. Can we talk about implementing some communication techniques that are designed to minimize misunderstandings, for example, paraphrasing, clarifying, rephrasing, repeating back for verification, and summarizing?

2. Focus on the solution rather than on the problem.

   Example 1:

   Statement: You do not think enough of me to notify me about upcoming meetings early enough that I can fit them into my schedule.

Response: Let's talk about ways you and others around here would like to be advised about upcoming meetings and deadlines.

Example 2:

Statement: If you would just do your share of the work around here, we would be finished on time.
Response: So, you would like to get out of here at quitting time and you would like more help, is that right?
Another response: Can we spend some time discussing what we all need to do to make sure that work is distributed differently, and together we ensure that we can all leave at quitting time?

3. Change the words to neutralize the negativity.

Example 1:

Statement: You are simply lazy and you are not willing to do what it takes to do your job.
Response: It sounds like you would like to discuss job expectations and ways to improve employees' job performances.

Example 2:

Statement: I want to address the organization's long-standing racist and sexist hiring practices.
Response: It sounds like you want to discuss the organization's hiring criteria and procedures.

4. Shift the focus onto underlying interests that can be met in a variety of ways, and away from specific demands that have to be either accepted or rejected.

Example 1:

Statement: I demand the organization give me another office, a new title, and an increase in salary that is commensurate with my responsibilities. Unless this is done I am going to court and accuse the organization of racial discrimination.
Response: It sounds like you are ready to sit down together and explore whether there are some additional ways we can show our recognition of your service.

Example 2:

Statement: I want to be reassigned to other duties. I am sick and tired of my supervisor micromanaging me and not giving me enough air to breathe.
Response: It sounds like you are ready to discuss your job description, and how you would like to be supervised to ensure some areas of greater autonomy.

Example 3:

Statement: This is bullshit. I will see you in court.
Response: Of course, we all have the option of turning this problem over to a court and taking the chance that a judge will see it our way.

Example 4:

Statement: I have never worked with such an inconsiderate and self-centered jerk.
Response: Can I assume that you would have an interest in discussing how to craft a more respectful and productive work relationship that works better for both of you?

Summary of Reframing

a. Frame issues so that multiple solutions are possible. Do not frame issues so that only one solution is suggested or implied.
b. Take the sting out of comments by neutralizing the |language.
c. Shift the focus away from the person being attacked to the underlying problem that is aggravating the other person.
d. Shift the focus from the problem to possible solutions.
e. Shift the focus away from past events or activities, which cannot be changed, to the future, when the problem can be prevented or avoided.
f. Shift the focus away from a solution that serves only the speaker to one that can be agreed to because it meets the mutual interests of all involved.

EXERCISES FOR CHAPTERS 5 AND 6   195

Some Additional Statements That Require Reframing

Assume that each of the statements below has just been made during a negotiation or mediation and you want to redirect the focus onto problem solving and away from accusations that will further polarize the parties engaged in the discussion. How would you reframe the following statements?

1. That's my final offer, take it or leave it!
2. I've been making concessions all night and you haven't moved at all. You are being completely unreasonable.
3. He's going to pay for the damage to my property, or there's nothing to talk about.
4. The law is on my side, and I am not budging.
5. My lawyer told me we are in the right, and I don't have to concede anything.
6. I'll see you in court.
7. That's a lie! You misrepresent everything. I can't believe a thing that you say.
8. You think you know everything.
9. I'm tired of listening to your self-serving excuses. Why don't you just admit that you did something wrong?
10. I demand an apology. If I don't get it, there is no way we will reach an agreement here.
11. You knew damn well I was angry. You did it just to irritate me.
12. You can't take a joke. You overreact to everything. You are so damn sensitive; it is impossible to work with you.
13. That's just the way those people are.
14. I have never seen her do a lick of work during the whole time she's been here, with the exception of making sure she leaves here by five o'clock.
15. I have never worked with such an inconsiderate, self-centered jerk.

Ways to Lower Resistance to Settlement Proposals

1. Continue to work with and to educate the other side.
2. Understand that it takes time and patience when building trust.

3. Develop an empathic understanding of the other party. Try to place yourself in her position. Anticipate her arguments and respond to those arguments before offering your proposal.
4. Ask open-ended and specific questions that are meant to reveal pertinent information. Engage in empathetic questioning and probing for additional information.
5. Listen carefully to the other party's statement and for what may exist between the lines. Be prepared to modify or change your own offer based on information and concerns disclosed by the other party.
6. Pay attention to the words the other party uses to get a deeper meaning or sense of intent.
7. Document or demonstrate how your proposal will satisfy the other party's interests.
8. Offer to speak with members of the opposing party who are not present about the merits of the proposal.
9. Emphasize the positive aspects of the proposal.
10. Validate and praise the other party for his creativity and constructive role in the negotiation.
11. Do not oversell the proposal. This may be viewed as suspect or coercive.
12. Do not pressure or intimidate the other party. Do not use the "I'm here to protect your interests, whether you like it or not" approach.
13. Be able to demonstrate or document your ability to make good on the settlement proposal.
14. When appropriate, and only if true, reveal your bottom line as the last offer you are able to make.
15. Emphasize the costs to the other party of not resolving the conflict as soon as possible.
16. Emphasize the benefits to the other party of putting an end to the conflict, and the benefits of being able to sit down together to increase understanding.
17. Present an unrelated proposal as a concession, and explain why it is being offered. In other words, enlarge the pie and offer a piece to chew on.
18. Offer the other party additional time to caucus and to consult with others.
19. Document or demonstrate how your proposal will satisfy the other party's interest.

20. Share with the other party that you place a high value on your values, beliefs, and interests, and that you are willing and prepared to go to any lengths to hold out for your values and interests.
21. Allow the other party to save face. Permit the proposal for settlement to become the other party's own idea. If appropriate, allow the other party to announce the settlement agreement.
22. Develop and incorporate a future dispute resolution clause into the settlement agreement.
23. Escalate your demands in order to demonstrate the seriousness of the situation. (But be prepared to revert to the previous position.)
24. Present implicit or explicit threats that are understandable and that you are capable of or willing to carry out. (This tactic is not recommended except in very serious situations.)
25. Demonstrate that time is on your side.
26. Demonstrate broad-based support for your side and increases in support from new constituencies as time goes on.
27. Convince, persuade, and influence people in the way they prefer to be convinced, persuaded, and influenced. (For example, if they are pragmatists, show how practical your proposals are. If they are convinced by facts, provide hard, supportive data. If they are idealists, appeal to higher values.)
28. Suggest bringing in a facilitator or mediator who enjoys credibility with both parties to provide greater order and some fresh new ideas about options for settlement.
29. If the other party wants to agree but needs to appear steadfast in the eyes of his constituents, he may agree to take the remaining unresolved issues to arbitration and prefer to be ordered by the arbitrator to do something that he wants to do but some of his constituents would oppose.
30. Suggest that the two primary spokespersons for each side take the proverbial walk in the woods (an informal personal discussion off the record and away from the table).
31. Suggest a change in venue for a break in the routine, to reduce the intensity, and to get a new perspective.
32. Suggest lowering the intensity by spending an evening out together devoted entirely to recreation and socializing—for example, dining together at a good restaurant, going to a movie together, etc.

33. Begin to question some of the assumptions on which the other party's positions are based—in order to create doubt and uncertainty in her mind about the viability of those positions.
34. Explain that your bosses who ultimately have to sign off and approve the agreement will not accept certain terms and conditions and suggest some ways these obstacles can be circumvented.

Can you think of other ways to lower resistance?

NOTES

Chapter 1

1. A thorough description of the Navajo Nation's Peace-making Program is available at its website, www.tribaljustice.org. In its own words, this program

> provides a traditional-culture alternative to Anglo-American justice practices by utilizing Diné wisdom, customs, and practices to resolve disputes. This program seeks justice for everyone involved by engaging the skills and perspectives of community members to come to a mutual solution. Community members (acting as Peacemakers) sit down with the disputing parties to talk through the issues rather than having a "disinterested" third party (e.g., judge) make the decision for them. The consensual agreement of the parties in peace-making emphasizes healing and lasting solutions rather than an adjudication of damages or punishment.
>
> It aims to mend interpersonal conflicts through harmony, using consensus-based agreement as the primary tool. Parties are encouraged to solve their own problems by opening communication through respect, responsibility, good relationships.... Detailed peace-making guidelines have been developed to ensure that the process is carried out properly. The guidelines are not rules, but are meant to prevent intrusion by the adversarial process and promote the utilization of traditional Dine dispute resolution.

The program "actively substitutes healing in place of coercion, helping people through a self-healing process of the mind, body, and spirit to end conflict. A peace-maker does not adjudicate or pass judgment on a dispute; rather he or she facilitates a dialogue so disputing parties can reach a decision for themselves." "The session ends with a closing prayer. Sessions often conclude with everyone eating together. The ceremonies before and after each peace-making session are holistic and connect each person to the elements, the seasons, the environment, and the heavenly bodies."

The "Navajo Nation Peace-making Program was developed in 1982 to revive traditional justice methods." It aims to serve any tribal member who has a dispute with another member or group. The program also contributes to legislative, program, and policy development; provides education curriculum and serves in schools and communities; and addresses conflicts and negotiations among agencies, Navajo and non-Navajo governments, and for the Navajo Nation.

The reader is encouraged to visit the Native American Rights Fund's (NARF) "Indigenous Peace-Making Initiative" website (peacemaking.narf.org) to learn more about efforts to restore traditional dispute resolution techniques throughout Indian Country. It include an extensive list of articles, books, and other resources on the various forms of indigenous justice throughout the United States.

Chapter 2

1. William Lincoln, renowned negotiator and mediator, offers the proposition that these three criteria determine whether consensus has been achieved. Bill was the founder and served as the executive director of the Conflict Resolution, Research, and Resource Institute (CRRRI) based in Tacoma, Washington. He is an internationally recognized practitioner of negotiations, mediated negotiations, and process coaching, as well as a teacher and trainer. He is the primary author of CRRRI's Training Manual in Dispute Resolution, in which consensus is discussed.

2. Originally derived from practices in the English Parliament, parliamentary procedures as they exist today have gradually evolved. Henry Martyn Robert first published his *Robert's Rules of Order* in 1876. It rapidly became accepted as the standard authoritative work on meeting rules. See Henry M. Robert III et al., *Robert's Rules of Order: Newly Revised in Brief* (Philadelphia: Da Capo Press, 2004).

3. The Indian Reorganization Act of June 18, 1934—the Wheeler-Howard Act—was federal legislation that dealt with the status of American Indians in the United States. It was the centerpiece of what has often been called the "Indian New Deal." (See Section 25 of the United States Code: Bureau of Indian Affairs.) Indian and other scholars have commented on the disruptive effects on tribes that govern by majority rule. "For the many American Indian Nations with histories and cultures of decentralized, consensus-oriented and deliberative methods of decision making, [the] IRA Constitutions' centralization of power in small tribal councils acting by divisive majority rules with few checks and balances has been a difficult transition." (Eric Lemont, "Developing Effective Processes of American Indian Constitutional and Governmental Reform: Lessons from the Cherokee Nation of Oklahoma, Hualapai, Navajo Nation and Northern Cheyenne Tribe," *American Indian Law Review* 26, no. 2 [2001–2002]: 147–76).

Duane Champagne also commented on the disruptive aspects of majority rule. In "Remaking Tribal Constitutions," he wrote, "The imposition of majority rule and delegated powers is often opposed by groups that continue to adhere to cultural worldviews and maintain their own sense of independence and autonomy from a constitutional government, especially in many communities where Indian administration constitutions were adopted with majority rule or methods that did not incorporate Native processes of consensus formation." He also observed, "Native peoples generally prefer consensus decision making when it comes to developing a governing document" or making other weighty decisions that affect the future of the tribe. Champagne further observed that the time and processes needed to create consensus and agreement may be well suited for solidifying community expectations, sustaining participation in decision making, and generating long-term support for constitutional reform. The chapter appeared in Eric D. Lemont, ed., *American Indian Constitutional Reform and the Rebuilding of Native Nations* (Austin: University of Texas Press, 2006), 11–34 (quotes on 30).

There has been some debate in the academic literature whether the IRA constitution was introduced as a template that was "imposed" on American Indian tribes. Elmer Rusco disagrees with what most IRA analysts have asserted about the federal government's "imposition" of a standard model constitution or boilerplate document for IRA tribes. He argues that there was never a written prototype constitution prepared and systematically promoted by the government, which implies that the Indian tribes at the time were free to develop their own governing systems without any pressure to standardize.

In reviewing Elmer Rusco's argument, it seems persuasive only up to a point. He has documented the intentions of John Collier, commissioner of Indian Affairs, and of Felix Cohen, the principal leader of the reform movement, which was advocating Indians governing themselves. Both gentlemen were at the forefront of designing and promoting the implementation of the Indian Reorganization Act (IRA); both were on record opposed to imposing a uniform template.

Nonetheless, there still has to be some explanation for why tribal constitutions, IRA and non-IRA, contain the same standard features. These features include centralized and concentrated power in small unitary tribal or business councils; the absence of a separation of powers among legislative, executive, and judicial branches; the democratic election of tribal leaders; usually fixed two-year and sometimes four-year terms in office; the principle of "one person, one vote"; decisions to be made by majority rule; etc.

We think that it is reasonable to assume that these similarities are due to a departure from Cohen's and Collier's policy at the point of the IRA's implementation. It also seems reasonable that the standardized template was due to the work of bureau superintendents and their technical and field staff who were working directly with the tribes during their transition to IRA constitutions.

Rusco himself points out that the bulk of his own research was on the period leading up to the IRA's implementation. Moreover, he explains that Congress did not appropriate funds to implement the bill, there was a shortage of paid staff specializing in implementation, staff was generally not informed about the concepts and provisions of the IRA, and many were antagonistic to the IRA's intention to support tribal self-government rather than preexisting U.S. policies of assimilation. The implementation of the IRA promised to translate into an enormous loss of these agency officials' discretionary power over tribal decision making. Moreover, those in charge of implementing the law were unfamiliar with the bill's authors' and supporters' repeated statements that the bill was the not intended to impose any form of government on any Native American society or to require any society to adopt a written constitution.

Finally, what seems particularly compelling was that the IRA required the secretary of the interior to formally approve all IRA constitutions. This was done largely by the same handful of inexperienced staff or bureau lawyers who could be expected to default to treating every tribe pretty much the same, rather than spending the time and making the effort to figure out how to tailor each tribal constitution differently to accommodate each tribe's unique culture and needs. We must ask why it would be any different in the 1930s and 1940s than now. Today, more often than not, the bureau follows a standard uniform approach when it reviews, revises, and approves tribes' government documents when they submit them for official approval. This is typical, whether for IRA or non-IRA tribes.

See Elmer Rusco's chapter, "The Indian Reorganization Act and Indian Self-Government," in Lemont, *American Indian Constitutional Reform and the Rebuilding of Native Nations*, 49–82. For a fuller account, see Elmer Rusco: *A Fateful Time: The Background and Legislative History of the Indian Reorganization Act* (Reno: University of Nevada Press, 2000).

David Wilkins comments on the relative lack of autonomy that tribes still experience. He wrote, "The U.S. government retains a significant direct and indirect presence in the internal affairs of Indian nations through the exercise of its trust responsibility. The federal government still sometimes defines its trust responsibility paternalistically, denying tribal government the right to make their own political and economic decisions. The distinctive and still oppressive and paternalistic system of internal colonialism that indigenous nations experience continues to be a plague on their self-governing aspirations" (Wilkins, "Seasons of Change of Reforms, Melees, and Revolutions in Indian Country," in Lemont, ed., *American Indian Constitutional Reform and the Rebuilding of Native Nations*, 16).

4. See the article by Robert D. Herring, in which he makes a case for the strong cultural value placed on respect and reverence for elders in Native American communities: "Nonverbal Communication: A Necessary Component of Cross-Cultural Counseling," *Journal of Multicultural Counseling and Development* 18, no. 4 (October 1990): 172–79. Also see Roger D. Herring, "Understanding

Native-American Values: Process and Content Concerns for Counselors," *Counseling and Values*, 34, no. 2 (October 1990): 134–37.

Deborah Wetsit writes that, to this day, the differences among cultural values between American Indian and European American students are very real. She cites differences in such areas as time management, group versus individual accomplishments, family orientation, sharing versus materialism, being versus doing, harmony with nature versus mastery over nature, the importance of tradition, humility versus arrogance, and reverence for elders. See Deborah Wetsit, "Effective Counseling with American Indian Students," in Karen Gayton Swisher and John Tippeconnic, eds., *Next Steps: Research and Practice to Advance Indian Education* (Charleston, WV: ERIC Clearinghouse on Rural Education and Small Schools, 1999), 181.

 5. John Ehle, *The Trail of Tears* (New York: Bantam Doubleday Dell, 1999).

 6. David H. Getches, Charles F. Wilkinson, and Robert A Williams Jr., *Cases and Materials on Federal Indian Law*, 4th ed. (St. Paul, MN: West Group, 1998), 165.

 7. According to Dorothy Hill, a series of forced marches took place in which Native Americans were driven off their ancestral lands in California. A representative example from this period is the formation of the Round Valley Indian Community in Covelo, California. On August 28, 1863, one of the most infamous forced marches began. The Conkow Maidu people were rounded up by armed soldiers and forced to march hundreds of miles from Chico, California, to Round Valley. Of the 461 Natives who began the journey, only 277 remained by the time they reached their destination. The others died of exhaustion, sickness, and starvation. See Dorothy J. Hill, "The Indians of Chico Rancheria" (State of California, Resources Agency, Department of Parks and Recreation, 1978).

 8. This information about lasting internal conflict due to divided loyalties comes from the personal experience of the author, who was involved in mediating a number of disputes, including helping to arrange a cease fire after violence broke out between factions within the tribe, leaving one member dead.

 9. See "Welcome to the Governors' Gallery!" California State Library, 2019, governors.library.ca.gov.

 10. According to historian James Rawls, who is quoted in the PBS Special, the American Experience, that aired on November 6, 2006, "California entered the Union with shining gold but dripping with blood."

 11. For additional insights on the long-term impacts of these federal policies, see the analysis by Dorothy Wetsit, "Effective Counseling with American Indian Students." Wetsit writes about the negative message conveyed in federal government boarding schools that Indian children and their parents were uncivilized and needed to be removed and remade in white persons' image. She wrote that these schools used a military model of discipline which created an

environment that contrasted harshly with the homes from which children as young as five years old had been removed.

12. For an extensive and very thorough review of the literature on historical trauma, see Tammy R. Barker, "The Psychological Impact of Historical Trauma on Native American People," *All Regis University Theses*, Fall 2013. Barker writes, "Historical trauma theory suggests that many American Indians are still affected by the cultural losses and injustices endured by the previous generations." The trauma "is deeply rooted within the psyches in the history of the population" and today persists as the "accumulation of genocidal acts, recycling epidemics of disease, war, and cultural destruction through forced relocation and assimilation over several hundreds of years." She maintains that these experiences "stripped them of their cultures, sources of self-worth, and mechanisms of coping" and that "the effects of the massive cultural trauma accumulated over time in individuals, family disruption, and health risk behavior such as drug and alcohol misuse" (61–62).

13. Adversarial forums of resolving disputes lead to a winner and a loser, someone who is penalized and someone who ends up deriving clear benefits. The parties are engaged in a zero-sum game. They presume that any gain the other side makes takes something from them and therefore cannot be conceded. This attitude is counterproductive in collaborative negotiation. In fact, it will unnecessarily limit the possibilities and virtues of the negotiation process by missing the opportunity to satisfy mutual interests.

14. The IDRS executive director was invited by Jon Townsend, mediator and trainer and principal with Cascade Mediation, to partner with him on his company's contract with the governor's office in 1998.

15. In his fascinating book, Thomas F. Crumm compares the Japanese martial art of Aikido with win-win negotiation and discusses how to neutralize the aggressor's attack. By using Aikido's defensive moves, the Aikido practitioner is advised to go along with the attacker's energy and direction without opposing force with force. The Aikido practitioner starts by facing the attacker and then neutralizes the attack by opening up the attacker and moving him to the position of standing side by side, looking in the same direction. Similarly, the negotiator tries to convert a frontal attack from his opponent by redirecting his energy and transforming him into a collaborator who then joins him in solving the problem together. See Crumm, *The Magic of Conflict* (New York: Simon and Schuster, 1987).

Chapter 3

1. Roger Fisher and William Ury, *Getting to Yes: Negotiating Agreement without Giving In*, 3rd ed. (New York: Penguin, 2011).

2. Abraham Maslow, *Motivation and Personality* (New York: Harper, 1954).

Chapter 4

1. The problem in the Paris Peace Talks with the shape of the table was a result of a disagreement over the status of the groups involved. North Vietnam wanted the United States to acknowledge that the war was not cast as a foreign invasion from the north but instead North Vietnam's support of the Viet Cong (from South Vietnam) who were involved in a "legitimate" civil war. A rectangular, four-sided table would have placed the negotiators from the United States and North Vietnam at the head of the table on opposite sides, appearing as the two main parties. But missing would be the presence and recognition of the Viet Cong and the negotiators representing South Vietnam having a separate distinguishable and legitimate role at the Peace Talks. An oval table was the agreed-upon solution.

2. Luis Cardenas, "Overcoming Cultural Barriers in Negotiations and the Importance of Communications in International Business Deals," Harvard Law School, Program on Negotiation, May 14, 2020. See also Jeswald W. Salacuse, "Negotiating: The Top Ten Ways Culture Can Affect Your Negotiation," *Ivey Business Journal* (March/April 2005): 1–6.

Chapter 5

1. Many of the elders and key tribal government leaders, along with the attorneys working with the Umatilla and Klamath Tribes, were of the opinion that they had been cheated of this land. They shared this belief with the author when he was working on other issues with the Umatilla Tribe in the 1990s and with the Klamath Tribes in 2004–11. In these discussions, the question was raised whether redress could be sought either through the courts or through government-to-government negotiations. In the end, the leaders and attorneys of both tribes concluded that it would be a long shot with little assurance that anything positive would come of the effort—after so many years had transpired since the execution of the surveys.

2. The chief provisions of the Dawes Act were, "(a) A grant of 160 acres to each family head, 80 acres to each single person over 18 years of age and each orphan under 18, and 40 acres to each other single person under 18; (b) a patent in fee to be issued to every allottee but to be held in trust by the Government for 25 years, during which time the land could not be alienated or encumbered; (c) a period of 4 years to be allowed the Indians in which they should make their selections after allotment . . . ; (d) citizenship to be conferred upon allottees and upon any other Indians who had abandoned their tribes and adopted 'the habits of civilized life'; and (e) reservation lands not allotted to individual Indians were declared surplus and offered for sale, sold mostly to non-Natives who wanted these Indian lands and resources for their own. See David H. Getches, Charles F.

Wilkinson, and Robert A. Williams, "A Century of Shifting Policy," in *Cases and Materials on Federal Indian Law* (St. Paul: American Case Book Series, 1998), 142–255, quote at 166.

3. Tribes lost more than forty-one million acres of their land base because of the General Allotment Act of 1887 (Dawes Act). See ibid., 166.

4. Russel Lawrence Barsh maintained that "the appropriation of Indian lands and the acculturation of Indian people have been the primary goals of the dominant society all along. See Barsh, "Progressive-Era Bureaucrats and the Unity of Twentieth-Century Indian Policy," *American Indian Quarterly* 15, no. 1 (Winter 1991): 9.

5. For an excellent account of how today's national parks are mainly made of lands that had been taken from the country's Native Nations, see Philip Burnham, *Indian Country, God's Country: Native Americans and the National Parks* (Washington, D.C.: Island Press, 2000). Burnham wrote, "Parkland was acquired many ways in the West. The Oglala (Badlands) and Ute (Mesa Verde) sold or traded treaty lands to the government under the threat of diminished rations, and Death Valley was created as a national monument by the stroke of the Presidential pen. In some cases, as at the Grand Canyon, Native people were forcibly removed from their homes so tourists would feel comfortable contemplating a true 'wilderness.' In many places that later became parks, as at Glacier, tribes were coerced into signing agreements that not only surrendered ownership of treaty lands but compromised their rights to use them for subsistence. Eventually the government came to control every conceivable aspect of park ownership—or management—the law would bear." All the Indian tribes affected "had ties to the parklands that go back centuries, not decades. The lands the ancestors lived on and used have been—and remain to this day—contested ground" (9).

6. Native Nations put more than 840,000 acres into trust status from 1998 to 2007, according to Timberly Ross of the Associated Press. The information was obtained from the BIA under the Freedom of Information Act. "Tribes say the purchases will help protect their culture and way of life by preserving burial grounds and areas where sacred rituals are held. They also provide land for farming, timber and other efforts to make tribes self-sustaining" (Timberly Ross, "Indian Tribes Buy Back Thousands of Acres of Land," Associated Press, December 27, 2009).

7. The identification and description of these three different dimensions of the negotiation process, in the context of operating in labor-management negotiations, appear in Thomas R. Colosi and Arthur Eliot Berkeley, *Collective Bargaining: How It Works and Why* (New York: American Arbitration Association, 1990). This concept is further elaborated in Colosi's *On and Off the Record: Colosi on Negotiation*, 2nd ed. (Washington, D.C.: American Arbitration Association, 2001).

8. According to most tribal constitutions, decisions that have significant impact on tribal resources ultimately have to be ratified by the general council,

which consists of all the voting tribal members. Most tribal constitutions delegate authority to tribal councils to run day-to-day matters, but when a decision concerns the big questions, they revert to the "people," i.e., all the enrolled members.

9. When the Klamath Tribes entered the Klamath River Basin Water Negotiations in 2001, the negotiation team prepared and distributed a survey questionnaire for the members to determine what they were interested in achieving in this transaction. The team subsequently held a membership meeting to share the survey results and discuss what seemed to be the more realistic expectations.

10. The author has worked with Native nations since 1979 as a community economic development consultant and later as a negotiator and mediator. During this time, he has attended many government consultations conducted by the Bureau of Indian Affairs (BIA), health agencies, and other federal and state agencies as both a facilitator and observer. While never taking an official survey, he has consistently found tribal leaders to harbor significant cynicism and resentment about the consultation process. Leaders who testify comment afterward that they thought it was a waste of time because they believed that the agency would go ahead and do whatever it intended to do in the first place. In contrast, these leaders prefer to meet with agency officials who are willing to sit down and reach a negotiated agreement. They are pleased to be regarded as equals rather than subjects in a more paternalistic process.

The statement that Joe Shirley, president of the Navajo Nation, made during congressional hearings is typical of many leaders' attitudes: "While the tribal leaders pour out their hearts talking about the needs of their people, the BIA bureaucrats sit there impassively listening. All the while the BIA officials know that the budgetary decisions have already been made and that consultation is nothing more than a pretense to being able to say that we listened and took notes but other priorities governed the process" (Hearings on HR 5608, To Establish Regular and Meaningful Consultation and Collaboration with Tribal Officials in the Development of Federal Policies That Have Tribal Implications, To Strengthen the United States Government to Government Relationship with Indian Tribes, And To Reduce the Imposition of Unfunded Mandates Upon Indian Tribes. April 9, 2008, Before the Committee on Resources, Supra note 102 at 25).

11. The author was intimately involved in these negotiations and takes partial responsibility for the failure to anticipate the importance of bringing the tribal membership into discussions while the negotiations were ongoing. It violated a cardinal principle in collaborative negotiation of avoiding surprises.

12. When Cesar Chavez was organizing Mexican American farmworkers in California in the 1960s and 1970s, a similar issue arose regarding the role of lawyers. There were some excellent, well-meaning, and dedicated attorneys working for the United Farm Workers Union and other support organizations.

Chavez, however, chose to limit these attorneys' roles because he observed that it was pre-empting the farmworkers themselves from taking leadership and building a self-reliant "movement." He wanted to build a strong organization in addition to winning. This information was gained by the author in the course of his work with the farmworker movement, his employment with the California Rural Legal Assistance (CRLA) program, and the fact that his twin brother was a lawyer who was employed by United Farm Workers at the time.

13. Thomas Colosi, negotiator and mediator, characterized these two orientations as being reflected in what he called the "destabilizer" and the "stabilizer." He describes what the team leader, in his role as quasi-mediator, must do with both types of negotiator to keep them engaged, maintain consensus on the team, and move the negotiation toward resolution (see *On and Off the Record*, 22–26).

14. Colosi, *On and Off the Record*, <??>.

Chapter 6

1. The author accompanied tribal leaders who were lobbying Congress to pass the Timbisha Homeland Act (2000). At that time, Senate Majority Leader Harry Reid of Nevada, the tribe's senator, refused to see them, asking the question, "Why would I want to talk to a bunch of Indians?" They also tried to meet with Senator Dianne Feinstein of California, who they believed would also be key to passing the legislation. She refused to meet, accusing them of really wanting to put a casino on reservation land, a pet peeve of hers and which the Tribal leaders had repeatedly denied. She sent the Director of her Washington D.C. staff to meet with them who treated them in a manner they found gratuitously "rude, dismissive and argumentative". It was clear that she did not regard them as members of her league. It was not a pleasant experience and they wrote a letter to the Senator to point that out.

2. Executive Order 13084 was annulled and replaced two years later with the same purpose and title by Executive Order 13175: "Consultation and Coordination with Indian Tribal Governments." See en.wikipedia.org/wiki/Executive Order 13175.

3. Executive Order 13175 states:

> The United States Government has a unique legal relationship with Native American Tribal governments as set forth in the Constitution of the United States, treaties, statutes and court decisions. . . .
>
> Each executive department and agency shall consult, to the greatest extent practicable and to the extent permitted by law, with tribal governments *prior to taking actions that affect federally recognized tribal governments*. All such consultations are to be open and candid so that all interested parties may evaluate for themselves the potential impact of relevant proposals.

Each executive department and agency shall assess the impact of federal government plans, projects, programs and activities on tribal trust resources and assure that tribal government rights and concerns are considered *during the development* of such plans, projects, programs and activities. . . .

Each executive department and agency shall take appropriate steps to remove any procedural impediments to work directly and effectively with tribal governments on activities that affect their trust property and/or governmental rights of the tribes.

This Executive Order by President Clinton was issued by the Department of Interior, Office of Collaborative Action and Dispute Resolution, and published in *Federal Register* 59, no. 85 (May 4, 1994) (italics added).

4. NAGPRA requires federal agencies, museums, and educational institutions (including state, local, and private institutions) receiving federal funds to prepare written summaries of their inventories of Indian human remains, funerary objects, and cultural items. Then these agencies and museums must notify Native nations that these inventories are available and reach agreements with Indian tribes and Native Hawaiian organizations regarding the process for repatriating or otherwise disposing of these remains and objects. Once lineal descent or cultural affiliation has been established, the culturally affiliated tribes and lineal descendants make the final determination about how to dispose of these items (e.g., from reburial to long-term curation).

5. See Francis P. McManamon, "An Introduction to the Native American Graves Protection and Repatriation Act (NAGPRA) 2003," at www.npd.gov. "The statute is to provide greater protection for Native American burial sites and more careful control over the removal of Native human remains, funerary objects, sacred objects, and items of cultural patrimony on Federal and tribal lands." It requires Native people to be consulted wherever archaeological investigations encounter or are expected to encounter these items. NAGPRA also requires that any excavation or removal must be done under procedures required by the Archaeological Resource Protection Act (Sec. 3 (c)(1)). "Any agency undertaking land modifying activities must engage in careful consultations with traditional users of the land and undertake intensive archaeological surveys to locate and then protect unmarked Native American graves, cemeteries or other places where cultural items might be located."

6. Two exceptions in the act have been used by those opposing repatriation requests made by the tribes: (1) Where the remains of objects are "indispensable for completion of a specific scientific study, the outcome which would be of major benefit to the United States," in such a case, the items must be returned within ninety days after the completing of the study; and (2) where more than one tribe or Native Hawaiian organization of descendants is making a claim, and the federal agency or museum "cannot clearly determine which

requesting party is the most appropriate claimant," in such a case, the federal agency or museum can retain the item until the parties agree or a court decides who should receive the item. See McManamon, "Introduction to the Native American Graves Protection and Repatriation Act (NAGPRA)."

7. See Barry Holt, "Archaeological Preservation on Indian Lands: Conflicts and Dilemmas in Applying the National Historic Preservation Act," *Environmental Law Journal* 15, no. 2 (Winter 1985): 413–53.

8. Federal Register, 11f: 1 Advisory Council on Historic 16 U.S.C. 470f (1996 Administrative Law).

9. See the National Park Service website (www.nps.gov) for a description of tribal heritage grants.

Chapter 7

1. Although the federal government has opted to regard consultation as the standard way of fulfilling President Clinton's Executive Order (EO 13175), it has been seriously criticized for not providing sufficient guidance to agencies and departments in developing consultant plans. Derek Haskew, a scholar at the University of Oklahoma College of Law, in a 2000 study predicted that it would be detrimental to the relationship between federal and tribal governments "because it is not enforceable and it establishes expectations ... that would go unmet and thereby perpetuate a sense of betrayal" within tribal communities. He concluded his criticism of EO 13175 by acknowledging that the EO itself was not a product of consultation with tribal leadership. Derek C. Haskew, "Federal Consultation with Indian Tribes: The Foundation of Enlightened Policy Decisions, or another Badge of Shame?" *American Indian Law Review* 24, no. 1 (2000): 21–74. Also see Colette Routel and Jeffrey Holth, "Toward Genuine Tribal Consultation in the 21st Century," *University of Michigan Journal of Law Reform* 46, no. 2 (2013): 417–75 for another article criticizing EO 13175.

2. For additional background on the troubled relationship between the tribe and the National Park Service, see Steve Crum, "A Tripartite State of Affairs: The Timbisha Shoshone Tribe, the National Park Service, and the Bureau of Indian Affairs, 1933–1994," *American Indian and Cultural Research Journal* 22, no. 1 (1998): 117–36.

3. In conversations with the author around this time, Fred Marr and Richard Boland, negotiators for the tribe, indicated that they were given assurances by Elizabeth Homer, director of the Office of American Indian Trust; Dr Catherine Vandemoer, special assistant to the assistant secretary of Indian affairs; and Dr Patricia Parker, chief of the NPS American Indian Liaison Office.

4. These observations expressed by the tribal team members were confirmed by two staff members who represented the Pacific Regional Office of the Bureau of Indian Affairs at the May 1995 meeting. Conversations with the author on November 15, 1999.

The letter to Secretary Babbitt from the Timbisha Shoshone Tribe was dated October 31, 1996, and signed by Frederick I. Marr, counsel to the Timbisha Shoshone Tribe. Quoting from the letter: "The Tribe rejects the present NPS and BLM 'study' in its entirety, as a sham. The 'study' was not done in 'consultation with the Timbisha Shoshone Tribe' or in 'consultation with relevant federal agencies.' As pointed out above, it is not a 'study.' Furthermore, the document omits any analysis of the vast Tribal ancestral homelands inside the Park in relation to the suitability of setting aside all or portions of these lands in trust for the Tribe. . . . It is a document created by NPS and BLM. It is in violation of the Desert Protection Act. It is an illegal document. We caution NPS and BLM not to complete their 'study' on the Timbisha or submit it to the Secretary, and again refer you to the Tribe's letter sent to the President dated September 8, 1996." A copy of this letter is on file with the author.

5. This assessment is based on discussions with staff members of this Senate committee held in September 1997.

6. These thoughts were expressed by John Reynolds in the author's presence at an American Bar Association convention in San Francisco on April 7, 2000. They appeared together on a panel to discuss the government-to-government negotiations between the tribe and the Park Service.

7. Four-page letter to Pat Parker from Steven Haberfeld for the tribe, dated November 1997. This document is in the author's files.

8. The December 22, 1997, letter from Patricia I. Parker, chief, American Indian Liaison Office, was addressed to Steven Haberfeld, executive director of the Indian Dispute Resolution Service. A copy of this letter is on file with the author.

9. Based on discussions between the author and Barbara Durham, tribal administrator, and Dorothy Alther, tribal attorney, following the meeting.

10. "Preamble and Framework for Achieving a Timbisha Shoshone Homeland," Timbisha Shoshone Tribe and U.S. Government Land Base Negotiation Meeting, Death Valley, California, January 15–16, 1998. Copy on file with author.

11. This is based on conversations with Richard Boland, tribal administrator, and Fred Marr, tribal attorney, at tribal planning meetings in Las Vegas in September 1997.

12. These were pared down from the eleven thousand acres that were discussed during the first round of talks because the BLM discovered that there were certain encumbrances, such as mining claims that prohibited trespassing.

BIBLIOGRAPHY

Ariely, Dan. *Predictably Irrational: The Hidden Forces That Shape Our Decisions.* New York: HarperCollins, 2008.
Augsburger, David W. *Conflict Mediation across Cultures.* Louisville, KY: Westminster/John Knox Press, 1992.
Barker, Tammy R. "The Psychological Impact of Historical Trauma on Native American People." *All Regis University Theses,* Fall 2013.
Barsh, Russel Lawrence. "Progressive-Era Bureaucrats and the Unity of Twentieth-Century Indian Policy." *American Indian Quarterly* 15, no. 1 (Winter 1991): 1–17.
Bingham, G. *Resolving Environmental Disputes: A Decade of Experience.* Washington, DC: Conservation Foundation, 1986.
Bowling, David, and David A. Hoffman, eds. *Bringing Peace into the Room: How the Personal Qualities of the Mediator Impact the Process of Conflict Resolution.* San Francisco: Wiley & Sons, 2003.
Burnham, Philip. *Indian Country, God's Country: Native Americans and the National Parks.* Washington, DC: Island Press, 2000.
Cardenas, Luis. "Overcoming Cultural Barriers in Negotiations and the Importance of Communications in International Business Deals." Presentation to Harvard Law School Program on Negotiation, Cambridge, MA, May 14, 2020.
Carpenter, S. L., and W. I. D. Kennedy. "A Practical Guide to Handling Conflict and Reaching Agreements." In *Managing Public Disputes,* ed. W. I. D. Kennedy, 197–223. San Francisco: Jossey-Bass, 1988.
Claro, Daya Schultz. *Conciliation in Industrial Disputes.* Geneva: International Labour Office, 1973.
Cloke, Kenneth. *Mediating Dangerously.* San Francisco: Jossey-Bass, 2000.
Collier, M. J., S. A. Ribeau, and M. L. Hechi. "Intracultural Communication Rules and Outcomes within Three Domestic Cultures." *International Journal of Intercultural Relations* 10, no. 4 (1986): 439–57.
Colosi, Thomas R. *On and Off the Record: Colosi on Negotiation.* Washington, DC: American Arbitration Association, 2001.

Colosi, Thomas R., and Arthur Elliot Berkeley. *Collective Bargaining: How It Works and Why.* Second ed. New York: American Arbitration Association, 1994.

Crum, Steve. "A Tripartite State of Affairs: The Timbisha Shoshone Tribe, the National Park Service, and the Bureau of Indian Affairs, 1933–1994." *American Indian and Cultural Research Journal* 22, no. 1 (1998): 117–36.

Crum, Thomas F. *The Magic of Conflict: Turning a Life of Work into a Work of Art.* New York: Simon and Schuster, 1987.

Dana, D. *Managing Differences: How to Build Better Relationships at Work and Home.* Wolcott, CT: MTI Publications, 1989.

Edelman, Joel, and Mary Beth Crain. *The Tao of Negotiations: How You Can Prevent, Resolve and Transcend Conflict in Work and Everyday Life.* New York: HarperCollins Business, 1992.

Ellison, Sharon. *Taking the War out of Our Words: The Art of Powerful Non-Defensive Communication.* Richmond, CA: Bay Tree, 2002.

Estes, R. W. *Labor Arbitration Advocacy.* Stoneham, MA: Butterworth's Legal Publisher, 1989.

Fisher, Roger, and Scott Brown. *Getting Together: Building Relationships as We Negotiate.* New York: Penguin, 1988.

Fisher, Roger, Elizabeth Kopelman, and Andrea Kupfer Schneider. *Beyond Machiavelli: Tools for Coping with Conflict.* Cambridge, MA: Harvard University Press, 1994.

Fisher, Roger, and Daniel Shapiro. *Beyond Reason: Using Emotions as You Negotiate.* New York: Penguin, 2005.

Fisher, Roger, and William Ury. *Getting to Yes: Negotiating Agreement without Giving In.* Third ed. New York: Penguin, 2011.

Folberg, J., and A. Taylor. *Mediation: A Comprehensive Guide to Resolving Conflicts without Litigation.* San Francisco: Jossey-Bass, 1988.

Folger, Joseph P., and Robert A. Baruch Bush. *The Promise of Mediation: Responding to Conflict through Empowerment and Recognition.* Revised ed. San Francisco: Jossey-Bass, 2005.

Gail, Linda. "Too Little to Celebrate: Dayton Continues to Fail Bosnia's Minorities." *European Voice*, November 21, 2012.

Getches, Donald H., Charles F. Wilkinson, and Robert A. Williams. "A Century of Shifting Policy." In *Cases and Materials on Federal Indian Law.* 4th ed., 190–257. St. Paul: West Group, 1998.

Glenn, E. S., D. Witmeyer, and K. A. Stevenson. "Cultural Styles of Persuasion." *International Journal of Intercultural Relations* 1, no. 3 (1977): 52–66.

Goldberg-Ambrose, Carole. *Planting Tail Feathers: Tribal Survival and Public Law 280.* Los Angeles: American Indian Studies Center, 1997.

Goleman, Daniel. *Emotional Intelligence: Why It Can Matter More Than IQ.* New York: Bantam, 2005.

Green, E., S. Goldberg, and F. Sander. *Dispute Resolution*. Boston: Little Brown, 1985.

Grey, Barbara. *Collaborating: Finding Common Ground for Multiparty Problems*. San Francisco: Jossey-Bass, 1989.

Haberfeld, Steven. "Government-to-Government Negotiations: How the Timbisha Shoshone Got Its Land Back." *American Indian Natural and Cultural Research Journal* 24, no. 4 (January 2000): 127–65.

Haberfeld, Steven. "Power and Dispute Resolution in Indian Country." *Mediation Quarterly* 10, no. 4 (Summer 1993): 405–22. (Special issue: Native American Perspectives on Peacemaking.)

Haberfeld, Steven. "The Process of Constitutional Reform." In *American Indian Constitutional Reform and the Rebuilding of Native Nations*, ed. Eric D. Lemont, chapter 8. Austin: University of Texas Press, 2006.

Haskew, Derek C. "Federal Consultation with Indian Tribes: The Foundation of Enlightened Policy Decisions, or another Badge of Shame?" *American Indian Law Review* 24, no. 1 (2000): 21–74.

Hechi, M. L., and S. A. Ribeau. "Ethnic Communication: A Comparative Analysis of Satisfying Communication." *International Journal of Intercultural Relations* 8 (1984): 135–51.

Herring, Roger D. "Nonverbal Communication: A Necessary Component of Cross-Cultural Counseling." *Journal of Multicultural Counseling and Development* 19, no. 4 (1990).

Herring, Roger D. "Understanding Native-American Values: Process and Content Concerns for Counselors" *Counseling and Values* 34, no. 2 (January 1990): 134–37.

Hill, Dorothy J., and Sandy Thornton. *The Indians of Chico Rancheria* (Chico, CA: Ka Ma Press, 1978).

Hines, B. L. *Arbitration and Mediation*. New York: Arbitration Forums, 1988.

Holt, Barry. "Archaeological Preservation on Indian Lands: Conflicts and Dilemmas in Applying the National Historic Preservation Act." *Environmental Law Journal* 15, no. 2 (Winter 1985): 413–53.

Kahn, R. L., and E. Boulding. *Power and Conflict in Organizations*. New York: Basic Books, 1964.

Kalt, Joseph P., and Joseph W. Singer. *Myths and Realities of Tribal Sovereignty: The Law and Economics of Indian Self-Rule*. Boston: Kennedy School of Government, 2004.

Kelly, Joan B. "Empirical Research in Divorce and Family Mediation." *Mediation Quarterly* 24. San Francisco: Jossey-Bass, 1996.

Keltner, John W. *Mediation: Toward a Civilized System of Dispute Resolution*. Annadale, VA: Speech Communication Association, 1987.

Kolb, Deborah M. *When Talk Works: Profiles of Mediators*. San Francisco: Jossey-Bass, 1994.

Kressel, R., and D. Pruitt. *Mediation Research: The Process and Effectiveness of Third-Party Intervention*. San Francisco: Jossey-Bass, 1989.

LeBaron, Michelle. *Bridging Cultural Conflicts: A New Approach for a Changing World*. San Francisco: Jossey-Bass, 2003.

Lemont, Eric D. "Developing Effective Processes of American Indian Constitutional and Governmental Reform: Lessons from the Cherokee Nation of Oklahoma, Hualapai, Navajo Nation and Northern Cheyenne Tribe." *American Indian Law Review* 26, no. 2 (2001–2002): 147–76.

Lemont, Eric D. "Remaking Tribal Constitutions." In *American Indian Constitutional Reform and the Rebuilding of Native Nations*, ed. Eric D. Lemont, chapter 1. Austin: University of Texas Press, 2006.

Lemont, Eric D., ed. *American Indian Constitutional Reform and the Rebuilding of Native Nations*. Austin: University of Texas Press, 2006.

LeResche, Diane, ed. "Native American Perspectives on Peace-Making." *Mediation Quarterly* 10, no. 4 (Summer 1993): 321–25.

Leritz, Len. *No-Fault Negotiating: A Simple Innovative Approach to Solving Problems, Reaching Agreements, and Resolving Conflicts*. Portland, OR: Pacifica, 1987.

Lewicki, Roy J., David M. Saunders, and John W. Minton. *Essentials of Negotiation*. Second ed. New York: McGraw Hill, 2001.

Lonowski, Delmer. "A Return to Tradition: Proportional Representation in Tribal Government."*American Indian Culture and Research Journal* 18, no. 1 (1994): 147–63.

Maslow, Abraham. *Motivation and Personality*. New York: Harper and Brothers, 1954.

Maslow, Abraham. "A Theory of Human Motivation." *Psychological Review* 50, no. 4 (1943): 370–96.

Mayer, Bernard. *The Dynamics of Conflict Resolution: A Practitioner's Guide*. San Francisco: Jossey-Bass, 2000.

Mayer, Richard J. *Conflict Management: The Courage to Confront*. Second ed. Columbus, OK: Battelle Press, 1995.

McCoy, Robert Ross, and Steven M. Fountain, eds. *The History of American Indians: Exploring Diverse Roots*. Austin, TX: Greenleaf, 2017.

McManamon, Francis P. "An Introduction to the Native American Graves Protection and Repatriation Act (NAGPRA)." www.npd.gov, 2003.

Miller, Robert James. "Consultation or Consent: The U.S. Duty to Confer with American Indian Governments." *North Dakota Law Review* 91, no. 1 (2015): 37–98.

Moore, Christopher M. *The Mediation Process: Practical Strategies for Resolving Conflict*. San Francisco: Jossey-Bass, 2004.

"National Park Service Guidance Regarding Determinations of Cultural Affiliation." Director's Order 28: Cultural Resource Management Guidelines, National Park Service, 1997.

Native American Rights Fund (NARF). "Indigenous Peace-Making Initiative." peacemaking.narf.org.
Navajo Nation Peacemaking Program. www.tribaljustice.org.
Northrup, Terrell A. "The Dynamic of Identity in Personal and Social Conflict." In *Intractable Conflicts and Their Transformation*, ed. L. Kriesberg. Syracuse, NY: Syracuse University Press.
Polley, R. B. "Coalition, Mediation, and Scapegoating: General Principles and Cultural Variation." *International Journal of Intercultural Relations* 13, no. 2 (1989): 165–81.
Rawls, James. "The Gold Rush." *An American Experience*. PBS. Aired November 6, 2006.
Raz, Tahl, and Beth Comstock. *Imagine It Forward: Courage, Creativity and Power of Change*. New York: Penguin, 2018.
Robert, Henry M., III *Robert's Rules of Order: Newly Revised in Brief*. Boston: Da Capo Press, 2004.
Routel, Colette, and Jeffrey Holth. "Toward Genuine Tribal Consultation in the 21st Century." *University of Michigan Journal of Law Reform* 46, no. 2 (2013): 417–75.
Rusco, Elmer. *A Fateful Time: The Background and Legislative History of the Indian Reorganization Act*. Reno: University of Nevada Press, 2000.
Rusco, Elmer. "The Indian Reorganization Act and Indian Self-Government." In *American Indian Constitutional Reform and the Rebuilding of Native Nations*, ed. Eric D. Lemont, 48–82. Austin: University of Texas Press, 2006.
Salacuse, Jeswald W. "Negotiating: The Top Ten Ways Culture Can Affect Your Negotiation." *IVEY Business Journal* (September/October 2004).
Schneller, R. "Intercultural and Intrapersonal Processes and Factors of Misunderstanding: Implications for Multicultural Training. *International Journal of Intercultural Relations* 13 (1989): 465–81.
Schwartz, S. H. "Individualism-Collectivism: Critique and Proposed Refinement." *Journal of Cross-Cultural Psychology* 21, no. 2 (1990): 139–57.
Shell, G. Richard. *Bargaining for Advantage: Negotiation Strategies for Reasonable People*. New York: Penguin, 1999.
Slaikeu, Karl A. *When Push Comes to Shove: A Practical Guide to Mediating Disputes*. San Francisco: Jossey-Bass, 1996.
Sterling Institute of Relationship. www.sterling-institute.com.
Stone, Douglas, Bruce Patton, and Sheila Heen. *Difficult Conversations: How to Discuss What Matters Most*. New York: Penguin, 2000.
Susskind, Lawrence, Sarah McKearnan, and Jennifer Thomas-Larmer, eds. *The Consensus-Building Handbook: A Comprehensive Guide to Reaching Agreement*. Los Angeles: Sage, 1999.
Tannen, Deborah. *Talking from Nine to Five: How Women's and Men's Conversational Styles Affect Who Gets Heard, Who Gets Credit, and What Gets Done at Work*. New York: William Morrow, 1994.

Tannen, Deborah. *You Just Don't Understand: Women and Men in Conversation* New York: Ballantine, 1991.
Thich Nhat Hanh. *The Miracle of Mindfulness: An Introduction to the Practice of Meditation*. Boston: Beacon, 1976.
Ting-Toomey, Stella, and John G. Oetzel. *Managing Intercultural Conflict Effectively*. Los Angeles: Sage, 2001.
Ury, William. *Getting Past No: Negotiating with Difficult People*. New York: Bantam, 1991.
Ury, William. *Getting Past No: Negotiating in Difficult Situations*. New York: Random House, 2007.
Ury, William. *Getting to Yes with Yourself (and Other Worthy Opponents)*. San Francisco: Harper One, 2015.
Ury, William *Power of a Positive No: How to Say No and Still Get to Yes*. New York: Random House, 2018.
Voss, Chris, and Tahl Raz. *Never Split the Difference: Negotiating as If Your Life Depended on It*. New York: HarperCollins, 2016.
Wetsit, Deborah. "Effective Counseling with American Indian Students. In *Next Steps: Research and Practice to Advance Indian Education*, chapter 8. Washington, DC: U.S. Department of Education, Office of Educational Research and Improvement, 1999.
White, Paul J. "Chuckwalla and the Belligerent Burro: Timbisha Shoshone Miners and the Footprints of Dispossession in the Panamints." Unpublished PhD thesis, Brown University, 2008.
Wilkins, David. "Seasons of Change of Reforms, Melees, and Revolutions in Indian Country." In *American Indian Constitutional Reform and the Rebuilding of Native Nations*, ed. Eric D. Lemont. Austin: University of Texas Press, 2006.
Zander, Benjamin, and Rosamund Zander. *The Art of Possibility*. Cambridge, MA: Harvard Business School Press, 2000.

INDEX

ACHP. *See* Advisory Council on Historic Preservation
Administration of Native Americans (ANA), 140
administrative hearings: adversarial nature of, 17; as conflict resolution strategy, 14–15
Advisory Council on Historic Preservation, 7, 117
agencies, negotiating teams of, 101
agency team, relations within, 100
Agency Working Groups, 92
agendas: agreement upon, 56; building of, 53–56; discussion of, 56; wording items for, 54–56
Agreement to Arbitrate, 14, 21
AIRFA. *See* American Indian Religious Freedom Act
alternates, roles of, 103
American Arbitration Service, 20
American Experiment, An (PBS), 34
American Indian Religious Freedom Act (AIRFA), 118
AM-FAC Corporation, 141
ANA. *See* Administration of Native Americans
arbitration: adversarial nature of, 17, 20; as approved dispute resolution process, 14; as conflict resolution strategy, 13–14; mediation versus, 20–21; primary purpose of, 21; roles of participants in, 21

arbitration agreements, 13–14, 20

Babbitt, Bruce, 144, 150, 154–55
Barry, Donald J., 149, 150, 151, 154–55
Best Alternatives to a Negotiated Agreement (BATNA), 77
BIA. *See* Bureau of Indian Affairs
Blackfeet Tribe, 147
BLM. *See* Bureau of Land Management
body language, 37
BOR. *See* Bureau of Reclamation
boycotts, 15, 22
Brunett, Peter, 34
Bureau of Indian Affairs (BIA), 2, 27, 136, 141: BIA, adjudication process in, 2; Fort Independence tribal elections dispute and, 5; Wilton Miwok Rancheria and, 3–4
Bureau of Land Management (BLM), 27, 83, 127, 136, 137, 139, 141, 142, 147, 151, 164
Bureau of Reclamation (BOR), 27, 126, 151

California: anti-Native actions in, 33–34; disruption of Native communities in, 33–34; federally recognized tribes in, 33; gold rush in, 33, 34; tribes' success in, 111
California Department of Transportation, 6–7

219

California Desert Protection Act, 135–36, 139–42
California Indian Legal Services (CILS), 6, 136, 141, 147
California Rural Legal Assistance, 120
California State Historic Preservation Office (SHPO), 7
casinos, 83, 85, 111, 208n1
caucuses, 20, 67, 105–6
Central California Area BIA Office, 5
China Lake Naval Air Weapons Station (NAWS), 7–8
CILS. *See* California Indian Legal Services
Clinton, Bill, 89–90, 112, 138, 148, 163
collaborative negotiation, 35
Colosi, Thomas, 108
Colville Confederated Tribes, 82
comanagement, 129–30
community organizing, 120–22
compromise, 1
concessions, 59–60
conciliatory gestures, as conflict resolution strategy, 12
Concow Tribe, 33
Concurrent Resolution 108 (Termination Act), 82–83
confidence-building measures, 36
confidentiality, 59, 74, 88, 106–7
confidentiality agreements, 67–69
conflict: agreements made in, under duress, 22–23; benefits of, 42–43; costs of, 41–42; internal, 23; origins of, 39–40; positive approach toward, x; problem of, in Indian Country, 1; reaction to, 11; stress relating to, 41
conflict aftermath, 72
conflict assessment, 39
conflict resolution: adversarial versus collaborative forms of, 17–20; judicial forms of, 17; Native strategies for, 29, 22; strategies for, 12–17
conflict resolution process: relationship building during, 36; trust building during, 36–37

consensus-based decision making, 21, 30–31, 35
consensus building: defined, 30; nonadversarial, 29
Conservation Fund, 128
consultation, vs. negotiation, 89–91
Coso Hot Springs (Calif.), management of, 7–8
courtroom procedures, reasons for, 63–64
Cultural and Historic Preservation Site, 7
cultural differences: negotiations and, 104–5; recognition of, 69–70
cultural resources, protection of, 115–17

Dawes Allotment Act (1887), 82
Death Valley: borax discovered in Furnace Creek, 138; as Timbisha Shoshone's ancestral homeland, 138
Death Valley National Monument, 26–27, 135, 139, 141
Death Valley National Park, 126, 158: desert inn at, 159–60; expansion to, 135–36, 139; public demonstrations and information marches in, 147–48; spiritual sites in, 161
decision making, consensus-based, 30–31
demands, 56. *See also* proposals
denial, as conflict resolution strategy, 11
Department of the Interior, 164
direct action: adversarial nature of, 17; as conflict resolution strategy, 15–16
disenfranchised groups, increasing negotiating power of, 120–23
dispute resolution. *See* conflict resolution
DWP. *See* Los Angeles Department of Water and Power

Eastern Sierra tribes, Coso Hot Springs management and, 7–8
economic development planning, 6–7

elders, keeping informed, during negotiations, 93–94
electoral support, 110
Endangered Species Act of 1973 (ESA), 113–14
Esteves, Pauline, 139, 158
ethnic cleansing, 148
Everglades National Park, 149–50
Executive Order 12875 (Executive Order 13175), 89–90, 138, 163
Executive Order 13084 (Executive Order 13175), 112
expectations: identifying, 52–53; management of, 88

facilitation: as collaborative form of resolution, 17–18; third parties' presence in, 17
facilitators: agenda setting and, 54; services of, 93
Feinstein, Dianne, 139–40, 142, 156–57
Fisher, Roger, 44
Five Sandoval Tribe, 147
forced relocation, 32–33
forests, comanagement of, 129
Fort Independence tribe: economic development project of, 6–7; elections dispute in, 5
Freedom of Information Act, 147
Fremont-Winema National Forest, 123–24
Furnace Creek (Death Valley, Calif.), 141, 156, 158–60
Furnace Creek Hotel, 27
Furnace Creek Inn, 141
future dispute resolution clause, 73–74

gaming tribes, political power of, 111
Getting to Yes: Negotiating Agreement without Giving In (Fisher and Ury), 44
government-to-government negotiations: additional studies resulting from, 106; addressing cultural differences, 104–5; authority in, 101; case-by-case handling of, 95–96; caucuses in, 105–6; confidentiality in, 106–7; differentiating between consultation and negotiation, 89–91; difficulty of federal agents speaking with tribal officers, 91–92; explicit agreement to, 151–52; federal record with, 91; increasing number of, 84–85; managing expectations during, 26; meeting places for, 105; no surprises in, 102–3; procedural agreements in, 103–7; ratification process for, 107; record keeping for, 105; schedules for, 105, 107; structural challenges of, 86–87; teams in, as quasi-mediators, 107–8
government-to-government relationships: codification of, 112; establishment of, 5; implementation of, 138; public commitment to, 138; reshaping of, 163
Greenpeace, 4, 149
ground rules, for negotiations. *See under* negotiation

Haberfeld, Steven J., 8
hierarchy of needs (Maslow), 47–49. *See also* Maslow, Abraham
higher good, commitment to, 23
historical oppression, 34
Hoover, Herbert, 135
horizontal negotiations, 86, 100–108; enrolling an agency in, 100–101; negotiating with people in authority, 101–2
Hualapai Tribe, 147

IBIA. *See* US Department of the Interior Board of Indian Appeals
IBN. *See* interest-based negotiation
IDRS. *See* Indian Dispute Resolution Services
ignoring, as conflict resolution strategy, 12

222   INDEX

Indian Country: conflict resolution approaches of, x; holistic relationships in, 36–37; kinship ties in, 36–37; majority rule introduced to, 31. *See also* Native Nations
Indian Dispute Resolution Services (IDRS), ix, 1, 8–9; focus of, 8; founding of, 1, 8; issues addressed by, 8–9; leadership training program, 30; mediating tribal disputes, 4, 5, 7–8; monitoring elections, 4–5; negotiation methodology of, 30; training by, 8, 34–35, 37; working with Klamath Tribe and Fremont-Winema National Forest, 123–24; working with Timbisha Shoshone Tribe, 141, 147
Indian Reorganization Act (IRA), 31, 38
Inouye, Daniel, 136
interest-based negotiation (IBN), x, 29, 152–53, 159–60; benefits of, 44–45; characteristics of, 23; Native approach to, 22
interests: flexibility and, 46, 48, 52; identifying, 45–52
internal team negotiations, 86–87, 94–100. *See also* tribal negotiation teams
IRA. *See* Indian Reorganization Act
issues, defining, 49–52

Kitzhaber, John, 37
Klamath Tribal Negotiation Team, 127
Klamath Tribes, 81–82; developing and promoting own forest management plan, 128–30; local agency supervisors and, 123, 124, 126; meeting with federal directors, 126–27; negotiations with Fremont-Winema National Forest, 123–24; water rights of, 114–15; Winona National Forest negotiations and, 8

land: ancestral, quasi–property right to, 112–13; communal ownership of, 82; significance of, to Native peoples, 83, 157
land management, attitudes toward, 142
land survey errors, 81–82
lawyers, tribal negotiation teams and, 94–95
letter-writing campaigns, 146–47
Lewis, Jerry, 140
listening, 42, 47, 49, 61
litigation, 13–14; adversarial nature of, 17, 18, 19; attorneys' behavior during, 18, 19; as conflict resolution strategy, 15; emotionality of, 63–64; lawyers and, 95; process of, 18–19
Little Lake Pomo Tribe, 33
Lomakatski Project, 129
Los Angeles Department of Water and Power (DWP), 6

majority rule, 23, 30
Maslow, Abraham, 45–49, 53, 57, 70
master stewardship agreement (MSA), 129–30
med-arb, 14. *See also* mediation-arbitration
mediation, 1, 4; acceptance of, 7–8; agenda setting and, 54; arbitration versus, 20–21; caucuses in, 20–21; as collaborative form of resolution, 17–18; as conflict resolution strategy, 12–13; forward-thinking orientation of, 21; ground rules for, 20, 21; primary purpose of, 21; third parties' presence in, 17
mediation-arbitration (med-arb): as conflict resolution strategy, 14; limited use of, 14; motivations for, 14
mediators, services of, 93
memorandum of understanding (MOU), 7
Miccosukee Tribe, 130, 147, 149–50
minorities, satisfying needs of, 31
motivation, understanding, 47, 48

MOU. *See* memorandum of understanding
MSA. *See* master stewardship agreement

NAGPRA. *See* Native American Graves Protection and Repatriation Act
NARF. *See* Native American Rights Fund
National Alliance to Protect Native Rights in National Parks, 130, 147, 149
National Congress of American Indians (NCAI), 147
National Historic Preservation Act (NHPA), 117–18
national leaders, appealing to, 126–27
National Marine Conservation Service, 113
National Park Denver Service Center, 159
national parklands, tribes adjoining, 147
National Parks and Conservation Association, 149
National Park Service (NPS), 27, 73, 126, 129, 164: involvement of, with Timbisha Shoshone Tribe 136, 137, 140, 141, 142, 146, 151–52; interest of, in Death Valley National Park, 158–60; leadership changes in, 149–50; political campaign against anti-Indian policy of, 136; public image of, 130; public pressure on, 148–49
Native American Graves Protection and Repatriation Act (NAGPRA), 115–17
Native American Rights Fund (NARF), 147, 154
Native Hawaiians, 147
Native nations: alliance of, 130; asset liquidation and, 82; behavioral norms in, 31–32; conflict resolution strategies of, 29; cultures destroyed by foreign forces, 30; development activities of, 84; dislocation of, 32–33; disruption of, in California, 33; efficiency in, 31; Endangered Species Act and, 113–14; forcible relocation of, 32–33; governance of, 31; government-to-government negotiations and, 84–85; historical and legal rights of, 111; internal conflict in, 31; inward looking, 85; land loss by, 81–84; leaders' selection in, 37–38; legislative tools for, 115–18; limited contact of, with government officials, 85; linked to ancestral lands and resources, 83; negotiation teams for, 86–87; peacemaking approach of, 13, 29–38; relationship building by, 37; selecting negotiators for, 38; as sovereign governments, xi, 26, 112, 114; traditional values in, 31; treatment of, during government decision making, 26; trust building in, 36; viewed as outsiders, 85; water rights of, 114–15. *See also* Indian Country; Native people
Native people: bringing issues to the public sphere, 118–34; dehumanization of, 34; excluded from America's political class, 109–10; federal government's trust relationship with, 111–12; governance of, 2; historical oppression of, 34; lacking political currency, 109–10, 131–34; leveraging rights and status, 111–12; messaging for, 119; political and public engagement of, 118–34; political resources for, 111–15; public opinion management of, 119–20; relations of, with federal agencies, 96; resources of, for extending influence, 132–34; self-respect of, 34
natural resource comanagement, 161
Nature Conservancy, 128, 129
Navajo Nation, 13, 147
NAWS. *See* China Lake Naval Air Weapons Station

NCAI. *See* National Congress of American Indians
needs, identifying, 45–49. *See also* hierarchy of needs (Maslow)
negotiated agreement, 137
negotiated regulations process, 91
negotiated rule making, 91, 96
negotiation: agenda for, 68; agreement language of, 71–75; as antidote to communications breakdown, xii; breaks during, 75; building framework for, 53–56; building relationships during, 75–76; as collaborative form of resolution, 17–18, 61; collaborative vs. positional, 35; as conflict resolution strategy, ix, 12; confrontational, 22–23; vs. consultation, 89–91; culture of, 18, 19–20, 69–70; defined, ix; distinguishing feature of, x; dynamic nature of, 88; emotions during, 64; expectations changing during, 24–25; expectations managed during, 25–27; frustration with, 44; ground rules for, 5, 34–35, 64–65, 67, 70–71; identifying interests during, 24; integrating parties' cultural preferences, 69–70; outcomes of, 68–69; participants in, 66; power disparities in, 137–38; procedural issues during, ix, 65–69; procedural rules for, 5, 34–35, 64–71, 98–99, 107; as process, 6–7, 29, 86; purpose of, 65; recording proceedings, 68; resistance toward, 1–2, 3, 44; satisfaction with, 150; setting of, 66–67; skills for, importance to Native nations, xi; stages in, 77–80; strategy formulation for, 52–53; third parties' presence in, 17; voluntary nature of, 44
negotiation teams, 86–87; authority of, 88–89; communicating with top decision makers, 89; during internal team negotiations, 87–88

negotiators: constraints on, 25–26; goals of, 150
news organizations, relationships with, 121
NGOs. *See* nongovernmental organizations
NHPA. *See* National Historic Preservation Act
Nomlacki Tribe, 33
non-engagement, as conflict resolution strategy, 12
nongovernmental organizations (NGOs), 128–30
no surprises, principle of, 102–3
NPS. *See* National Park Service

observers, roles of, 103
Office of Economic Opportunity (OEO), x–xi
Oglala Sioux Tribe, 147
Oregon, Native negotiations in, 37
Owens Valley (Calif.) Tribal Water Commission, 5–6

Paris Peace Talks (1968), 65
peacemaking, as conflict resolution strategy, 13
personality disputes, 6
Pit River Tribe, 33
political action, 15
political currency, 110
political influence, 110
political interest groups, 109–10
political leverage, Native tribes lacking, 109–10
positional negotiation, 35, 56, 159
procedural agreements, 35; benefits of, 70–71; in government-to-government negotiations, 103–7; negotiation of, 63–71
procedural issues, during negotiations, 65–69
procedural satisfaction, 63–71
process negotiations, between Timbisha Shoshone and government parties, 151–54
property, violence against, 16

INDEX 225

property rights, as political resource, 112
proposals: conciliatory gestures leading to, 62; conditional phrasing of, 60; developing and exchanging, 56–62; explaining or justifying, 57; getting stuck on, 58; justification for, 59; language used for, 60–61; offered in confidentiality, 59; questioning merits of, 59, 62; responding to, 62; secondary and tertiary, 58; tentative agreements on, 62; in win-win negotiations, 58–59
PSAs. *See* public service announcements
public agencies: diverse cultures of, 125–26; interests of, 124–25; vulnerabilities of, 124–25
public opinion, influencing of, 16, 120–22, 130–31
public relations campaigns, 131
public service announcements (PSAs), 130–31

quasi-mediators, 107–8
quid pro quos, 60

regional leaders, appealing to, 126–27
relational satisfaction, 75–76; Timbisha Shoshone Tribe meetings and, 162–64
relationship building, 162; importance of, 75–76; in Native negotiating, 36–37
religious, traditional, 118
reservations, 81, 82
resources, cooperative management of, 137
restorative justice, 13
Reynolds, John, 149, 150, 153, 154
Robert's Rules of Order, 31
Round Valley Indian Tribe, 33
rules of engagement, 5, 20

sabotage, 22
San Francisco Regional NPS office, 143–44, 145, 149, 150

satisfaction: creation of, 63; types of, 63
SCORE, 131
secretary of the interior, 148
self-actualization, 47–48
self-determination, goal of, 95
Senate Committee on Indian Affairs, 127
settlements, noncompliance with, 22
SHPO. *See* California State Historic Preservation Office
Stanislaus County Tenants Rights Association, 120–22
striking, 22
substantive agreements, between Timbisha Shoshone Tribe and NPS, 159–61
substantive satisfaction, 71–75; Timbisha Shoshone Tribe meetings and, 156–59

terrorism, 16
third parties, 17–18; as facilitators, 153–54; involved in mediation, 12–13
THPOs. *See* Tribal Historic Preservation Offices
Timbisha Homeland Act, 135
Timbisha Shoshone Natural and Cultural Preservation Area, 137, 161
Timbisha Shoshone Tribe, 8; agreeing to negotiate, 92; Death Valley as ancestral homeland of, 138–39; establishing homeland in Death Valley National Park, 130; establishing procedural rules for federal negotiations, 65; federal government study reports on, 143–45; food sources for, 160; land act agreement of, with United States, 135; land desired by, 26–27, 141–44, 157–59, 161; meeting with federal representatives, 136–37, 140–46, 150–64; national political organizing campaign of, 146–50; negotiation team changes in, 150; prohibited from cultural,

Timbisha Shoshone Tribe (*continued*) spiritual, and food source sites, 139; requesting BOR's participation in negotiations, 126; reshaping government-to-government relationship, 163; spiritual sites for, 161; squatting at Furnace Creek, 135; tribal council election conflict in, 2; tribal village for, 159–60
Timbisha Tribal Homeland Act (2000), 27
Torres Martinez Tribal Elections Procedures Agreement, 4
Torres Martinez Tribe: contested elections in, 4; dispute in, regarding toxic dumping, 4–5
toxic dumping, 4–5
Trail of Tears, 32
tribal constitutions, 2, 112
tribal councils: elections of, 2–3; makeup of, 94
Tribal Forest Protection Act (TFPA), 127
Tribal Historic Preservation Offices (THPOs), 117–18
tribalism, 82
tribal lands, dumping on, 4–5
tribal leaders: and structural barriers to political influence, 110; successes of, 110–11
tribal negotiation teams: agreements of, during federal negotiations, 91; appointment of, 94–95; differences within, 97; internal ground rules for, 98–99; job of, 97; lawyers and, 94–95; leader of, 97–98; meeting with agency directors or nonagency personnel, 92–93; meeting with federal team leaders, 92; quasi mediators, 107–8; relationship building among, 99; requesting agency directors and program managers, 101; sizes of, 104; technical staff members on, 96–97
tribal ratifiers, talking with, during negotiations, 93–94

trust: conflict resolution and, 36–37; effects of, on negotiations, 37; undermining of, 151
Trust for Public Lands, 128
trust land, alternatives to, 157, 159

Umatilla Tribe, 81–82
unions, 15
United States: imposing white culture on Natives, 34; lobbying in, 109–10; as Natives' legal trustee, 81; negotiating with Native tribes, 83–84; polarization in, xii; political class in, 109–10; politics in, as positional negotiation, 56; taking Native lands, 81–84; trust relationship of, with Native tribes, 111–12
Ury, William, 44
U.S. Congress: approach of, to Native American issues, xi; meeting with members and staff of, 127–28
USDA. *See* U.S. Department of Agriculture
U.S. Department of Agriculture, 120, 136
U.S. Department of the Interior, 6, 135, 136, 140, 144, 145, 146;
U.S. Department of the Interior Board of Indian Appeals (IBIA), 2
U.S. Department of the Navy, 7
U.S. Fish and Wildlife Service, 113
U.S. Forest Service (USFS), 84, 136, 141; comanagement with, 129; Executive Policy Group, 127; Klamath Tribe meeting with, 127; Native American Liaison Office, 127
U.S. House Natural Resources Committee, 127
U.S. Institute of Environmental Conflict Resolution, 7
U.S. Rancheria Act (1958B), 3
U.S. secretary of the interior, 113–14
U.S. Senate Committee on Indian Affairs, 116, 144, 149, 150

vertical negotiations, 87–93
violence, adversarial nature of, 17; against persons, as conflict resolution strategy, 16; against property, as conflict resolution strategy, 16

Wailacki Tribe, 33
war, as conflict resolution strategy, 16–17
water issues, 6, 151; Furnace Creek and, 142–43
water rights, 27; as political resource, 114–15
Wilkinson, Charles, 153–54, 162–63
Wilton Miwok Rancheria, factional dispute within, 3–4
Winema National Forest, restoring health of, 129–30
Winnemucca tribe, tribal council election disputes in, 3
winning, assessment of, 23–25, 27–28
win-or-lose strategy, consequences of, 23

Winters Doctrine, 114
Winters v. United States, 114
win-win approach, implementation of, 163–64
win-win negotiations, 21–28, 137–38; expectations for, 27–28; outcomes of, 57–58, 91; providing value to both parties, 22
win-win outcomes, commitment to, 35
win-win principle, x
work slowdowns, 15, 22
work stoppages, 15
written agreements, 5, 80; addressing all agenda items, 72–73; avoiding vague language in, 73; balance in, 72; conclusions and preambles to, 74–75; confidentiality of, 74; expressing promises in behavioral terms, 72; importance of, 71–72; reality testing of, 73

Yuki Tribe, 33
Yurok Tribe, 147

www.ingramcontent.com/pod-product-compliance
Lightning Source LLC
Chambersburg PA
CBHW050156150425
25134CB00003B/133